**The Language of Thought**

A New Philosophical Direction

# The Language of Thought

A New Philosophical Direction

Susan Schneider

The MIT Press

Cambridge, Massachusetts

London, England

For information about special quantity discounts, please email special_sales@mitpress.mit.edu

This book was set in Stone by the MIT Press. Printed and bound in the United States of America.

Library of Congress Cataloging-in-Publication Data

Schneider, Susan, 1968–
The language of thought : a new philosophical direction / Susan Schneider.
    p.   cm.
Includes bibliographical references and index.
ISBN 978-0-262-01557-8 (hardcover : alk. paper)
1. Philosophy of mind. 2. Cognitive science—Philosophy. 3. Thought and thinking—Philosophy. 4. Fodor, Jerry A. I. Title.
BD418.3.S36 2011
153.4—dc22
                                                    2010040700

10   9   8   7   6   5   4   3   2   1

To Rob, Jo, Denise, and Ally

# Contents

# Preface

This project started when certain of the language of thought program's central philosophical commitments struck me as ill conceived. It might have ended after several lengthy arguments with Jerry Fodor, but I am more stubborn than he is.

The idea that the mind is computational pervades contemporary cognitive science and philosophy of mind. Within cognitive science, it has become something like a research paradigm. And over the years, I've been very happy with that research paradigm—thrilled, actually. Who would deny that the last thirty or so years have witnessed an amazing beginning for cognitive science? But I must confess that computationalism's philosophical credentials always struck me as weaker than the science behind it. For what is it to say that the mind is computational? We cannot merely assume that if the *brain* is computational, the *mind* is as well. There are substance dualists who accept the former while repudiating the latter, after all. No, we need to reflect on whether the mind is computational even on the assumption that computationalism about the *brain* is promising. Here, philosophers have ventured two sorts of computational approaches to the mind: one that is based on a connectionist, or neural network, approach, and one—the language of thought (LOT) approach—that takes thinking to consist in the algorithmic manipulation of mental symbols.

Now, I thought to write a book-length exposé of the flaws in connectionist approaches to higher cognitive function, but someone already had (Marcus 2001). And in any case, it struck me that, philosophically speaking, connectionism is actually far better off than LOT, for its leading proponents are at least bona fide computationalists. Fodor, in contrast, is not. So I decided to sit down and ponder the scope and limits of the LOT approach, to determine if it is even a well-conceived computational approach to begin with. In this book, I do not intend to rule out non-computationalist options (e.g., biological naturalism, substance dualism): I trust many readers have arrived at views on this matter; they pick up this book because they find computationalism about the mind to be prima facie attractive. Yet even to those who sympathize with the computational approach, LOT seems to be in deep philosophical trouble: in the last several years, numerous cracks have emerged in its conceptual foundations. Its theory of meaning conflicts with its theory of computation; its theory of concepts is too emaciated—too nonpsychological—to be a satisfactory theory of concepts; Fodor's recent books on LOT actually argue that the cognitive mind is noncomputational; and even LOT's conceptual cornerstone—the very notion of a symbol—is poorly understood.

So here, I grapple with these problems, and at the end of the philosophical day, I believe you will find that the LOT I arrive at is quite different from the orthodox philosophical LOT. For the new LOT seeks integration with cognitive and computational neuroscience—indeed, LOT's naturalism requires it. And I repudiate Fodorian pessimism about the capacity of cognitive science to explain cognition. Further, in my hands LOT becomes a *pragmatist* theory: I argue that LOT couldn't have been otherwise, and that even the mainstream, Fodorian LOT made hidden appeals to pragmatism, while officially embarking on a massive attack on it, quite ironically. Relatedly, I advance a pragmatist version of conceptual atomism: *pragmatic atomism.*

I imagine that you will care about all this if you've signed on to the LOT program. And if you are vehemently opposed to LOT, you may want to know whether the LOT you are opposed to is really one that requires all the philosophical wares commonly associated with it, which you've come to know and hate. I am claiming that LOT is different than you think.

But before I launch into all this, allow me to give credit where credit is due. First and foremost, I would like to thank Jerry Fodor for his many thought-provoking ideas, and for numerous philosophical discussions. I'm afraid he will disagree with much of this book, but I hope my reworking of LOT inspires fruitful lines of inquiry. I am also grateful to the National Endowment for the Humanities for their financial support, to Philip Laughlin at MIT Press for his efficient editing and helpful advice, to Melanie Mallon and Katherine Almeida at MIT Press for their thorough copyediting, and to the audiences at various departments who hosted me at their colloquia in which chapters of this book were presented (the University of Maryland, Washington University at St. Louis, the University of Pennsylvania, Lehigh University, and the University of Cincinnati).

This book drew from several earlier papers of mine: "The Nature of Symbols in the Language of Thought," *Mind and Language* (Winter 2009): 523–553; "LOT, CTM and the Elephant in the Room," *Synthese* (Winter 2009): 235–250; "Fodor's Critique of the Classical Computational Theory of Mind" (with Kirk Ludwig), *Mind and Language* 23 (2008): 123–143; "Direct Reference,

Psychological Explanation, and Frege Cases," *Mind and Language* 20, no. 4 (September 2005): 223–447; "Conceptual Atomism Rethought," *Behavioral and Brain Sciences*, 33 , pp 224–225; and "Yes, It Does: A Diatribe on Jerry Fodor's Mind Doesn't Work That Way," *Psyche* 13, no. 1 (Spring 2007): 1–15. I would like to thank the editors and reviewers at these journals for their useful suggestions.

I am especially grateful to Mark Bickhard, Gary Hatfield, John Heil, Michael Huemer, and Gerald Vision. Not only did they give insightful feedback on parts of the manuscript, but they provided valuable practical advice and words of encouragement as well. I am also very grateful to the following people for their helpful comments on certain chapters: Murat Aydede, David Braun, Adam Croom, Matt Katz, Jonathan Cohen, Frances Egan, Michael Huemer, Brian McLaughlin, Carlos Montemayor, Jesse Prinz, Philip Robbins, Andreas Scarlatini, Murray Shanahan, Whit Schonbein, Bradley Rives, Jacob Beck, and Gualtiero Piccinini. The work of many of these people has played a significant role in the development of this book. Kirk Ludwig was also key to this project, to say the least, as he coauthored one of its chapters. I've enjoyed working with Ludwig, and indeed, all of these people, immensely. Needless to say, despite help from such a stellar crowd, I am sure errors have inevitably crept in, and that these are all due to me.

Last but most significantly, I am grateful to my family. I am especially indebted to my mother-in-law, Jo Marchisotto, and sister-in-law, Denise Marchisotto, who watched my young one while parts of the book were being written, and to both my husband and daughter, Rob and Alessandra Marchisotto, who tolerated an all-too-often distracted writer in their midst.

# 1  Introduction

Minds, whatever these are, are the bearers of mental states. And it is the primary ambition of philosophy of mind to figure out the nature of minds and their states. No matter what one thinks of the language of thought program, it is clear that it offers an influential theory of the nature of thoughts and the minds that have them. With respect to minds, the program says that they are symbol-manipulating devices of an ultrasophisticated sort. With respect to mental states, these are said to be mental symbols—ways in which we conceive of the world—strung together by operations of an inner grammar, the behavior of which is to be detailed by a completed cognitive science.

And this brings me to the very reason that I sat down to write this book. Despite the language of thought program's enormous influence, I wasn't sure that if you thought any of this through—if you hadn't already—you would say that you *really* know what it means. Hence, the three central puzzles of this book, which I shall now describe.

*Problem One.* Consider what the language of thought (LOT) approach says about the nature of mind, at least within philosophical circles. Jerry Fodor, the main philosophical advocate of LOT and the related computational theory of mind (CTM), claims that while LOT is correct, the cognitive mind is likely noncomputational (2000, 2008). This is perplexing, to say the least, because LOT is supposed to be a computational theory, and CTM quite obviously is supposed to be such as well (Fodor 1975).[1] Further, as I'll illustrate, insofar as Fodor even entertains the idea that cognition is computational, he employs a view in which cognitive processing is entirely sequential, and in which the biological underpinnings of cognition are ignored. Herein, I dismantle Fodor's case against computationalism, and provide LOT with a superior account of the computational character of the cognitive mind, at least in rough outline.

*Problem Two.* What about mental states? Of course, LOT and CTM say that mental states are *symbolic*; but what is a symbol? Strangely, LOT, a position that claims that thinking is *symbol* processing, has never clarified what a symbol is (Anderson 2007, Ch 1; Marcus 2001, 147). Indeed, the issue has been "largely neglected" (Pessin 1995, 33). Yet symbols are the conceptual cornerstone of the LOT program. They are supposed to capture our ways of conceiving the world, figure as kinds in explanations of thought and behavior, and enable LOT to integrate thought into the world that science investigates. Indeed, Fodor has voiced the worry that without a coherent theory of symbols ". . . the whole [LOT] project collapses" (Pessin 1995, 33). I agree. In this book I single out a conception of a symbol for LOT—it is the only notion of a symbol suitable to play the important philosophical

---

1. CTM holds that the mind is computational, with thinking being the algorithmic manipulation of semantically interpretable symbols in LOT. LOT and CTM are close kin—so much so that CTM generally consists in a philosophical commitment to LOT, together with an added semantic dimension that many build into LOT in any case. For this reason, following Fodor, I'll refer to the *philosophical* program surrounding both as simply the "LOT program," or simply "LOT."

and scientific roles that symbols are summoned to play. Yet once symbol natures are understood, elements of the current philosophical LOT program must be discarded. And LOT becomes a pragmatist theory.

*Problem Three.* Central to any account of the nature of mentality is a story about the representational nature of thought. So how is it that LOT's mental states come to represent, or be about, entities in the world? Here, many advocates of LOT appeal to a theory of meaning or mental content that is (to a first approximation) referential: e.g., the content or meaning of both the mental symbols #Cicero# and #Tully# is just the man, Cicero, despite the fact that the symbols differ in their cognitive significance.[2] (This kind of content has been called *broad content*). But here's the rub: as I'll explain, this approach to content conflicts with the view that thinking is symbolic, at least insofar as a leading, neo-Russellian theory of belief ascription is employed; and this is the view that mainstream LOT currently favors (Aydede and Aydede 1998; Aydede and Robbins 2001; Fodor 1994; Schneider 2005). For the standard LOT faces *Frege cases*: counterexamples to intentional generalizations arising from intentional laws that are sensitive to broad contents, rather than being sensitive to the particular ways the individual conceives of the referent. Frege cases undermine LOT's ability to explain thought and behavior. Further, Frege Cases suggest that LOT's account of mental states is deeply mistaken: mental states may very well be symbolic and computational, but it is unclear whether, as such, they can also

2. Although LOT's position on content is referential in the case of proper names, indexicals, and demonstratives, note that the content of a predicate is a property, rather than an extension at a world. The literature on LOT tends to ignore this subtlety (and I'll follow). Note that I will designate LOT expressions by enclosing the relevant expression with the symbol "#" (e.g., #dog#).

have the sort of semantic features that the standard LOT claims that they have.

I must confess that these three problems have been grating on me for some time, so permit me a rant: I have an ambivalent relationship toward LOT and CTM. They are immensely problematic, at least in their philosophical incarnation, being both divorced from the rest of cognitive science and plagued by serious problems. And I am quite interested in connectionist and dynamical systems approaches to the brain. Yet something seems unfair about LOT's philosophical predicament: in cognitive science proper, the symbol-processing view is alive and well. The notion of a symbol requires clarification, admittedly, but overall, there are sensible symbolic approaches in cognitive science, including, for instance, Gary Marcus's recent survey of why connectionism, if it is to explain cognition, must employ symbolic resources (2001). Even an influential computational neuroscience textbook respects the need for symbolic resources in models of higher cognitive function (O'Reilly and Munakata 2000). And the symbol-processing approach is the leading view of the format of thought in information-processing psychology; in this domain, LOT is thriving.

But as you've surely noticed, the philosophical LOT troubles me. For one thing, it turns away from the symbol processing tradition in cognitive science, as I've indicated. For Fodor, as brilliant as he is, is at heart not a computationalist. His latest books include several chapters arguing that LOT's *central system*—LOT's expression for the system responsible for higher cognitive function—will likely defy computational explanation (2000, 2008).[3] Astonishingly, he implores cognitive science to stop research on

3. Fodor also advances this position at the end of an earlier book, *The Modularity of Mind* (1983).

the central system. For another thing, the standard LOT wages an all-out war with concept pragmatism. In the literature on concepts, LOT famously opposes "pragmatist" accounts of the nature of thought, where by "pragmatist views" Fodor means claims that one's abilities (e.g., one's recognitional, classificatory, or inferential capacities) determine the nature of concepts (Fodor 2004, 34). In fact, Fodor proclaims that pragmatism is the "defining catastrophe of analytic philosophy of language and philosophy of mind in the last half of the twentieth century" (2003, 73-74). And he declares in his *LOT 2* that LOT's favored theory of concepts and, indeed, LOT itself, represents an important alternative to pragmatism (2008, 12).

After careful consideration of Fodor's positions on these matters, I will argue that Fodor situates LOT on the wrong side of both of these battles; indeed, I will develop a LOT that is firmly rooted in both pragmatism and computationalism. Back in 1975, Fodor noted in his *The Language of Thought* that characterizing the language of thought "is a good part of what a theory of mind needs to do," and this classic book was a brilliant exposition and defense of the symbolicist position in cognitive science (1975, 33). But a good deal of work still needs to be done. So here is what I propose to do: my reflections on Problem One will give rise to a LOT that is squarely computationalist, being integrated with current findings in cognitive science. And my solution to Problem Two will reveal that LOT cannot oppose pragmatism, for a symbol is individuated by what it does, that is, by its psychological role: the role it plays in one's mental life, including the role it plays in recognition, classification, and inference.[4] This leaves LOT with an account of symbols—LOT's neo-Fregean

4. In particular, symbols shall be individuated by their role in computation.

"modes of presentation"—that is pragmatist in an important sense. Further, this result extends to LOT's theory of concepts (*conceptual atomism*) as well, generating a superior version of the view. And concerning Problem Three, this new understanding of symbols, together with argumentation that I suspect is even palatable to the current LOT, provides a solution to the problem of Frege cases.

It is largely due to Fodor's insights that philosophers of mind have come to appreciate LOT. But if you ask me, LOT has been straying from its rightful path. Lost afield, it cries out for a philosophical overhaul.

## Some Background

But I am skipping ahead a bit, presupposing background knowledge of the terrain. I should now like to provide a brief survey of the LOT approach for those who are relatively uninitiated. Then—for my connectionist friends and other critics of the LOT program—I should like to make clear why it is worth bothering to devise solutions to these three problems, refurbishing LOT, rather than just throwing our hands up in the face of them and embracing one of *their* views instead. For I suspect that if you are a critic of LOT, then this is your reaction to our three problems. I shall then trace the dialectical path through which the chapters proceed.

According to the LOT program, conceptual thinking occurs in an internal languagelike representational medium. However, this internal language is not equivalent to one's spoken language(s). Instead, LOT is the format in which the mind represents concepts. The LOT hypothesis holds that the mind has numerous mental "words" (called *symbols*) that combine into mental sentences according to the grammatical principles of the language. When one thinks, one is engaged in the algorithmic processing of strings of these mental symbols.[5] The LOT program and the connectionist program are often viewed as competing theories of the format, or representational medium, of thought.[6]

As you may have surmised, the idea that there is a language of thought is commonly associated with the work of Jerry Fodor, who defended this hypothesis in an influential book, *The Language of Thought* (1975), and who has continued to do so in the context of a steady and influential stream of books and articles.[7] The philosophical literature on LOT focuses on the LOT program as it is developed by Fodor, in which the idea that we think in an inner symbolic language is developed in tandem with a constellation of related issues concerning meaning, modularity, concepts, CTM, and more. Fodor's writings on these topics are commonly part of the graduate and undergraduate canon in philosophy of mind. I mention this because readers in other fields of cognitive science may not realize that within philosophy, Fodor's program *is* for the most part the philosophical face of LOT and CTM. This book is a philosophical treatment of the language of thought approach, so quite naturally, it is a close

5. By "algorithm" I mean an effective, step-by-step procedure that manipulates strings of symbols and generates a result within finitely many steps.

6. But this latter issue is actually more subtle than this, as I explain shortly. For very readable overviews of connectionism, see Churchland (1996), which focuses on philosophical issues, and Hawkins (2005). The latter author is a scientist who provides a fairly up-to-date, broad-ranging discussion of the connectionist-based approach to intelligence.

7. Some would say that the LOT position dates back to Plato, who obviously was not a computationalist, but who held that each of us has innate concepts of universals, or forms, that we recall, at least to a degree.

treatment of, and reaction to, Fodor's ideas. This being said, the reader should bear in mind that those theorists who ascribe to LOT but reject the views that happen to be under fire in a given chapter (e.g., anti-computationalism) are not the targets of my criticisms.

According to Fodor, LOT was inspired by the ideas of Alan Turing, who defined computation in terms of the formal manipulation of uninterpreted symbols according to algorithms (Turing 1950; Fodor 1994). In Turing's "Computing Machinery and Intelligence," he introduced the idea that symbol-processing devices can think, a view that many in cognitive science are sympathetic to, yet which has also been the focus of great controversy (e.g., Searle 1980; Dreyfus 1972; Turing 1950). Indeed, the symbol-processing view of cognition was very much in the air during the time when Fodor's *Language of Thought* was published (1975). Two years before the publication of *The Language of Thought*, Gilbert Harman published his *Thought*, in which he argued that mental states "have structure, in the way that sentences have structure. . . . Mental states are part of a system of representation that can be called a language of thought" (1973, 65).[8] And three years before *The Language of Thought* came out, Allen Newell and Herbert Simon suggested that psychological states could be understood in terms of an internal architecture that was like a digital computer (Newell and Simon 1972). Human psychological processes were said to consist in a system of discrete inner states (symbols), which are manipulated by a central processing unit (CPU). Sensory states serve as inputs to the system, providing the "data" for processing according to the

8. Harman's book does not wed LOT to pessimism and anti-pragmatism, and I am sympathetic to it.

rules, and motor operations serve as outputs. This view, called *classicism*, was the paradigm in the fields of artificial intelligence, computer science, and information-processing psychology until the 1980s, when the competing connectionist view also gained currency. LOT, as a species of classicism, grew out of this general trend in information-processing psychology to see the mind as a symbol-processing device. The classicist tradition stressed an analogy between cognition and digital computers while downplaying the relevance of neuroscience to understanding cognition. Even today, the symbol-processing approach is at the heart of information-processing psychology and philosophy of mind, being one of two leading computational theories of the nature of thought (the other being connectionism).

Now, let us ask: Why believe in the language of thought? The most important rationale for LOT derives from the following observation: any empirically adequate theory of mind must hold that cognitive operations are sensitive to the constituent structure of complex sentencelike representations (Fodor 1975; Fodor and Pylyshyn 1995; Marcus 2001). This observation has been regarded as strong evidence for a LOT architecture. Consider the sentence "The cappuccino in Italy is better than in China." Despite never hearing this sentence before, you are capable of understanding it. Thought is *productive*: in principle, you can entertain and produce an infinite number of distinct representations. How can you do this? Our brains have a limited storage capacity, so we can't possibly possess a mental phrase book in which the meaning of each sentence is encoded. The key is that the thoughts are built out of familiar constituents and combined according to rules. It is the *combinatorial* nature of thought that allows us to understand and produce these sentences on the basis of our antecedent knowledge of the grammar and atomic constituents (e.g., *China*, *Italy*). This allows for the construction of potentially infinitely many thoughts given a finite stock of primitive expressions (Chomsky 1975; Fodor 1975, 31; Fodor and Pylyshyn 1988, 116; Fodor 1985, 1987).

Relatedly, consider the phenomenon of systematicity. A representational system is *systematic* when the ability of the system to produce (or entertain) certain representations is intrinsically related to the ability to produce (or entertain) other representations (Fodor and Pylyshyn 1995, 120). Conceptual thought seems to be systematic; e.g., one doesn't find normal adult speakers who can produce "Mary loves John" without also being able to produce "John loves Mary." How can this fact be explained? Intuitively, "Mary loves John" is systematically related to "John loves Mary" because they have a common constituent structure. Once one knows how to generate a particular sentence out of primitive expressions, one can also generate many others that have the same primitives (Fodor 1987; Fodor and Pylyshyn 1988; Fodor and McLaughlin 1990).

Systematicity and productivity are commonly regarded as providing significant motivation for LOT. Whether any connectionist models can explain these important features of thought is currently very controversial (see, e.g., Fodor and Pylyshyn 1988; Fodor and McLaughlin 1990; Elman 1998; van Gelder 1990; Marcus 2001; Smolensky 1988, 1995). Connectionist models are networks of simple parallel computing elements with each element carrying a numerical activation value, which the network computes given the values of neighboring elements, or units, in the network, employing a formula. In very broad strokes, critics claim that a holistic pattern of activation doesn't seem to have the needed internal structure to account for these features of thought (Marcus 2001; Fodor and Pylyshyn 1988). Critics have argued that, at best, certain connectionist models would model how symbol structures are implemented in the brain; they cannot really represent genuine alternatives to the LOT picture, however (Fodor and Pylyshyn 1988). There is currently a lively debate between this "implementationalist" position and radical connectionism, a position that advances connectionism as a genuine alternative to the language of thought hypothesis.

Now let us turn to a more detailed discussion of LOT's fundamental claims. We've noted that LOT holds, first and foremost, that *thinking is the algorithmic manipulation of mental symbols*. This view, when fleshed out more fully, is generally taken to involve the following three claims.

(1) *Cognitive processes consist in causal sequences of tokenings of internal representations in the brain.*

Rational thought is said to be a matter of the causal sequencing of tokens—patterns of matter and energy—of representations that are realized in the brain. Rational thought is thereby describable as a physical process, and further, as we shall see below, as both a computational and a semantic process as well.

In addition:

(2) *These internal representations have a combinatorial syntax and semantics, and further, the symbol manipulations preserve the semantic properties of the thoughts* (Fodor 1975; Fodor and Pylyshyn 1988).

Although technically, the LOT hypothesis does not require that symbols have a semantics, in practice, that symbols have a semantics has, in effect, become part of many elaborations of LOT (but see Stich, 1994). This being said, claim (2) has three components:

(2a) *Combinatorial syntax.*

As noted, complex representations in the language of thought (e.g., #take the cat outside#) are built out of atomic symbols (e.g., #cat#), together with the grammar of the language of thought.

(2b) *Combinatorial semantics.*

The meaning or content of a LOT sentence is a function of the meanings of the atomic symbols, together with their grammar.

(2c) *Thinking, as a species of symbol manipulation, preserves the semantic properties of the thoughts involved* (Fodor 1975; Fodor and Pylyshyn 1988).

To better grasp (2c), consider the mental processing of an instance of *modus ponens*. The internal processing is purely syntactic; nonetheless, it respects semantic constraints. Given true premises, the application of the rule will result in further truths. The rules are truth preserving. John Haugeland employs the following motto to capture this phenomenon:

*Formalist Motto:* If you take care of the syntax of a representational system, the semantics will take care of itself (Haugeland 1989, 106).

    And finally:

(3) *Mental operations on internal representations are causally sensitive to the syntactic structure of the symbol* (Fodor and Pylyshyn 1988).

Computational operations work on any symbol/symbol string satisfying a certain structural description, transforming it into another symbol/symbol string that satisfies another structural description. For example, consider an operation in which the system recognizes any operation of the form (P&Q) and transforms it into a symbol of the form (P). Further, the underlying physical structures onto which the symbol structures are mapped are the very properties that cause the system to behave in the way it does (see Fodor and Pylyshyn 1988, Macdonald 1995, ch. 1; Marcus 2001, ch. 4; Smolensky 1988, 1995).[9]

Claims (1)–(3) are the primary tenets of the LOT position. Further, they underlie a view that is closely related to LOT, the aforementioned computational theory of mind (or "CTM").

*CTM*: Thinking is a computational process involving the manipulation of semantically interpretable strings of symbols, which are processed according to algorithms (Newell and Simon 1976; Fodor 1994; Pinker 1999; Rey 1997).

Steven Pinker nicely captures the gist of the manner in which (1)–(3) give rise to CTM:

Arrangements of matter . . . have both representational and causal properties, that is, . . . [they] simultaneously carry information about something and take part in a chain of physical events. Those events make up a computation, because the machinery was crafted so that if the interpretation of the symbols that trigger the machine is a true statement, then the interpretation of the symbols created by the machine is also a true statement. The Computational Theory of Mind is the hypothesis that intelligence is computation in this sense. (1999, 76)

This statement aptly connects the CTM hypothesis to the classic question, "How can rational thought be grounded in the brain?" According to LOT and CTM, rational thought is a matter of the causal sequencing of symbol tokens that are realized in the brain

---

9. It turns out that this feature of classical systems—that the constituents of mental representations are causally efficacious in computations—plays a significant role in the debate between LOT and connectionism, for in contrast to symbolic systems, connectionist systems do not operate on mental representations in a manner that is sensitive to their form.

(thesis 1). These symbols, which are ultimately just patterns of matter and energy, have both representational (thesis 2b) and causal properties (thesis 3). Further, the semantics mirrors the syntax (thesis 2c). This leaves us with the following picture of the nature of rational thought: thinking is a process of symbol manipulation in which the symbols have an appropriate syntax and semantics (roughly, natural interpretations in which the symbols systematically map to states in the world).

Advocates of LOT and CTM mine this account of the nature of rational thought in their attempt to solve an important puzzle about intentional phenomena. By *intentional phenomena* I mean a thought's "aboutness" or "directedness"—that it represents the world as being a certain way. Thought has long been suspected of being somehow categorically distinct from the physical world, being outside the realm that science investigates. For how is it that thoughts (e.g., the belief that the espresso is aromatic, the desire to drink Merlot), which, as we now know, arise from states of the brain, can be about, or directed at, entities in the world? In essence, advocates of LOT and CTM approach this question in a *naturalistic* way, trying to ground intentionality in the scientific world order. Now, I've already noted that symbols have a computational nature. As such, they are part of the scientific domain. But the proponent of LOT has a naturalistic story about the aboutness, or intentionality, of symbols as well: Symbols refer to, or pick out, entities in the world in virtue of their standing in a certain causal or nomic relationship to entities in the world. Simply put, the symbols are "locked onto" properties or individuals in virtue of standing in a certain nomic or causal relationship specified by a theory of meaning or mental content. So the intentionality of a thought is a matter of a nomic or causal, and ultimately physical, relationship between mental symbols and entities in the world.

This naturally brings me to the matter of LOT's standard line on semantics. I have just mentioned, somewhat vaguely, that the LOT program posits a "locking" relationship between symbols and referents. As it turns out, LOT's semantic side is multifaceted. Bearing in mind that Problem Three concerns the relationship between symbols and psychological generalizations sensitive to semantic properties, the reader may benefit from more detail.

Proponents of LOT are generally *externalists* about mental content, holding that thought content is not solely determined by one's internal states; instead, content depends upon entities in the world as well. Further, advocates of LOT often have a specific sort of externalist mental content in mind, *broad content*, which, as observed, is basically referential.[10] Why would one hold this unintuitive view? One reason is that individuals having different types of inner states—in the context of LOT, this amounts to different types of symbolic states—can nonetheless have thoughts with the same content. Content individuation becomes a species of the metaphysics of object and property individuation. To be sure, these are big ticket items in metaphysics, but every theory of meaning relies on a manner of individuating such entities in any case. Worries that content will be as idiosyncratic as thought threatens to be drop out of the picture. Different thinkers, and indeed, different kinds of minds, can, at least in principle, have thoughts that refer to the same entities.

10. Here I'm following Fodor's usage of "broad content" (Fodor 1994, 7). There is another usage in which it is taken as being synonymous with *wide content*.

I've mentioned that LOT's semantic story is multifaceted. In addition to appealing to broad content, the standard LOT adopts a related position called *neo-Russellianism*. According to neo-Russellianism, the proposition expressed by the sentence "Cicero is Tully" is an entity that consists in the relation of identity, the man, Cicero, and the man, Tully. Further, the sentence "Tully is Tully" expresses the same proposition. On this view, individuals are *literally* constituents of neo-Russellian propositions. As Bertrand Russell commented to Gottlob Frege, "Mont Blanc itself is a component part of what is actually asserted in the proposition 'Mont Blanc is more than 4000 meters high'" (Frege 1980, 169). Crucially, neo-Russellians hold that "believes" expresses a binary relation between agents and propositions. They therefore hold the surprising view that anyone who believes that Tully is Tully also believes that Cicero is Tully.[11] I explore neo-Russellianism in chapter 8; for now, observe that a LOT that is wedded to neo-Russellianism adopts the following claim about psychological explanation:

(PE) Sentences in one's language of thought that differ only in containing distinct primitive co-referring symbols (e.g.,

---

11. This view has also been called the *naïve theory*, *Russellianism* and *Millian-Russellianism*. By *neo-Russellianism*, I am of course not referring to Russell's other, descriptivist, account of names. Neo-Russellianism has been defended by (*inter alia*) David Braun, Keith Donnellan, David Kaplan, Ruth Marcus, John Perry, Mark Richard (in one incarnation, at least), Bertrand Russell, Nathan Salmon, Scott Soames, and Michael Thau. In addition to providing an account of proper names, neo-Russellians typically extend their account to other expression types. To keep matters simple, I focus on the case of proper names. For a helpful overview of neo-Russellianism and other theories of attitude ascription, see Richard (1990).

#Cicero#/#Tully#) are to be treated by intentional psychology as being type-identical and are thereby subsumable under all the same intentional laws (Fodor 1994).

The position sketched in these last paragraphs is often referred to as *referentialism*.[12]

Now, nothing in this book argues that referentialism, or even externalism, is correct, although I am sympathetic to these positions, at least when it comes to the content of thought. Again, the task of this book is to determine the scope and limits of the LOT program—to lay bare its key problems, to respond to them, and in the course of advancing these responses, to identify new contours to the intellectual landscape. In this vein, the third problem concerns whether referentialism is even compatible with LOT to begin with, for Frege cases suggest that LOT's neo-Russellian-inspired generalizations—that is, generalizations conforming to (PE)—face counterexamples and are thus not viable. If Frege cases cannot be solved, something is deeply wrong with LOT's current thinking about mental states.

## Discarding LOT?

I have now discussed the basic elements of the LOT program, including the family of doctrines that have come to be associated with the LOT position in its philosophical incarnation: naturalism, intentionality, neo-Russellianism, broad content, and more. Bearing all this in mind, recall our earlier discussion of the three problems that LOT faces. These problems threaten the very

12. In this book I reserve the expression "referentialism" for the neo-Russellian position, not the hidden indexical theory, although the hidden indexical view also appeals to broad content.

fabric of the LOT program: its drive to explain thinking computationally in terms of the manipulation of mental symbols deriving their meaning, or "aboutness," from nomic relations to the world. Surely if the cognitive mind is not even computational, if the very notion of a symbol is empty, or if its intentional generalizations have counterexamples, LOT should be discarded.

Perhaps the weight of these problems is simply too staggering. Given the prominence of connectionism, for instance, shouldn't the verdict be that we must finally put LOT to rest? There will be some who are eager to draw this conclusion; I suspect, however, that doing so would be premature. For one thing, cognitive science is increasingly making progress on higher cognitive function, and models of higher cognition seem to be precisely the terrain in which one would expect to see validation of the symbol-processing approach, if validation is to come. As connectionists Randall O'Reilly and Yuko Munakata admit in a recent computational neuroscience textbook, the symbolic approach to higher-level cognition has a "long history of successful models," for "in symbolic models, the relative ease of chaining together sequences of operations and performing arbitrary symbol binding makes it much more straightforward to simulate higher-level cognition than in a neural network." In contrast, "neural network models of higher-level cognition are in their relative infancy" (O'Reilly and Munakata 2000, 379). And although representation in the prefrontal cortex (PFC) is still poorly understood relative to many other brain regions, as they point out, representation in the PFC appears to be combinatorial and discrete. If this turns out to be correct, it would support an appeal to symbolic models to explain higher-level cognition (perhaps implemented by connectionist networks, perhaps not). The combinatorial and discrete representations of the PFC are distinct from the more distributed modality-specific representation of the posterior cortex; prima facie, this latter representation seems more straightforwardly amenable to traditional connectionist explanation.[13] And all this comes from the latest computational neuroscience textbook, not just from symbolicists like Fodor and Marcus.

Add to this the fact that the precise relationship between LOT and connectionism is extremely subtle. The proponent of LOT has an important rejoinder to the connectionist attempt to do without mental symbols: to the extent that the connectionist can explain the combinatorial nature of thought, then connectionist systems would, at best, merely provide models in which symbols are implemented in the cognitive mind. Such systems do not really represent genuine alternatives to the LOT picture. For the networks would ultimately be the lower-level implementations of symbolic processes. This view was briefly mentioned earlier; it is often called *implementational connectionism*.[14]

Further, our reflections shall have implications for philosophy of cognitive science more generally, bearing on the scope and limits of naturalistic approaches to the mind. For instance, any sort of theory of mind appealing to referentialism will likely face the third problem, which involves the presence of counterexamples to intentional generalizations. And although other approaches will not experience problems with the nature of mental *symbols*, similar issues with the individuation of mental states arise in the context of both narrow content and connectionism, and computationalists of any stripe face the kind of problems that motivated

13. For a discussion of the distinct processing in the PFC and posterior cortex, see O'Reilly and Munakata (2000, 214–219).
14. For discussion, see Fodor and Pylyshyn (1988), Pinker and Prince (1988), Marcus (2001).

Fodor to conclude that the cognitive mind is likely noncomputational (Churchland 2005; Fodor and LePore 1992; Fodor 2000).
These issues will not simply disappear on their own.

Hence, the insight that symbolicism is still central, even for
those who appreciate connectionism, is my point of departure.
Fortunately, I suspect that the problems before us can be solved,
and in what follows, I provide a synopsis of how the book shall
endeavor to do so.

## Overview of the Chapters

Making progress on important theoretical questions, such as that
of the nature of mind, involves discarding inadequate theories
as well as generating new, more plausible ones. This being said,
little reason remains for upholding a LOT framework while also
denying that conceptual thought is itself computational. Fodor
may be right: the central system may not be computational, but
then thought simply isn't symbolic. For this reason, chapters 2
and 3 aim to solve the first problem, setting aside Fodor's pessimistic concerns and developing a genuinely computational
approach to the central system.

Fodor's pessimism is motivated by two problems that are commonly known as the relevance and globality problems. Chapter
2 focuses on the relevance problem: the problem of if and how
humans determine what is relevant in a computational manner.
Fodor suggests that there is an absence of viable computational
approaches, indicating that the cognitive mind is likely noncomputational. I contend that a more fruitful way to proceed is
to assume that the presence of a relevance problem in humans
is not terribly different from relevance problems confronting
other computational systems. In the case of human cognition,

however, the "solution" is a matter of empirical investigation of the brain mechanisms underlying human searches. I then sketch the beginnings of a solution to the relevance problem that is based on the global workspace (GW) theory, a theory of consciousness that extends to higher cognitive function more generally, and that is well received in psychology, cognitive neuroscience, cognitive robotics, and philosophy.[15]

Chapter 2 then develops a positive account of the central system, outlining a computational theory that is based on the GW approach. I provide only an outline because the research I discuss is just now under development. Still, a distinctive element of this approach is that it frames a LOT that embraces work in cognitive and computational neuroscience to sharpen its understanding of the central system—in fact, as mentioned, I urge that LOT *must* pay close attention to neuroscience if it is to be a bona fide naturalistic theory. Further, I argue that the popular doctrine of multiple realizability should not discourage interest in neuroscience on the part of the proponent of LOT.

The defense of LOT from pessimistic worries continues into chapter 3, where Kirk Ludwig and I respond to Fodor's globality problem. *Global properties* are features of a sentence in the language of thought that depend on how the sentence interacts with a larger plan (i.e., a set of LOT sentences). Fodor believes that the fact that thinking is sensitive to such properties indicates that thought is noncomputational. In response, Ludwig and I argue that not only is Fodor's version of the globality problem self-defeating but other construals of the problem are also highly problematic.

15. The GW theory is also called the *global neuronal workspace theory*. Researchers in neuroscience often use this expression instead.

Chapters 4, 5, and 6 tackle the second problem, developing a theory of symbols and employing it to reshape LOT. I propose that symbol natures are a matter of the role they play in computation, and more specifically, they are determined by the symbol's *total computational role*—the role the symbol plays in the algorithm that is distinctive to the central system. I will call this position on symbol natures the *algorithmic view*. The algorithmic view is not new: in the past, both Fodor and Stich have appealed to it (Fodor 1994; Stich 1983). However, because both of their discussions were extremely brief, neither philosopher offered arguments for the position nor defended it from objections. And, as will become evident from my discussion of his objections to my proposal, Fodor came to repudiate it.[16] My case for the algorithmic view is twofold: first, chapter 4 identifies the central and commonly agreed upon philosophical functions that symbols are supposed to play and determines whether any competing conceptions do in fact fill these nonnegotiable roles. The answer is: none do.

Then, more positively, chapter 5 provides three arguments for the algorithmic view. Readers familiar with debates over functionalism about mental states are likely already concerned about the notorious problem of *publicity* that attaches to individuating mental states in terms of their total functional or computational roles. Indeed, both Fodor and Prinz have separately responded to the arguments I offer in chapter 5, employing an argument that I call the *publicity argument*, which contends that because symbols are determined by the role they play in one's entire cognitive economy, different individuals will not have symbols of the same type. For people differ in the memories and cognitive

16. Stich himself is no longer sympathetic to LOT.

abilities they possess—indeed, even the same person may do so at different times.[17] Generalizations that are sensitive to symbols will not then be "public": different individuals, or even the same individual at distinct times, will not satisfy the same generalizations (for a similar criticism, see Aydede 2000).

In chapter 6, I offer an extensive reply to this objection, as well as responding to related objections, and in doing so, I also illustrate how my theory of symbols reshapes LOT. Here, I develop LOT's approach to neo-Fregean modes of presentation, which LOT views as nonsemantic and, in particular, symbolic. And in chapter 7 I summon the algorithmic conception of symbols to devise a theory of concepts. *Pragmatic atomism* is a version of conceptual atomism that draws from both concept pragmatism and referentialism, believe it or not. I argue that pragmatic atomism is far superior to mainstream conceptual atomism, for it can satisfy more of the desiderata that many believe a theory of concepts should satisfy. This is due to the fact that pragmatic atomism introduces a much-needed psychological element to conceptual atomism.

Finally, chapter 8 turns to the third problem, the problem of Frege cases. When individuals lack certain knowledge that is relevant to the success of their behaviors, they can fail to behave as LOT's neo-Russellian-based intentional laws predict, for again, such laws are sensitive to broad contents and are insensitive to the particular ways in which the referents are represented. Critics suggest that Frege cases illustrate that psychological explanation must be sensitive to one's ways of conceiving things (Aydede

17. Fodor and Prinz separately offered this objection in personal correspondence and discussion. This issue is closely connected to debates concerning functional role theories of concept and content individuation (see, e.g., Fodor and LePore 1992, Fodor 2004).

and Aydede 1998; Aydede and Robbins 2001). In this chapter, I attempt to solve this problem, and in doing so, I put the algorithmic conception of symbols to work to further refine the LOT program's account of the causation of thought and behavior. I also provide some background on the relation between broad content and theories of belief ascription, such as neo-Russellianism and the hidden indexical theory; it is crucial that readers appreciate fully why Frege cases arise in the first place, and why solving them is important to many philosophical advocates of LOT.

I would be delighted if the discussion of Frege cases, together with the chapters on symbol individuation, proved useful to philosophers of language interested in the nature of propositional attitude ascription. The attitude ascription literature, as sophisticated as it is, tends to work against the backdrop of a rather impoverished conception of cognition in which vague discussions of "guises" and "tokens in belief boxes" are commonplace. As philosophers of language know, these expressions are fudge words that urgently need fleshing out. It is my hope that this book spells out these important ideas in the context of one influential theory of mind.

## Reconfiguring the Language of Thought Approach

This, then, is my game plan. Now assume for a moment that my budget of solutions *works*. One thing should be clear already: this reconfigured LOT aspires to explain the computational nature of the central system instead of holding the suicidal position that computationalism stops at the modules. Other results are equally significant. For example, LOT was developed in the absence of a theory of symbols, despite the ironic fact that LOT's key contention is that cognition just *is* the processing of symbols. On the other hand, the theory of symbols that I defend *reshapes* LOT. For if this book is correct, then LOT finally has a concrete theory of modes of presentation (or "MOPs"), as recall, LOT's MOPs are just symbols. Moreover, once symbols are individuated, computational theories can, at least in principle, better determine how proprietary entities (e.g., activation patterns) relate to symbolic processes. Further, the algorithmic view generates an improved version of conceptual atomism.

And now, I would like to offer a disclaimer. This book is obviously not intended to be a full treatment of current answers to the question, "If and how is the brain plausibly computational?" For instance, it does not treat the connectionist or dynamical approaches to cognition. But one must approach massive questions piecemeal: LOT is one influential approach to answering the question, so let's see if it is even a good approach. So what I offer you herein is an assessment of the scope and limits of the LOT program, including considerations for rethinking certain key issues that the program currently addresses. Thus, in lieu of a firm endorsement of LOT and CTM, I venture that, assuming the problems laid out herein can be tackled, the program offers an important and prima facie plausible proposal concerning the nature of conceptual thought. Of course, I happen to suspect that the solutions work and that this is indeed the present state of things; barring that, I am happy to write an exposé of the problems that LOT and CTM face. At the very least, it will inspire a new appreciation of the problem space. That's progress too.

# 2 The Central System as a Computational Engine

The language of thought program has a suicidal edge. For we have just observed that Jerry Fodor, of all people, has argued that although LOT will likely succeed in explaining modular processes, it will fail to explain the central system, the system responsible for our ability to integrate material across sensory divides and generate complex, creative thoughts. A fundamental characteristic of the central system is that it is *informationally unencapsulated*: its operations can draw from information from outside of the system, in addition to its inputs. And it is *domain general*, with inputs ranging over diverse subjects. The central system is the holy grail of cognitive science, for our ability to connect apparently unrelated concepts enables the creativity and flexibility of human thought. But according to Fodor, the holy grail is out of reach, for the central system is likely to be noncomputational (Fodor 1983, 2000, 2008). Cognitive scientists working on higher cognitive function should abandon their efforts. Research should be limited to the modules, which for Fodor rest at the sensory periphery (2000).[1]

1. Mainstream LOT contrasts the central system with the more domain-specific sort of processing that the "modules" engage in, where modules

Cognitive scientists who work in the symbol-processing tradition outside of philosophy would surely reject this pessimism,
but ironically, it has been influential within philosophy itself,
most likely because it comes from the most well-known proponent of LOT. I imagine this makes the standard LOT unattractive
to those philosophers with a more optimistic approach to what
cognitive science can achieve. Compared to connectionism, for
instance, the standard LOT is simply no fun, lacking an account
of that which it was originally most interested in explaining:
the computational format of higher thought itself. Abysmally, it
doesn't even strive for such an account.

In this chapter and the next, I overturn Fodorian pessimism,
developing a genuinely computational LOT. In doing so, I go over
to the dark side, embracing LOT's traditional enemies, cognitive

---

are understood as being (inter alia): (1) informationally encapsulated—
the module's internal operations cannot draw on information from
outside of that module, over and about the input to the module; (2)
fast—modules are able to perform a particular function very quickly; (3)
domain specific – modules get inputs of only a particular, restricted,
subject matter (e.g., only edges, only faces); (4) mandatory—the algorithms that the modules compute are automatically applied (Fodor
1983, 47–99). Fodor intends (1) to be an essential feature of modules but
stops short of saying whether features (2)–(4) are essential. He simply
says that a module has "most or all" of these features (p. 47).

It is important to note that the central system is not modular, on
Fodor's view, because, by definition, the central system is informationally unencapsulated. Fodor explains, "As Kant pointed out, something
in your head has to integrate all this stuff, and it's non-modular by definition" (e-mail correspondence, Aug. 2006). Herein, to keep things
clear, I will work with Fodor's rough definitions of a module and central
system. Many cognitive scientists have a looser definition of a module.
Nothing hangs on this; we could reframe the discussion in terms of a
weaker conception of a module.

and computational neuroscience. Although the standard LOT program views neuroscience as being ill suited to explaining the mind, this dismissive attitude is deeply mistaken. The brain is an excellent computational system to study—the best one I know of. But before I develop an alternative approach, because Fodor's pessimistic arguments have proven to be so influential in philosophical circles, I must put these arguments to rest. In broad strokes, the dialectical strategy of the next two chapters is the following: (1) negatively, I illustrate that Fodor's two arguments for pessimism are unsound; (2) employing insights from my response to one of Fodor's arguments, I outline a computational theory of the central system. I provide only an outline because the research on the central system is young. Still, the research is both exciting and impressive. In discussing it, I hope to encourage its further exploration by advocates of LOT. This, then, is how I shall attempt to solve the first of the three problems that I have identified.

In the first section of this chapter, I overview Fodor's two arguments, called the *globality argument* and the *relevance argument*. Section 2 provides a brief response to each and identifies an additional flaw with the globality argument. Then, section 3 responds to the globality argument as it is presented in Fodor's recent book, *LOT 2* (2008). As we'll see, the globality argument appearing in Fodor's *LOT 2* differs from the earlier formulation that appeared in *The Mind Doesn't Work That Way* (2000), so it is important to respond to it. (In the next chapter, Kirk Ludwig and I examine the 2000 version of the argument in detail, urging that it is self-refuting.) Then, in section 4 I argue that although the relevance problem is a serious research issue, its presence does not justify concluding that the central system is likely noncomputational. After highlighting some neuroscientific research on the central system that indicates that the mind is computational, I sketch the beginnings of a solution to the relevance problem that draws from the global workspace (GW) theory, a theory that is well received in psychology, cognitive neuroscience, cognitive robotics, and philosophy. I then outline a computational theory of the central system that is based on the GW theory. In section 5 I further explore the GW approach to centrality in the context of discussing the advantages that it has over the traditional characterization of the central system. In section 6 I argue that the LOT program's commitment to naturalism *requires* a computational, and neuroscientifically based, approach to centrality, and that further, the popular doctrine of multiple realizability does not suggest that the LOT program take a disinterested stance toward neuroscience. Finally, section 7 responds to an important objection.

Perhaps I should underscore how philosophically novel the present approach to LOT's central systems is. Although Bernard Baars and Murray Shanahan advance a solution to the relevance problem in their 2005 *Cognition* paper, their discussion concerns only the relevance problem. And they do not discuss the GW approach in the context of the larger constellation of philosophical issues surrounding LOT's central system. Further, although philosophers have appealed to the GW account as a computational account of consciousness, LOT's philosophical advocates have not employed the GW approach as the basis for a more up-to-date conception of LOT's central system.[2] I believe we have a

2.  Peter Carruthers appeals to the GW view at several points in his (2006) book, but the GW theory is not the basis of his account of massive modularity. And he distinguishes his view from the GW view in his (2003). To the best of my knowledge he is the only philosopher, besides myself, to discuss the GW approach within the context of LOT's central system.

significant scientific resource before us: an established approach that draws from the most current understanding of higher cognitive function. So I shall reject Fodor's dated conception of the central system in favor of its being a GW that is a pancortical structure managing inputs from the brain's multiple parallel nonconscious computational processes.[3] Contra the standard LOT, the brain does not have a central processor through which all cognitive processes are shuttled, for many computations do not meet the threshold for global activation. But some do: namely, those that are the focal point of deliberation and planning. LOT should draw from this research to put flesh on the bones of its skeletal central system.

We have a good deal to accomplish in this chapter. So let us begin.

## 1 Two Puzzles

Pessimism about centrality is based on the following two arguments:

(a) *The globality argument. Global properties* are properties of a LOT sentence that are supposed to be determined by the nature of the larger group of sentences that the sentence is entertained with. Consider, for instance, the LOT sentence *the espresso machine broke*. On the one hand, if you consider it in tandem with sentences about your plan to vacation in London next year, it will likely not alter the plan. On the other hand, if the sentence is entertained together with mental sentences that concern a plan to make espresso tomorrow morning, it will ruin the plan. The

---

3. Caveat: certain processes not in the GW at a given time are part of the central system as well; namely, those that are not modular (by Fodor's understanding of "module"); I save such details for Section 4.

role the sentence plays in computation is *context sensitive* then, depending upon what other mental sentences are under consideration. And the problem with LOT and CTM is that cognition, being computational, is sensitive only to the "syntax" of the particular mental representation. Syntactic properties are *context insensitive* properties of a mental representation. That is, what a mental representation's syntactic properties are does not depend on what the other mental representations in the plan happen to be. But whether a given mental representation has the global properties that it has will depend on the nature of the other sentences in the relevant group. If this is correct, then global properties do not supervene on syntactic properties. Hence, LOT and CTM are untenable as a general account of how the cognitive mind works (Fodor 2000, 23-26, 2008; Ludwig and Schneider 2008; Schneider 2009a; Horgan and Tienson 1996; Sperber 2005).[4]

(b) *The relevance argument.* Like many critics of the symbol-processing view, Fodor suspects that for a symbol-processing device to determine whether a given fact is relevant, the device would need to walk through virtually every item in its database. But "the totality of one's epistemic commitments is vastly too large a space to have to search" (Fodor 2000, 31). This would be a huge computational task, and it could not be accomplished

---

4. This statement of the problem is based on Fodor's most detailed discussion of the globality argument (Fodor 2000). Unfortunately, his discussions of this matter are somewhat obscure (Fodor 2000, 2008). As noted, chapter 3 shall provide an in-depth discussion of the argument as presented in his 2000; the rough argument of his 2008 is discussed in the present chapter. The statement of the globality argument in this chapter abstracts from certain details of Fodor's 2000 that will be discussed in chapter 3.

quickly enough for a system to act in real time (Shanahan and Baars 2005, 163; Fodor 2000, 31-37; 2008, 118-120; Dennett 1984, 129; Carruthers 2003, 505; Horgan and Tienson 1996, 40). However, humans clearly make quick decisions all the time about what is relevant. Yet it is doubtful that such determination can be made in real time if we suppose that humans compute in LOT. Hence, unencapsulated, domain general thought—the kind of thinking that the central system engages in—is likely noncomputational, at least when computation is understood symbolically.[5]

If these two arguments are correct, then they spell the end of the LOT program. For we've already observed that the central system is the primary domain that LOT characterizes. And LOT is supposed to be a computational theory, at least in its contemporary incarnation (Fodor, 1975; Harman 1973; Carruthers 2006). So, again, how can LOT even purport to characterize the central system if the central system is not, in fact, likely to be computational to begin with? And how can CTM be upheld?

Perhaps there is an escape route for LOT and CTM, however. Perhaps the central system is itself "massively modular", having numerous domain-specific modules within it (Carruthers 2005, 2006, 2008; Pinker 1997; Sperber 2005). The phenomena of globality and the problem of relevance do not warrant an appeal to massive modularity, however, even assuming the problems they

5. I will not refer to this problem as "the frame problem of AI," although Fodor calls it that (2000, 38; 2008, 118). It is not the same problem: it isn't formulated in the context of formal logic, and it doesn't specifically concern the noneffects of actions (Shanahan 2010; Shanahan and Baars 2005). For an extensive response to AI's frame problem, see Shanahan's book on this topic (1997).

pose are well founded. For globality and relevance problems can even apply to uncontroversially computational systems, including encapsulated domain-specific ones, as I urge in the following section. If (a) and (b) are sound arguments, they would, in fact, also have versions that apply to modules within a central system as well.

In essence, no matter what landscape you attribute to the central system, if (a) and (b) are sound, they rule out the plausibility of LOT and CTM. Clearly this is an important issue: If LOT is noncomputational, I suspect that few of its current proponents would be interested in it any longer. So are (a) and (b) indeed correct?

## 2 Flaws in Both Arguments

As it happens, both arguments possess multiple flaws. For one thing, neither is valid. Consider: what if one could show that both problems appear in the context of uncontroversially computational processes? Intuitively, if this could be accomplished, then the presence of a globality or relevance problem would not suggest that the system in question is likely to be noncomputational. So the conclusions of the respective arguments would not follow from the premises. Now, bearing in mind this observation, let us consider a simple chess-playing program. Suppose the human makes the first move of the game, moving a pawn one square forward. To respond, the program must determine which move to execute, given the information about what the previous move was.

But observe:

(i) *A globality problem emerges.* Suppose that there are two game strategies in the program's database, plans A and B, and the program must select the simplest one, given the first move. We can now formulate a globality problem, for the impact that the addition of the information about what the opponent's first move was on the simplicity of each of the two plans fails to supervene on the type identity of the string of symbols encoding the information about the opponent's first move. Instead, the impact of the addition of the string of symbols to the simplicity of each plan depends on the way that the string interacts with the other sentences in the plan. Thus, the processing of the chess program is not syntactic. So it is not computational. It thereby appears that a globality problem emerges even in the context of highly domain-specific and encapsulated computing. But if a globality problem can emerge in an uncontroversially computational process, it cannot be the case that the globality problem suggests that the system in question is likely noncomputational.

(ii) *A relevance problem emerges.* Skillful chess playing involves, among other things, the ability to select a move based on the projected outcome of the move as far into the future of the game as possible. Chess programmers routinely face the challenge of intractability, for massive combinatorial explosion threatens to make determining an optimal move extremely difficult, given the constraints of real time. Indeed, to quickly determine the best move, clever heuristics must be employed. This is precisely the issue of locating algorithms that best allow for the quick selection of a future move from the greatest possible projection of potential future configurations of the board (Marsland and Schaeffer 1990). And this is just the relevance problem, as Fodor and others have articulated it.

The situation is thus: both problems emerge at the level of relatively simple, modular, and uncontroversially computational processes that involve the rule-following manipulation of uninterpreted symbols. And if both problems can occur in the context of uncontroversially computational processes, the presence of a globality or relevance problem does not suggest that the system in question is likely noncomputational. And recall that this was the conclusion that was needed to undermine LOT and CTM.

Now let us briefly revisit the globality argument in particular. We have observed that the argument is not valid. Further, it has a flawed premise: the argument claims that because a mental representation has global properties, and such properties are context dependent, mental processing does not supervene on syntactic properties. But this is not the case. Suppose that a given LOT sentence is global, differing in the effect it has depending on the nature of the other sentences in the plan. Upon reflection, this is actually compatible with the requirement that syntax be context insensitive: that is, the requirement that tokens of the same symbol type will make the same syntactic contribution to every belief set that they figure in. The same mental sentence can do so, for all that a sentence contributes to a computation is its type identity, and this may have a different impact on different plans. The impact depends on the type identity of the added sentence, the type identity of the other sentences in the group, and the nature of the program. For instance, consider a situation in which one adds a new premise to an existing argument in first-order logic. Put into a different argument, the same premise may have a different impact: for instance, it may now bring about a contradiction. But the difference in impact, while not being a matter of the type identity of the premise alone, is still syntactic. For it depends on the type identity of the premise, together with the type identity of the other sentences in the argument, and the rules. Fodor has thereby failed to establish that global properties lead to a failure of mental properties to supervene on syntax.[6]

As mentioned, in the following chapter Kirk Ludwig and I provide an extensive response to the version of the globality argument appearing in Fodor's *The Mind Doesn't Work That Way* (2000), arguing that it is self-defeating. The version of the argument appearing in Fodor's (2000) is much like the globality argument stated above, although it has the added dimension of relying on a stipulative definition of simplicity, which, as we shall see, leads to the argument's demise, for the argument, given this definition, becomes self-refuting. Ludwig and I also examine alternative formulations of the argument along the lines of that which is stated above that are not self-defeating. These are found to also face deep problems. I believe that our discussion, when coupled with the considerations raised in this chapter, provides strong reason to reject the globality argument as stated above.

However, Fodor has recently reconsidered the globality problem in chapter 4 of his *LOT 2*. This discussion does not rely on a stipulative definition of simplicity but leaves simplicity intuitive.

6. We can further observe that massive modularity would not constitute an exit strategy if one did indeed find (a) and (b) compelling. For I've just noted that both problems apply even to modular, encapsulated systems. Indeed, as Fodor himself remarks, globality problems emerge even for a small number of beliefs (2008, 122). And concerning relevance determination, notice that domain-specific encapsulated systems, such as human facial recognition, have an astronomically large number of mental representations to sift through in real time. So if one is convinced that the phenomena of globality and relevance plague computational explanations of the central system, one cannot appeal to central modules as an escape strategy. However, as I argue herein, both problems are flawed to begin with.

And the argument, although somewhat rough, appears to be different from the above argument. So, in the spirit of leaving no stone unturned, let us briefly consider his remarks.

## 3    The Globality Argument of LOT 2

Fodor writes,

The Globality Problem is that I can't evaluate the overall simplicity of a belief system by summing the intrinsic simplicities of each of the beliefs that belongs to it. In fact, there is no such thing as the intrinsic simplicity of a belief. . . . Nothing local about representation—in particular, nothing about the formal relations between the representation and its constituent parts—determines how much I would complicate or (simplify) my current cognitive commitments if I were to endorse it.

Notice that unlike the problem of relevance, this sort of worry about locality holds even for the very small systems of belief. . . . Suppose that my sole belief is that P, but that I am now considering also endorsing either the belief that Q or the belief that R. What I therefore want to evaluate, if I'm to maximize simplicity overall, is whether P&Q is simpler than P&R. *But I can't do that by considering P, Q and R severally; the complexity of P&Q isn't a function of the simplicity of P and the simplicity of Q.* So the operations whereby I compute the simplicity of P&Q can't be local. (Fodor 2008, 122; italics mine)

Fodor's general point is relatively clear, although it may be difficult to appreciate in the context of a system that merely has the belief that P. He once remarked to me in conversation that the globality problem involves a common fallacy in reasoning in which one (say) mistakes the strength of an army for the mere addition of the strength of each of its members. Like army strength, simplicity is not additive: the simplicity of a plan is not a matter of the simplicity of each mental sentence. Nor is it the case that one's assessment of which of two plans is simpler, given the choice of the addition of a new LOT sentence, is determined only by the constituents of the two plans and the added sentences alone.

Nonetheless, the rough argument in the second passage is flawed, for it requires the following implicit premise: if LOT is true, then one's evaluation of the relative simplicity of P&Q and P&R is entirely determined by the simplicity of the constituents, P, Q, and R and the conjunction operator alone. And this premise radically underestimates the resources of the LOT/CTM position. To see this, consider a more realistic case than one in which a system has only the belief that P; consider the case of a normal adult. It is plausible that a judgment that the plan P&Q is simpler than P&R will involve other LOT sentences in one's database as well as P, Q, and R; for instance, those concerning one's means for carrying out the plans. In addition, individuals may employ heuristics for deciding which competing plans are simpler. (Such are, according to LOT, lines of code in the cognitive mind's "program.") That LOT holds that the cognitive mind processes symbols in accordance with a larger algorithm is uncontroversial. Notice that these additional elements are all local, syntactic features of mental processing, but they go beyond P, Q, R, and the conjunction operator.

For example, I (quite pathetically) find the proximity of coffee a deciding factor in adjudicating the simplicity of a travel plan. You, I hope, do not. But if the cognitive mind is symbolic, then this tendency to add beliefs about the proximity of caffeine to practically any plan I entertain can be explained in terms of the LOT sentences I happen to have and the algorithm that governs my cognitive system. Just as an estimate of the strength of an army requires additional principles beyond mere facts about the members—it requires organizational principles, for instance—so too the simplicity of a plan requires an appeal to more than just the type identity of its members and the conjunction operator. LOT obviously has more than this at its disposal.

Fodor will likely retort that the problem is how we select these other beliefs (e.g., the location of a Starbucks) as being relevant to the simplicity of the given plan. Here, it is important to bear in mind that the issue of what beliefs a system identifies as being relevant is a separate problem: in fact, it is the aforementioned relevance problem. Indeed, although Fodor conflates the two problems in *The Mind Doesn't Work That Way* (2000), he had distinguished them in his earlier *The Modularity of Mind* (1983). Here, he observes that the central system is characterized by two puzzling features:

*Being Quinean*: certain epistemic properties are defined over a larger set of attitudes. (1983, 107)
*Being Isotropic*: any member of an attitude set is potentially relevant to any other. (1983, 105)

The globality problem is a more detailed version of the problem that Quinean properties are said to pose for CTM. The concern is that there are global properties of belief that seem to be defined over a larger set of attitudes, and as such, they seem to depend on the nature of the other beliefs in the set. In contrast, isotropy concerns the relevance problem. Notice that the globality problem is an in principle objection to the success of CTM. If there are, in the relevant sense, global properties, cognition is supposed to fail to supervene on symbolic computations. In contrast, the relevance problem is not an in principle objection to CTM. The problem is not that properties relevant to cognition might not supervene on the syntax of mental representations; it is instead that the serial-based computing that CTM appears to rely on makes relevance determination too time consuming. The relevance problem is thereby an empirical puzzle rather than an in principle or a priori objection. It is not the sort of problem that, in contrast to the globality problem, would urge us to give up without further effort. Confusion of the two is dangerous, for it may lead either to seeing the globality problem as just an empirical problem, which it is not, or to seeing the relevance problem as an in principle difficulty that makes embarking on further empirical work futile.[7] Further, these observations indicate that the objector's response, which reframed the globality problem as one of relevance, is unwise, for they are separate problems. Conflating them may make the problems seem more difficult than they are, obscuring the possibility of a divide-and-conquer strategy that tries to solve each of the problems separately. This is the strategy taken herein.

Even setting aside the objector's conflation, the critic's concern that a problem of relevance arises does not, in fact, indicate that the cognitive mind is likely noncomputational, for, as I have already argued, Fodor's relevance problem is not valid. I shall now turn to a more in-depth response to it as well; importantly, this response will be summoned later in this chapter to outline the beginnings of a computational account of the central system. Our discussion begins by considering a response that Fodor and other pessimists may venture.

## 4   The Global Workspace Approach to the Central System

It is likely that Fodor will respond that cognitive science will fail to explain relevance determination in the central system, for the failures of AI during the 1970s and 1980s indicate that human relevance determination is likely noncomputational (Fodor 2000, 37–38). So let us ask: is this a viable justification

7. This is discussed in more detail in Ludwig and Schneider (2008). Fodor has recently acknowledged that they are distinct problems (Fodor 2008, 122).

for giving up the idea that the central system is computational? I believe that Fodor's apprehension derives from conflating certain issues, making the relevance problem appear to be a more serious obstacle to computationalism than it actually is. For the relevance problem that CTM faces can be distinguished from the one that AI faces in crucial ways. Consider what we might call the *AI challenge*:

*The AI challenge*:   Build computational systems that engage in domain-general, commonsense reasoning.

The relevance problem, as it relates to AI, is a challenge to engineer such a system. To solve the AI challenge, an actual system must be built. To merely solve the "CTM challenge," in contrast, one needs to illustrate that human domain-general thought is likely to be computational.

Cognitive science could discover the principles that humans use to decide what is relevant long before machines are built that do these things. We should look to these accounts, rather than to the classicist AI programs of the 1970s and 1980s, for the most up-to-date information about the computational basis of relevance. For after all, classical AI of the past borrowed little from concrete research on the brain, and indeed, far less information about the brain was available.[8] A further reason why the AI and CTM problems differ is that in AI, one might build a system that determines what is relevant that is nothing like a human brain. Technically, this would constitute a solution to the relevance problem for AI, but it would not solve the challenge for CTM. It

8. However, I suspect that in the near future, the development of AI will borrow heavily from, and proceed roughly in parallel with, empirical discoveries about human and nonhuman brains. There is currently a massive amount of interest in getting machines to compute algorithms describing actual brain processes. AI is booming again.

is thus crucial to keep the AI and CTM issues separate. Indeed, the history of failures of classical AI to build a system that decides what is relevant is daunting. These failures may wrongly encourage one to conclude that the brain is not computational. The problem that CTM faces is less overwhelming when it is separated from the AI problem.

So let us ask: what sort of considerations are needed for the relevance objection to the central system to succeed? Here, the pessimist needs to argue that cognitive science will likely fail to explain the underlying process that humans employ when they determine what is relevant. Merely gesturing at the history of AI will not suffice. It is doubtful that this can be illustrated, however. For advocates of the GW theory have offered a plausible outline of a solution to the relevance problem as it arises for CTM and LOT (Shanahan and Baars 2005). The GW theory is one of the most influential scientific theories of the workings of consciousness, entering into the undergraduate curriculum in cognitive psychology and being endorsed by numerous philosophers and scientists. Daniel Dennett, for instance, observes that "Theorists are converging from quite different quarters on a version of the global neuronal workspace model" (Dennett 2001). And Peter Carruthers remarks that it has "robust empirical evidence" in its favor (2006, 220).

The key idea behind the GW theory is that during a conscious effortful task, special workspace neurons become coactivated, creating representations in a global workspace that mobilize neurons from multiple brain processes and that are subject to regulation by attention neuromodulators and to selection by reward signals.[9] The representations in the workspace selectively

9. The workspace itself is not in a single location but is instead a pancortical system. The expression "workspace" is a bit misleading.

gate a subset of processor neurons in a top-down fashion. A representation selected by the GW remains active, insofar as it receives positive reward signals. If it is instead negatively evaluated, it can be updated or replaced via trial-and-error processing by another representation in the GW (Baars 2007; Shanahan and Baars 2005; Dehaene and Naccache 2001; Changeux and Michel 2004). The GW theory gains much of its support through experiments employing the method of contrastive analysis, an experimental paradigm that tests closely matched nonconscious and conscious conditions (Baars 2002, 2007) as well as computer models (Shanahan 2008b; Dahaene et al. 2003; Dehaene and Changeux 2005).

To appreciate the GW approach to the relevance problem, let us first consider the predicament that the standard LOT faces. Suppose that a classical system needs to make a relevance determination. The standard concern is that it must engage in serial computations that examine each member of a long list of alternatives, one by one (see figure 2.1). Assuming that the database is large, and knowing what we do about the speed of neural processing, it is difficult to grasp how a relevance determination can be made in real time.

Peripheral Processes (Modules)

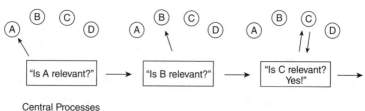

Central Processes

**Figure 2.1**
The standard LOT model of information flow in the central system. Reprinted from Shanahan and Baars (2005, 12).

Upon reflection, something is deeply wrong with the standard model: the view that all mental processing involving relevance determination is serial is outdated. Fodor is taking the computer metaphor too literally, regarding cognitive processing as being sequential, like the CPU in a standard computer (Fodor 1994, 109; 2000, 30-31, 105, note 3).[10] This is mistaken: although cognition, being upstream, involves integration across sensory divides, and certain conscious processing seems to be sequential, the brain (including much of cognition itself) is massively parallel, a feature of mental processing that cognitive scientists working in the symbol-processing tradition are well aware of.

In contrast to the outdated model of information flow that the standard model accepts, the GW view of relevance determination holds that a global workspace facilitates information exchange among multiple specialized unconscious processes. When there is a state of global activation in the workspace, information is broadcast back to the rest of the system (Baars 1988, 1997, 2007). At any given moment, there are multiple parallel processes going on in the brain that receive the "broadcast." Access to the global workspace is granted by an attentional mechanism and is then processed in a serial manner. (And this seems intuitive, as many of our conscious and deliberative thoughts seem to be serial.) So, when the brain asks what is relevant to a given fact, multiple unconscious processes search and compete

10. Cognitive scientists may suspect that I am setting up a strawman in claiming that Fodor holds that all cognitive processing is sequential. After all, who still believes this? But Fodor explicitly states that the relevance problem emerges because every fact in one's database must be considered sequentially (Fodor 2000, 31). Indeed, the Fodorian central system is commonly construed as sequential and CPU-like in the literature (e.g., Dennett 1991; Perry 1993, 312; Shanahan and Baars 2005).

for access to the global workspace. From the first-person perspective, the contents of the workspace seem to unfold serially, but each step is the result of massive parallel processing. Information may then be broadcast back to the specialist processes for further searching. As Murray Shanahan explains:

To my mind, one of the attractions of GW Theory is that there is no such central processor [CPU]. Rather, we find that high-level cognitive processes are the emergent product of a blend of serial and parallel processing. The serial procession of states in the global workspace can be thought of as the trace of a high-level cognitive process. But this serial procession of states . . . reflects the combined contributions of massively parallel competing and co-operating processes. (Shanahan, e-mail correspondence, January 2007)

Now, Baars and Shanahan's account is clearly intended to be an outline of an answer to the relevance problem, rather than a complete account. But bearing in mind the significant empirical support for GW, I suspect that their suggestion reflects, in very broad strokes, what the brain is doing. Couple this with the earlier observation that the relevance problem does not even involve a sound argument to begin with and we can see that it is far from clear how to justify the pessimist's extremely strong claim that work on the central system will likely fail to explain how humans determine relevance.

So let us press on with a positive, computational, approach to centrality.

## 5  An Alternative Approach to the Central System

In advancing this solution to the relevance problem, I have been taking a different methodological line than the standard LOT program does, one that frames the central system by reference to research in cognitive science rather than by features that set it apart from cognitive science altogether. In this section, I further explore this approach in the context of outlining two relative advantages that a GW-inspired approach brings to the table. Then, in the subsequent section, I argue that the LOT program's naturalism actually *demands* such an approach.

Before highlighting these advantages, a general observation. Contrary to Fodor's sense of the terrain, in which explanation in cognitive science stops at the modules, cognitive science suggests that the brain regions underlying what Fodor calls "the central system" are computational. Consider what brain regions correspond to the central system: again, LOT's central system is by definition the system that integrates material from different modules. By this rough definition, the central system extends beyond the prefrontal cortex to encompass the multimodal association areas that integrate material from multiple sensory modalities. It also encompasses the highly abstract and combinatorial processing of the hippocampus. Now, given this demarcation of the central system, it is worth appreciating that there is a fair amount of ongoing research on it. Concerning the association areas, in particular, agile computational theories of multimodal processes are under development (Spence and Driver 2004; Calvert, Spence, and Stein 2004). Indeed, according to Charles Spence and Jon Driver, in their introduction to a recent collection on multisensory processing, such processes are "increasingly being related to higher level mental processes (such as selective attention and/or awareness) rather than only being studied at the level of lower-level sensory interactions."[11]

11. Spence and Driver (2004, vii). See also Stein et al. in Spence and Driver (2004), for discussion of particular types of algorithms that multisensory neurons compute for transforming modality-specific inputs into a unified multisensory output.

There is also impressive work on the processing of certain parts of the hippocampus, even to the point of isolating combinatorial and discrete representations of concepts like [fear] and [nest] in hippocampal area CA1 in rats.[12] And consider the amazing work on neural connectivity by Olaf Sporns and his associates. By using diffusion brain-imaging techniques that allow for the noninvasive mapping of pathways of neural fibers, they constructed neural connection maps spanning the entire cortical surface. Computational analyses of the resulting large-scale brain connectivity networks revealed a "structural core" within the cortex: regions of cortex that are both highly central and connected. Brain regions within this core constitute connector "hubs" that link major structural (i.e., neuroanatomical) modules, including a module in the prefrontal cortex (Sporns et al. 2004). (Sporns and his associates, like many others, have a less restrictive notion of a "module" than Fodor does, in which a module need not be encapsulated. They are thereby describing what the proponent of LOT considers to be the central system.) These hubs are important to the development of the GW theory, as we shall see. Further, consider that neuroscience textbooks routinely discuss the six-layer structure of neocortical processing, differentiating the computational work that each of the neurons in these layers performs.

Now, cognitive scientists generally regard these bodies of research as constituting important computational work on what LOT considers to be the central system. Is the standard LOT suggesting that all this work is incorrect? Fodor often laments that we haven't a clue how the central system works. I am happy to concede that when it comes to higher cognitive function,

12. See, e.g., Lin, Osan, and Tsien (2005).

our understanding lags far behind our understanding of the modules. But this is due to the unavailability of animal models and sufficiently high-resolution brain imaging, as well as the fact that understanding such high-level processing requires the integration of computational accounts of processing at the relatively lower levels. Why is the relative scarcity of information supposed to show that the central system is noncomputational? Fodor hasn't explained—that is, he hasn't engaged with neuroscience on its own terms. In contrast, the new account of centrality draws from the GW theory, which itself draws from the latest scientific findings on higher cognitive function. Further, the new account features the following two advantages over the standard position.

First, it rejects an antiquated sense in which the brain is computational. I have noted that the standard LOT has said very little about the central system. To the extent that anything has been said at all, the central system is said to be CPU-like, or it is characterized by the properties *being isotropic* and *being Quinean* (Fodor 1986, 2000, 2008). Since these two properties are the very features that inspired the two arguments against computationalism about cognition, the central system was said to be, on the one hand, not even genuinely computational. Yet on the other hand, it was supposed to be like the CPU of a standard computer. This ambivalent approach to the central system is unilluminating. Ambivalence aside, to the extent that the standard LOT takes the central system to be computational at all, as noted, the central system is supposed be like a CPU, processing every state sequentially. In contrast, the new account draws from current cognitive science, rejecting this crude picture for an account of the computational nature of the central system in terms of a GW-based architecture.

Second, the GW-based account avoids the charge of homuncularism that arises for the Fodorian conception of the central
system. Explanation in cognitive science generally employs the
method of functional decomposition, a method that explains
a cognitive capacity by decomposing it into constituent parts,
specifying the causal relationships between the parts, and
then decomposing each part into further constituents, and so
on (Cummins 1975; Hatfield 2009). A common problem with
accounts of cognitive function is that they can be homuncular, positing a functional decomposition featuring a centralized
process that is a sort of central executive or cognitive command
center that turns out, upon reflection, to merely be the very cognitive phenomenon to be explained. In the case of explanations
of consciousness, for instance, the homunculus is the conscious
agent itself (Dennett and Kinsbourne 1995, 185). Such accounts
are obviously uninformative. Now, the standard LOT is a para-
digmatic homuncular theory, positing a mysterious central system that carries out cognitive tasks yet is itself not explained.
Indeed, Daniel Dennett subjects LOT's central system to the following attack in *Consciousness Explained*:

By giving this central facility so much to do, and so much non-modular
power with which to do it, Fodor turns his modules into very implausible agents, agents whose existence only makes sense in the company of
a Boss agent of ominous authority. . . . Since one of Fodor's main points
in describing modules has been to contrast their finite, comprehensible,
mindless mechanicity with the unlimited and inexplicable powers of
the nonmodular center, theorists who would otherwise be receptive to
at least most of his characterization of modules have tended to dismiss
his modules as fantasies of a crypto-Cartesian. (Dennett 1991, 261)

The standard LOT certainly invites such charges. Like Dennett's Cartesian Theater, there is a mysterious command center
in the brain where the contents from various sensory domains

(i.e., the modules) converge. How the integration occurs—how reasoning itself operates—is *terra incognita*. The central system has simply been an inexplicable epicenter, characterized by the mysterious features *being isotropic* and *being Quinean*.

LOT can do better than this. To begin with, notice that it is not the nonmodular nature of the central system, in and of itself, that makes LOT's central system homuncular—it is that there is no underlying explanation of cognition itself. A non-modular central system can in principle be computationally structured, consisting in algorithms discovered by an ultimate cognitive science; it can even be subject to further functional decomposition.[13] Bearing this in mind, how does the GW view of centrality banish the homunculus? The central system is not regarded as an inexplicable command center but a cortex-wide communications infrastructure that allows information in different regions of the brain to be broadcast pancortically by long-range pathways of white matter (Shanahan 2008a, 2008b). Stanislas Dehaene, Jean Pierre Changeux, and Lionel Naccache have been investigating the neurobiological implementation of the GW, providing a basic understanding of how the central system can be realized by underlying neural processes, rather than disappointingly terminating in a homunculus. As they explain, the research builds on Fodor's distinction between the vertical "modular faculties" and a distinct "isotropic central and horizontal system" capable of sharing information across modules (Dehaene and Changeux 2004; Dehaene and Naccache 2001). In particular, they have been investigating neurons with

13. Functional decomposition of the central system is possible even if its subprocesses themselves do not qualify as Fodorian modules. There just needs to be identifiable subcomponents standing in causal relations with each other.

long-range connections that play a role in multimodal, or central, thought (such neurons are pyramidal neurons of cortical layers II and III, among others). Such neurons are said to "break the modularity of the cortex by allowing many different processors to exchange information in a global and flexible manner" (Changeux and Michel 2004). Being distributed across the cortex, the long-range neurons physically integrate multiple processors by being able to receive signals from and send signals to homologous neurons in different cortical areas through long-range excitatory axons. The horizontal projections interconnect at distant areas in the same hemisphere and via the corpus callosum, across hemispheres.

This helps banish the homunculus. Indeed, the new conception of the central system is no less homuncular, and no more sequential, than Dennett's own position on consciousness. For at the very core of Dennett's theory of consciousness is an explicit appeal to GW theory as well (Dennett 2001; Schneider 2007). This is an intriguing convergence: that both a proponent and a critic of LOT can agree on the GW view is quite possible. The GW model itself is neutral concerning whether the format of thought is symbolic or connectionist. More specifically, although those working on the GW approach are often connectionists, that Shanahan and Baars have a paper with the key task of arguing for a resolution to the relevance problem within the classical computational approach to mind obviously indicates that they intend their approach to apply to the symbolic view as well.[14] (As these authors know, the format of thought issue is

14. Of course, Dennett famously rejects the symbolic conception, but that is a separate issue; the point is that the GW theory itself is compatible with both approaches.

very subtle, for as we noted in the introduction, some say certain connectionist networks implement symbolic representations.)

Now, the critic may react that I am overplaying the differences between the new and old LOT, as I too regard the processing of the central system as sequential, for the processing in the GW itself is sequential. And this may lead one to suspect that homuncularism is not really avoided. This point raises an important subtlety that can now be introduced, bearing in mind Fodor's division between the modules and the central system (1983; see note 1 of this chapter). On his view, the central system is by definition that which is nonmodular. And Fodorian modules, recall, are generally limited to the sensory periphery, such as sentence parsing and early vision (Fodor 1983; Carruthers 2007). All of cognition, on the other hand, is within the purview of the central system (Fodor 2000b, 496–497). This leaves us with a conception of the central system that is more extensive than just the GW. The central system also includes certain parallel processing that lies behind the workspace, competing for access into the workspace, where it would be the focus of deliberation, conscious activity, and planning. Such behind the scenes activities are normally considered to be nonmodular by the Fodorian tradition.

The upshot is that in contrast to the Fodorian LOT, which views the entire central system as a sequential processing device, I am suggesting a view of the central system in which sequential processing occurs in only part of the central system—the GW. (It is fair to say that the heart of the central system is the GW however, as it is the seat of our reasoning activities, and its contents are closely related to the contents of working memory and attention. It is the core of our conscious experience and intellectual lives. This is a key element of the traditional conception of a central system as well (Fodor 1983). My discussion has understandably focused on this core.) Further, unlike the CPU-based conception, the GW account ventures a more biologically realistic sense in which mental processing has a sequential aspect, and this sequential element itself promises to be cashed out in terms of its biological substrate.

These, then, are two important dimensions in which the new approach reshapes LOT's perspective on the central system. There is a more general methodological lesson here as well: LOT can and should be combined with the most recent neuroscientific innovations to update and sharpen its conception of the central system. For the first part of this chapter illustrates that globality and relevance concerns fail to undermine computationalism. Further, in doing so LOT rightly moves away from an account of the central system that was developed back in 1975, at a time when far less was known about higher cognitive function. By moving in this direction, LOT draws from the latest developments in cognitive science, diffuses homuncularism, and offers a superior, if initial, sense in which the central system computes.

## 6   Changing LOT's Attitude toward Neuroscience

Indeed, it is worth pausing to marvel over the philosophical LOT program's incredible lack of interest in the workings of the brain. While those working on the symbol-processing tradition in other subfields of cognitive science are keenly interested in the brain, philosophers working in the LOT tradition, with certain exceptions (Peter Carruthers, for one), have largely ignored neuroscience. Where might this disinterest, and even antagonism, toward neuroscience come from? I suspect that it is due to the influential position, inspired by Hilary Putnam, that mental properties are multiply realizable, and for this reason, their essence is not neural. It is likely also due to the closely related position that thought possesses a sort of explanatory autonomy over the lower-level details of its neural implementation. Indeed, you may be uncomfortable with my appeal to neuroscience for these very reasons.

I will not challenge the Putnam-inspired positions herein; I agree with the gist of them in any case. So let us assume that symbolic thought is multiply realizable by (say) both carbon-based and silicon-based systems, and that furthermore, symbolic explanations of the causation of thought and behavior do constitute an autonomous level of explanation. Even so, paying attention to the implementational-level details of symbolic processing is crucial to investigating issues of primary concern for LOT. For doing so helps determine whether the following commitments of the LOT approach are correct: (1) whether intentionality is naturalizable—a commitment that both the new and the standard LOT share; and, assuming you are on board with a cognitive science–oriented approach to centrality, (2) whether the GW theory correctly characterizes the central system, and if so, what the details of such an account are. I'll discuss each of these points in turn.

First, I've observed that LOT's naturalistic program contends that intentionality is a matter of a nomic or informational connection between symbolic representations in the brain and entities in the world. These symbolic representations are supposed to be grounded in neural structures that are themselves ultimately physical in nature. The question of whether symbolic representations are genuinely grounded in neural structures is of great import to LOT's naturalism. Now, in chapter 4, I will urge that LOT requires a plausible understanding of a mental symbol in order to answer this question, for to determine whether there are symbolic representations in the brain one must know what symbols are. And in chapters 5 and 6, I will defend a theory of the nature of symbols. Assuming that LOT does indeed arrive at a plausible conception of mental symbols, for LOT's naturalistic agenda to hold, symbols must ultimately be part of the domain that science investigates. It will not do to simply claim that thinking is symbolic. The relationship between symbolic structures and lower-level neural structures must be well understood: neural structures must be shown to realize symbolic manipulations.

Here, it is important to determine if any neurocomputational models of higher cognitive function truly implement symbolic processing, for if the ultimate neuroscientific theory of the workings of the cognitive mind does not connect with symbolic processing, then something's got to give: either the brain does not engage in symbolic processing, or LOT's naturalism fails, for science will not fully explain the workings of the mind. Clearly, LOT should be interested in determining whether either of these situations obtains. The upshot: LOT's naturalism requires the explanatory success of neuroscience. An antagonistic attitude toward neuroscience works against LOT's naturalistic program.

Second, engagement with work in neuroscience is required to further investigate the GW approach. Several intriguing bodies of research are of particular interest in refining the GW approach to the central system. For instance, the aforementioned ongoing brain-connectivity research by Olaf Sporns and his associates will likely add important detail to the GW theory. Scattered throughout the cortex, cortical wiring seems to possess features of a "small world network," which, in the present context, means that there are numerous specialized anatomically segregated regions that connect to each other via highly connected nodes called "hubs." Although cortical networks segregate into tightly coupled neighborhoods, due to short pathways linking hubs, information can quickly travel to different nodes in the network. Hubs and their pathways can thereby facilitate rapid connectivity to other specialized cortical regions and, when suitable conditions are met, be broadcast into the GW. Fascinatingly, due to the small world structure of cortical representation, any single representation is only about six or seven processing steps from any other. (Sporns, Honey, Kötter 2007; Sporns and Zwi 2004; Hagmann et al. 2008; Watts and Strogatz 1998; Shanahan 2008b). I anticipate future refinements to the GW approach in dialog with this research on hubs.[15]

Other important recent work on the GW theory includes the implementation of a GW architecture in a sophisticated artificial system based on our current understanding of human cognition (Franklin 2003b) as well as on Dahaenne, Michel, Naccache, and Changeux's aforementioned work, which is intended to provide detail on the biological underpinnings of the global workspace—a project that may bolster LOT's naturalism. As noted, they concentrate on special "workspace" neurons with long-distance axons that exchange signals in a fluid fashion, enabling the manipulation of information across the modules. This allows for the mobilization of various brain areas, bringing their contents to attention, working memory, and consciousness (Dahaenne and Changeux 2004; Dehaene and Naccache 2001; Changeux

15. Murray Shanahan has in fact recently developed a model of cognition in which certain minicolumns that form a type of hub node called a *workspace node* feature neurons that facilitate the flow of information into and out of the GW (2008a).

and Michel 2004). These long-range connections minimize the average path length in large-scale cortical networks, enabling integration between the aforementioned hubs.

So why ignore the brain? After all, it is the most efficient computer we've encountered. The symbol-manipulation view need not stand in opposition to neuroscience. Philosophers in the symbolic camp are making claims about the nature of mental processing—they should roll up their sleeves and engage with cognitive and computational neuroscience. In the spirit of this task, I have tried to better understand the workings of the central system by employing the GW theory rather than by following the mainstream LOT in relegating computationalism to the modules only. Given the immensity of the cognitive mind, this is only a humble beginning—a small piece of the cognitive puzzle—but I believe that it is a direction well worth investigating. And it is an improvement over the standard LOT to be sure.

## 7  Objection

It is now time to consider an important objection to my account of centrality. One might suspect that there is an underlying tension in my approach to the central system, for I appeal to a LOT framework, on the one hand, and a framework that draws heavily from neuroscience, on the other. In more detail: the GW theory is grounded in cognitive and computational neuroscience, and computational neuroscience, in particular, is connectionist through and through. Many working within the connectionist tradition have little interest in the symbol-processing approach. Given these considerations, if the new LOT is in fact willing to give neuroscience its due, why should it even purport to be the format of thought in the central system? For computational neuroscience does not itself seem to appeal to LOT. Why not see the central system as a sort of neural network, rather than as a symbol-processing engine?

It is easy to get caught up in the antagonistic atmosphere that surrounds debates over the format of thought within philosophical circles. LOT is not opposed to contemporary computational and cognitive neuroscience, or at least it should not be: instead, the symbolicist can be keenly interested in connectionism yet suggest that the ultimate computational neuroscience will likely need to be symbolic, at least in part (Schneider 2009b; Marcus 2001). For computational neuroscience to succeed in uncovering the workings of the neural basis of cognition, it will need to employ symbolic representations in its models. To see this, let us briefly consider the relationship between the symbolic conception and the neural network approach.

Advocates of LOT question whether purely connectionist models can fully explain the combinatorial and language-like nature of higher thought. They also point out that it is currently unclear how very simple models of isolated neural circuits are supposed to "come together" to give rise to a larger picture of how the mind works (Anderson 2007; Schneider 2009b). Further, as the introduction noted, models of higher cognition are the terrain in which one would expect to see validation of the symbol-processing view, for when it comes to higher-level cognition, the symbol-processing approach has a history of successful models—symbolic models excel in chaining together sequences of operations and performing arbitrary symbol binding (O'Reilly and Munakata 2000, 379). In contrast, recall that characterizing the sort of mental operations featured by the prefrontal cortex is a challenge to traditional connectionist explanation (O'Reilly and Munakata 2000).[16] So I would urge that both sides be modest. It is still very early in the game. LOT is still quite relevant, despite connectionist success stories. It may be wrong. But it may be right.

A further consideration to bear in mind is that, as noted, the relationship between LOT and connectionism is nuanced: proponents of LOT claim that insofar as the connectionist can explain the combinatorial and language-like nature of thought, then connectionist systems would merely yield models in which symbols are implemented in the cognitive mind (Fodor and Pylyshyn 1995; Pinker and Prince 1988; Marcus 2001). If connectionism and symbolicism represent genuine alternatives, then radical connectionism must be correct. But existing connectionist models of higher cognitive function are few, and there are persuasive arguments that putative radical connectionist models in fact make covert use of symbolic representations (Marcus 2001). So again, there is reason to look to the language of thought approach, even if one is sympathetic to connectionism.

The state of play is thus: the concerns about how connectionism can handle certain properties of the cognitive mind are quite serious.[17] If connectionist models ultimately fail to explain higher-level cognition, then there is reason to turn to the symbolic approach.[18] This may very well be the way that events

16. For discussion of this matter, see O'Reilly and Munakata (2000, 214–219).

17. Here I have in mind concerns detailed by, inter alia, Marcus (2001), Fodor and Pylyshyn (1995), and Fodor and McLaughlin (1990).

18. I am not leaving out dynamic systems approaches as an option—in practice, dynamical approaches are frequently employed by connectionist modelers and are assimilated into the connectionist program. As Scott Kelso remarked to me, there is not really a "dynamical systems theory" per se but a toolkit of resources that connectionists employ. (You may ask: are the items in the toolkit computational? How to define "computational" is of course the fodder for yet another book-length

unfold. On the other hand, should connectionism succeed in cognitive domains, then given an implementationalist framework, symbolicism is in business as well. (Indeed, connectionism strengthens symbolicism by supplying the neurocomputational basis of symbolic processing. As I've noted, such details bolster naturalism.) But things will likely not be this black and white. The cognitive mind may be a sort of hybrid system, consisting of certain neural circuits that compute according to connectionist principles, not satisfying symbolic operations at all (for instance, these circuits may lack representations that combine in language-like ways), while having other circuits that satisfy such operations. In fact, several connectionists actually adopt hybrid positions in which symbol-processing plays an important role (Wermter and Sun 2000). Many of these models employ connectionist networks to model sensory processes and then rely on symbol-processing models for the case of cognition, but perhaps even the cognitive mind will be a mix of different formats.

So we have observed that LOT can comfortably appeal to computational neuroscience. Unlike radical connectionism, LOT sees neuroscience as being at least partly symbolic. When it comes to the neural basis of cognition, for computational neuroscience to succeed in uncovering its workings, it will need to employ symbolic representations in its models.

## 8    Conclusion

The foregoing is only a sketch; as I've emphasized, higher thought is not terribly well understood. Yet we do see the outlines of the

project, but the short answer is yes, insofar as the context in which they are employed is a connectionist account of part or all of a cognitive or perceptual capacity. Further, they explain the relevant mental function using formal resources, i.e., differential and difference equations.)

biological underpinnings of what the LOT theorist would call the *central system*. And if you ask me, all this research is utterly fascinating. Too bad it has been largely ignored by the mainstream LOT program, the focus of which has instead been on arguments that prematurely conclude that the central system will likely defy computational explanation.

But this chapter has done something about this. Herein, I provided a comprehensive response to pessimism about centrality, setting aside the relevance and globality problems and establishing LOT as a genuinely computational theory. After distinguishing between the two problems, I observed that global properties are instantiated by uncontroversially computational systems, thereby showing that the presence of such features does not suggest that the central system is noncomputational. Using the example of a simple chess program, I also observed that relevance problems are routine challenges that even highly domain-specific computations face. Simply put, the brain has found, and programmers seek to find, judicious algorithms. Further, I noted that the globality problem has a flawed premise and responded to a slightly different version of the argument from Fodor's recent *LOT 2*.

Treating the relevance problem in more detail, I advanced a solution to the problem that appealed to the GW theory. Further, I urged that LOT take a more neuroscientifically based approach to the central system; indeed, LOT's naturalism requires it. After all, it would be perplexing if naturalistically inclined philosophers insisted that LOT was correct yet failed to integrate LOT with our scientific understanding of the neurobiological basis of thought. Neither multiple realizability nor the fact that computational neuroscience is generally connectionist speaks against an integrative approach. Then, drawing from a widely respected theory in the consciousness studies literature, I developed an account of LOT's central system as a pancortical network of long-range neurons responsible for the global activation of information throughout the brain's massively parallel subprocesses and for the bottom-up delivery of information from these low-level subprocesses to the attentional and working memory systems. The serial unfolding of events that we experience in our ordinary lives—put metaphorically, the world of experience as it shines forth under the illumination of the attentional spotlight—is underwritten by these massively parallel nonconscious computational processes in the brain. In sum: I've urged that the LOT program reject Fodorian pessimism and mine this research as it further unfolds, developing a genuinely computational picture of the central system.

There is one final task to accomplish before Fodor's pessimistic view of the central systems can be set aside, however. Recall that we have yet to address the globality problem of Fodor's *The Mind Doesn't Work that Way* in any detail. Pessimism about centrality is a central thread of Fodor's book, so it is important to respond to this discussion. In light of this, in the following chapter, Kirk Ludwig and I provide an extensive reply to it.

# 3 Jerry Fodor's Globality Challenge to the Computational Theory of Mind

Before us is the following puzzle. Cognition seems sensitive to global properties. Suppose you are in Rome, and you learn that tomorrow's ride to Florence has been canceled. Your belief that tomorrow's ride to Florence has been canceled may not complicate your plan to visit London next year, but it ruins your plan to visit the Uffizi the next day. The role a given belief plays in cognition is *context sensitive*, depending on the nature of the other mental sentences in a given plan. And the problem is that CTM holds that cognition, being computational, is sensitive only to the syntax of a mental representation, and syntactic properties are *context-insensitive* properties of mental representations. That is, what a mental representation's syntactic properties are does not depend on what the other mental representations are that are in the plan. But whether a given mental representation has the global properties that it has will depend on the nature of the mental representations in a given plan that the representation is being considered with.[1] If this is right, then global properties

1. Not *all* global properties are context sensitive. For example, belonging to a set of attitudes is a global property that every attitude carries with it from set to set. But evidently, many global properties will be context sensitive. And these will raise a problem for CTM if Fodor is

are not, and do not supervene on, syntactic properties. Thus, the pessimist concludes, cognition cannot be wholly explained in terms of computations defined over syntactic properties. So CTM cannot explain mental processing in the central system.

Chapter 2 offered a brief objection to this argument and responded to a version of the argument that appeared in Fodor's *LOT 2* (2008). In this chapter, we provide a detailed response to Fodor's longer discussion of the globality argument, which appeared in his *The Mind Doesn't Work That Way* (2000) (henceforth, *MDW*). This version of the argument differs from the rough argument above in matters of detail and substance; it is therefore natural that the pessimist would urge that the discussion of the globality argument in chapter 2 has failed to provide a sufficiently rich exegetical discussion of Fodor's globality argument, especially in light of the fact that it was treated extensively in his *MDW*. So herein we set ourselves this task, illustrating that this version of the argument, like the ones discussed earlier, is unsuccessful. Worse yet, this version is self-defeating.

Our discussion proceeds in the following manner. The first section outlines the notion of syntax that is relevant to Fodor's argument and explains why it must be construed as being context insensitive. Section 2 then explores Fodor's argument in more detail, providing a reconstruction from the text. This reconstruction follows Fodor in formulating the argument in terms of his example of a putatively context-sensitive property that is said to be relevant to cognition, *the simplicity of a belief* (roughly, the measure of a belief's contribution to how complicated or simple a theory or plan is). We then show that the argument has a false

---

right that some global properties that are context sensitive are relevant to cognition. It is these context-sensitive global properties that we are specifically concerned with.

premise, and, in particular, that the premise can be shown to be false using only definitions and assumptions Fodor himself has introduced and endorsed in the argument. The argument is, therefore, self-defeating.

In section 3, we consider whether Fodor has merely stated his argument infelicitously, and whether there is another, more successful, argument in the vicinity of the one we criticize. We offer one possibility that might be suggested by the text, showing that this version of the argument is also unsound. Then, in section 4, we consider whether the lesson generalizes to properties other than that of simplicity. We argue that in the end it is an empirical question whether there are properties relevant to cognition of the sort that Fodor thinks make trouble for CTM, but also that it is highly plausible that there are not.

## 1 Syntax and Context Insensitivity

Given that the globality problem pays careful attention to the notion of the syntax of a mental representation, it is crucial, at the outset, to explain the relevant sense in which computational properties are said to be "syntactic." Speaking of "LOT syntax" is a bit misleading because the operative notion is not the well-known sense of "syntax," which involves principles governing well-formed expressions. Although constituents in the language of thought combine to form thoughts in ways that are "syntactic" in this familiar sense, by *syntactic properties in the language of thought* philosophers of mind frequently mean

(i) grammatical properties of the vocabulary items, and

(ii) other properties that type individuate the vocabulary items.

Any notion of syntactic properties requires (ii) in addition to (i) for the following reason. Consider the case of the type individuation of primitive vocabulary items in LOT. Grammatical properties alone will not suffice for type individuating primitive symbols because any primitive vocabulary item having the same grammatical properties (e.g., *being a noun*) would be the same symbol. So there would be no way to distinguish between expressions that are grammatically the same but have different meanings or referents (e.g., *dog/tree*), or are different ways of representing the same referent (e.g., *Cicero/Tully*). As a result, LOT would have no chance of accounting for cognition computationally. Hence, (i) alone would not yield an adequate theory of primitive expressions in LOT.

Several proposals concern what features of a primitive vocabulary item, in addition to its grammatical category, should type individuate it. Indeed, this important issue is the topic of the subsequent chapter. However, deciding between the various views is not really the concern of the globality problem because on any of the existing proposals for individuating LOT syntax, Fodor's problem seems to emerge. This is because at the heart of the globality problem is a tension between a common requirement on any theory of LOT syntax—that syntactic types be context insensitive—and that there are cognitively relevant global (hence, context-sensitive) properties like simplicity. The problem can be put as follows. There are properties like the simplicity of a belief that are relevant to cognition and that are context sensitive because they are global. Syntax is not context sensitive. Therefore, cognition cannot be entirely a matter of computations defined over syntax.

Now, before developing the globality argument in further detail, we should ask: Why must syntax be context insensitive? For if syntax can be *context sensitive*, then there is no obstacle to simplicity supervening on syntax even if it is context sensitive, and the problem does not arise. So let us suppose that a sentence in LOT syntax is type individuated in part by the relations it has to the larger plan that it happens to figure in. Then we face the following dilemma: either mental representations are individuated independently of their syntactic type, so that the same mental representations may be parts of different systems of representations, or not. If they are, then generalizations over syntax will not capture generalizations over mental representations. For the syntactic type of a mental representation will change from one system to another, and there will be no generalizations in terms of syntax that capture what we are interested in, namely, what difference a given mental representation makes to mental processes of which it is a part. If mental representations are not individuated independently of their syntactic type, then, on this proposal, mental representations would not in general be shared between different sets of attitudes. This would have the *consequence* that generalizations over mental representations, so understood, would not capture the generalizations about mental process we are interested in because those are processes that can involve the same mental states in different plans, or groups of beliefs. For syntax to do the explanatory work it is supposed to do, it must not vary depending on the system of attitudes of which it is a part. It is necessary that the very same sentence of LOT can preserve its syntactic type through changes in a thinker's set of attitudes and be identified across different sets of attitudes.[2] LOT syntax must therefore be context insensitive. More

2. Indeed, this requirement is related to the publicity objection that arises for the theory of symbols defended in chapter 5. That conception of a symbol does not individuate a symbol with respect to the other items in the system's data set, however, let alone the particular items in a plan. It individuates a symbol with respect to the algorithm that describes the central system. This view of symbols does not in fact violate context insensitivity.

explicitly, the following is a requirement on LOT syntax if it is to do the explanatory work required of it:

*Context insensitivity* (CI):   The syntactic properties of a mental representation are invariant across contexts; that is, the properties that individuate an expression in the language of thought are independent of what plan a given symbol happens to figure in.

## 2   The Globality Argument in More Detail

It is crucial to grasp the precise way in which simplicity is supposed to present a challenge to CTM in the light of (CI). First, Fodor defines a notion of simplicity of a belief, for the purposes of the argument roughly sketched above, as follows:

The simplicity of a [belief is] whatever determines for any given theory that you add it to, how much it complicates (/simplifies) that theory (*MDW*, 26).

He then claims that if the simplicity of a belief is a context-insensitive feature of a mental representation, then, intuitively, it can only contribute to the simplicity of a theory by contributing a "constant increment (/decrement)" to the overall simplicity of a theory (p. 26). So, for a given sentence in the language of thought, *the overall contribution made by the simplicity property of the syntactic expression to each belief set must be the same.* But, Fodor continues, if this is so, then it seems that adding a belief to one set of attitudes cannot make a small difference to the simplicity of a plan, while adding the same belief (a belief of the same type) to another set of attitudes makes a significant difference to the simplicity of a different plan. And, unfortunately, this sort of thing happens all the time. So it seems that (CI) is violated on the assumption that the simplicity of a belief is a syntactic feature of it, or that simplicity supervenes on its syntactic properties.

Now we will put the above observations together with some basic facts in order to provide a more formal version of Fodor's argument:

The Globality Argument

1. A belief can contribute to the complexity/simplicity of a theory. [fact]

2. The complexity/simplicity of a theory is relevant to cognition. [fact]

3. What a belief contributes to the complexity/simplicity of a theory is relevant to cognition. [1, 2]

4. Def: "The simplicity of a [belief is] whatever determines for any given theory that you add it to, how much it complicates (/simplifies) that theory" (p. 26).

5. The simplicity of a belief is relevant to cognition. [3, 4]

6. If the computational theory of mind is true, then the simplicity of a belief must be a context-invariant feature of it.

7. If the simplicity of a belief is a context-invariant feature of it, then it can only contribute to the complexity of a theory by contributing a "constant increment (/decrement) to the overall simplicity of" the theory (p. 26).[3]

8. If adding a belief can contribute to the complexity of a theory only by contributing a constant increment or decrement, then adding a belief to one set of attitudes cannot make a minimal difference to the complexity of an agent's theory,

3. This is weaker than the claim Fodor makes, which is a biconditional. We need only the left-to-right direction for the argument.

while adding the same belief (a belief of the same type) to another set of attitudes makes a significant difference to the complexity of the agent's theory.

9. However, adding a belief to one set of attitudes can make a minimal difference to the complexity of an agent's theory, while adding the same belief to another set of attitudes makes a significant difference to the complexity of an agent's theory.

10. Therefore, CTM is false. [6–9]

Before we evaluate this argument, we want to make a few remarks about its general character. This is what might be called a classic "armchair argument." It purports to establish its conclusion on the basis of general considerations available to anyone on reflection—from the armchair. An armchair argument is not necessary purely a priori, that is, it does not necessarily rely only on purely a priori premises, though it often involves a priori elements together with what are taken to be obvious facts. In this argument, the underived premises are 1, 2, 4 and 6–9. Premises 1 and 2 are taken to be obvious facts, and indeed may plausibly be claimed to be conceptual truths about beliefs, and 4 is definitional in character, but it is a reference-fixing definition rather than a concept-giving definition. It fixes the denotation of "the simplicity of a belief" as the property that is the denotation of a certain description. It stipulates what, if anything, "the simplicity of a belief" should refer to, and Fodor appears to entertain no doubts about whether it could fail to refer. Premise 6 is a priori because it just draws out a consequence of CTM, and 7 is a crucial premise. What is its status? It is introduced in the text as if it is obvious. It is not a premise derived from an induction on the failure of CTM, because it is a premise in an argument for the conclusion that CTM must fail. Nor is it presented as derived from a more general principle that has been inductively supported. It appears therefore to be presented to us as a premise that can be known a priori. Premise 8 is clearly a priori, and 9 has the same status as 1 and 2. The argument as a whole, then, is presented as largely a priori. The question whether it is purely a priori hinges on whether 1, 2, and 9 are a priori, and whether "the simplicity of a belief" can be known a priori to refer given the definition. They are, in any case, clearly taken to be obvious or nearly self-evident truths. The argument looks to be presented, then, as an in principle challenge to CTM, and that is what we take it to be. It is thus a very significant objection, for prior to any further empirical investigation, it purports to tell cognitive science that it cannot offer a classical computational theory of the central system.

Fodor would object to characterizing the argument as aspiring to be a priori or largely a priori because he follows Quine in rejecting the analytic/synthetic distinction, and, along with this, the a priori/a posteriori distinction. However, even for a Quinean, there is a distinction between arguments that draw on assumptions central to the web of belief, like the law of noncontradiction, and ones that do not. Those that do have the character of in principle arguments, and we might call them "in principle" arguments. It is, then, for a Quinean, presented as an "in principle" argument, as opposed to an in principle argument. However, this will have no practical effect on the style of evaluation that is appropriate, or its practical significance if it is correct.

We have dwelt on the character of the argument because Fodor sometimes presents himself, in his framing remarks, as merely pointing out a pattern of failure in attempts to understand the mind computationally. For example, in the introduction to *The Mind Doesn't Work That Way* (p. 6), he writes:

Over the last forty years or so, we've been putting questions about cognitive processes to Nature, and Nature has been replying with interpretable indications of the scope and limits of the computational theory of the cognitive mind. The resultant pattern is broadly intelligible; so, at least, I am going to claim.[4]

We are going to evaluate the argument as an in principle (or "in principle"—henceforth we omit the qualification) argument against CTM. If it is meant merely as a kind of induction on the failure of attempts to get a handle on how beliefs contribute to such properties of systems of beliefs as their simplicity, then responding to it as an in principle argument would be mistaken. However, when we get to the details of the globality argument, it is clear that the argument is not a matter of drawing attention to repeated failures to come to grips with how simplicity and complexity of theories figure in cognition. Rather, the observations appealed to can be put in the form of a deductive argument, the premises of which are introduced as if they were obvious independently of any detailed information about the history of attempts to make the CTM work, and, indeed, the central premise is introduced in the fashion in which one normally introduces an assumption that is self-evident, like the law of noncontradiction. Notwithstanding Fodor's framing remarks, then, the globality argument is appropriately taken as an in principle argument against CTM. The framing remarks can be interpreted in the following fashion. First, a Quinean would regard all these arguments as broadly a posteriori, even if some are relatively more a priori than others, and so any conclusion we reach

4. Also, in his "Reply to Steven Pinker 'So How *Does* the Mind Work?'" Fodor says, "TMD offers a diagnosis of a pattern of failures whose self-evidence it takes to be glaring" (2005, 25), suggesting the argument he mounts is inductive.

can be construed as in a sense something that Nature teaches us. Second, the framing remarks refer not to the specific, and crucial, argument we focus on in this chapter, but to the larger argument of *MDW*, in which Fodor considers the relevance problem, which has been distinguished from the globality problem in the previous chapter, for which the pattern of failure remark would be appropriate.

We now turn to our evaluation of the globality argument. The argument begins with some basic, obvious, and perhaps conceptually grounded facts: (1), beliefs contribute to the complexity or simplicity of plans; (2) the complexity or simplicity of plans is relevant to cognition. We regard these as obvious. A further obvious conclusion of (1) and (2) is that what a belief contributes to the simplicity of a plan is relevant to cognition. The argument then relies on Fodor's definition of simplicity of belief for the purposes of the argument. We then draw the conclusion that simplicity, understood in this way, is relevant to cognition. So far, so good. Premise 6 says that if CTM is true, simplicity must be context invariant. As argued above, this must be so. So if simplicity is not context insensitive, it cannot supervene on syntactic properties.

But now we arrive at what we believe is a false premise: 7. Here, Fodor seems to think that a given sentence in LOT must contribute a constant increment or decrement, or the same overall result, to every belief set. That is, a given sentence must result in the same increase or decrease in the overall simplicity of a plan, no matter what plan is involved. This is incorrect, however, because a *constant result* is not required by context insensitivity. *Only a constant contribution is.* A LOT expression may make the same contribution to any attitude set, where the contribution is simply its syntax. So (CI) is satisfied. But the same mental representation may differ in its effect, depending on the context or nature of the other beliefs in the set. In other words, the contribution may be constant while the interaction effect is not, since that depends on its interaction with the constant contributions of the other different elements it is combined with. To see this, let us reconsider premise 7. However, this time, let us substitute Fodor's definition of "simplicity":

7.* If the property of a belief that determines for any given theory that you add it to how much it complicates (/simplifies) that theory is a context-invariant feature of it, then it can only contribute to the complexity of a theory by contributing a constant increment or decrement.

When we put in the definition, whatever prima facie appeal the premise had dissipates, and for good reason. For clearly there can be intrinsic features of things that when added to some systems have a small effect on certain global properties, but that when added to others have a significant effect. Adding a small amount of mass, say, a gram, to the Moon will not have much effect on its size. But adding the same amount of mass to a star that is on the brink of collapsing in on itself due to its mass may have an enormous effect on its size. So the size of some systems may be minimally affected by the addition of a quantity of mass, while the same quantity significantly affects the size of others. (Indeed, chaos theory is based on related phenomena: e.g., the falling of a tree would not generally have much effect on weather patterns in a far-away region, but it is not out of the question that in certain conditions, it would have a significant effect.)

Part of what makes premise 7 seem plausible, to the extent that it is, is the introduction of the term "simplicity of a belief." For this suggests that we are thinking of a measure of this simplicity taken by itself. And thinking about that, it may seem puzzling how any intuitively reasonable conception of the simplicity of a belief could contribute in any other way than incrementally to the simplicity or complexity of a theory. It makes it look as if we were discussing a property of a system like mass, and the contributions of the same sort of property of its parts to that global property of it, where the contributions of the masses of the elements is additive. That is why substituting the definition changes the premise from one that looks at least plausible to one that looks, to say the least, dubious.

Fodor's globality argument employs a definition of the simplicity of a belief as whatever property of it determines for any given theory how much it complicates that theory. This is a technical term. It is not supposed to express any intuitive notion of the simplicity of a belief taken by itself. Indeed, it is clear that its definition rules this out. The parallel case in our example is defining the size of a quantity of mass as whatever property of it determines how it contributes to the size of any object to which it is added. Clearly, it doesn't follow that the contribution to the size of an object must be incremental, and clearly the property so defined has nothing to do with the ordinary notion of the size of something.

But even more significantly, if we consider how *simplicity* was defined, we can see that it is guaranteed to be a context invariant property that also does the right job. As Fodor writes:

The simplicity of a [belief is] whatever determines for any given theory that you add it to, how much it complicates (/simplifies) that theory. (*MDW*, 26)

Rewriting this to make it clearer (and taking a theory to be a set of beliefs):

The simplicity of a belief B = the property P of B such that for any theory T, and any change in complexity R, if R is the change in the complexity of T on adding B to it, then that B has P determines that the change in complexity of T on adding B to it is R.

This is clearly not a property of B that changes depending on what theory it is embedded in: by definition, in fact, it is not, because it is defined in terms of what effect B's having P has on the change of complexity of any theory to which it is added. This requires P to be a property B possesses *independently* of what belief set it is a member of. Thus, the definition of the simplicity of a belief rules out that it is, in Fodor's terms, a context-sensitive property. Thus, in the light of premise 9, we can deduce that 7*, and hence 7, is false. Thus, Fodor's own definition of the simplicity of a belief and other premises of his argument show that the central premise of the argument dealing with the contribution of the simplicity of a belief to the simplicity of a theory to which it is added is false. The globality argument of Fodor's *MDW* is therefore self-defeating.

### 3  The Revised Globality Argument

The problem we have identified hinges on the manner in which Fodor introduces the term "simplicity of a belief." Given the definition, the simplicity of a belief is guaranteed to be a context-insensitive property of it which also does the right job. It is reasonable to ask whether this is really what Fodor intended. That is, does our criticism of Fodor's challenge rest on taking advantage of a careless formulation? The definition itself cannot, we think, be read in a way that does not result in "the simplicity of a belief" picking out a context-insensitive property. For the phrase introduced is a definite description, and it is meant to be read as "the degree of simplicity of a given belief." Fixing the belief, there can be only one degree of simplicity for it, absent any further relativization, and none is provided.

We might try to introduce at this point a different definition of simplicity that would avoid this problem. However, it will be more profitable, we think, to consider whether we can construct an alternative argument from considerations in the text leading up to the official argument. We noted above that premise seven appears more plausible if we suppose that the simplicity of a belief is a determinate of the same determinable as that we apply to a theory or plan in calling it simple or complex, that is, if we assume that relevant property of a belief is being simple to a certain degree in the same sense in which a theory or plan is simple to a certain degree. As we have pointed out, the way that Fodor fixes what property the "simplicity of a belief" refers to does not at all require that this be so. It might be thought, however, that whatever property of a belief would contribute to the simplicity or complexity of a theory to which it was added would be a determinate of the same determinable that theories or plans have when we call them simple. In the paragraph prior to that, in which he gives the definition of "simplicity of a thought," Fodor entertains a simple model of what an intrinsic syntactic measure a mental representation's simplicity might come to: "as it might be, the number of [primitive] constituent representations it contains" (*MDW*, 26). The same measure might then be applied to a system of representations. On this model, the contribution of a belief to the simplicity of a system to which it belongs would be additive. In *MDW*, Fodor points out that this would not account for the fact that the same belief may complicate one plan and simplify another. Thus, *number of primitive constituents* cannot be the syntactic property that simplicity of a theory or plan supervenes on. In this book, Fodor rightly does not suggest that this is the only way to think of what syntactic properties of a sentence of LOT that might determine what they contribute to the simplicity of a system of which they are a part. There is no reason why we should not appeal to the "logical form" of LOT sentences and what type individuates particular symbols in explaining how a LOT sentence contributes to the simplicity of theories or plans. This is the reason Fodor goes on to give a general argument, which doesn't depend on this model, for the conclusion that the syntax of mental representations cannot account for their contribution to the simplicity of systems to which they are added. Yet, it might be suggested that he is still assuming that a belief contributes to the simplicity of theories or plans by way of having a degree of simplicity of the same sort as the degree of simplicity of the plans or theories to which it contributes, and that this is what underwrites the assumption that whatever syntactic (or other context-insensitive) property that degree of simplicity supposedly supervenes on would have to contribute a constant increment or decrement.

Can we use these assumptions to provide a sound argument for the context sensitivity of what a belief contributes to the complexity or simplicity of a theory? If we can, then there will be considerations in the immediate vicinity of the official argument that can be marshaled for the conclusion, and Fodor's charge that CTM cannot serve as a general account of how the mind works will be vindicated. The official argument may then be seen as an unfortunate misstatement of the underlying considerations that make trouble for CTM. The two assumptions around which we need to construct the argument are, first, that beliefs (thoughts) contribute to the simplicity or complexity of theories or plans by way of a degree of simplicity of the same type as the theories or plans have, and, second, if the property of an element and the property of a system to which it is added are determinants of the same determinable, then the contribution is additive. If we combine this with the observation that if CTM is true, the degree of simplicity of a thought must supervene on its syntax, we get the conclusion that beliefs must contribute a constant increment or decrement to any theory to which they are added. More formally:

The Revised Globality Argument

1. A belief can contribute to the complexity/simplicity of a theory. [fact]

2. The complexity/simplicity of a theory is relevant to cognition. [fact]

3. What a belief contributes to the complexity/simplicity of a theory is relevant to cognition. [1, 2]

4. If a belief contributes to the complexity/simplicity of a theory, then it does so by way of having a degree of simplicity of the same sort as the degree of simplicity the theory has.

5. If the property of an element and the property of a system to which it is added are determinants of the same determinable, then the contribution of that property of the element to that property of a system to which it is added is additive.

6. What a belief contributes to the complexity/simplicity of a theory is additive. [4, 5]

7. If the computational theory of mind is true, then what a belief contributes to the complexity/simplicity of a theory must be a context-invariant property of it. [CTM, 3]

8. If the computational theory of mind is true, then what a belief contributes to the simplicity of a theory is always a constant increment/decrement. [6, 7]

9. If a belief can only contribute to the complexity of a theory by contributing a constant increment or decrement, then

adding a belief to one set of attitudes cannot make a minimal difference to the complexity of an agent's theory, while adding the same belief (a belief of the same type) to another set of attitudes makes a significant difference to the complexity of the agent's theory.

10. However, adding a belief to one set of attitudes can make a minimal difference to the complexity of an agent's theory, while adding the same belief to another set of attitudes makes a significant difference to the complexity of an agent's theory.

11. Therefore, CTM is false. [8–10]

Unlike the official argument, this argument is not self-defeating. However, we can show that, like the official argument, it is unsound. Our main objection is to premise five. But prior to explaining that, we wish to raise two questions about premise four.

The first is whether there is indeed an appropriate notion of simplicity that applies to both beliefs and theories or plans or reasoning indifferently. This is a presupposition of premise 4. If there is not, then in light of premise 1, premise 4 cannot be true. It is not clear that a belief that it is windy, for example, is simple or complex in the same sense in which a plan or a deliberative process to which it is added is simple or complex. What makes for complexity in planning depends both on what one aims at and on what one believes about the world, particularly about the means to ends available to one. The measure of complexity might be the number of independent steps that one must take to reach one's goal. There is no analog to this in a belief considered by itself. Beliefs don't involve steps or goals. Perhaps in the case of beliefs and theories (here a set of beliefs), it may be argued that the same notion of simplicity applies, because a set of beliefs in certain propositions is equivalent to a belief in the conjunction of those propositions. However, this is not true, for beliefs in propositions come in different degrees. And this affects how we adjust what we believe when we acquire a new belief. To hold onto a particular belief in light of a new observation, one may have to complicate one's theory considerably. If the degree of belief in it is high, then one's theory must be complicated; if it is low, it may be discarded. So the degree of belief matters to the effect new beliefs have, and a system of beliefs is not equivalent to a belief in the conjunction of the propositions believed. Further, this additional element that plays a role in assessing the simplicity in theories, the relative strengths of beliefs, has no applicability in the case of a single belief. We do not mean to settle the issue of whether the same notion applies to beliefs and systems of which they are components. To do this, we would need to provide clear and intuitively adequate accounts of the notions of simplicity that apply to theories, plans, deliberation, reasoning, and individual attitudes. Our goal here is to draw attention to the nonobviousness of this presupposition of premise 4, and to what would be needed to establish it. Fodor does not provide any analysis of the target notion of simplicity or complexity. In the absence of that, one cannot establish 4, and there are, as we have indicated, some prima facie reasons to doubt that the presupposition is true.

The second question about premise 4 is whether, even if there is a notion that applies to both, we must think of the way a belief contributes to the complexity or simplicity of a theory or plan as going wholly by way of the corresponding measure of the belief. Let us recur to our earlier example involving the addition of some mass to an object. The size of the object added may be relevant to the resulting size of the system to which it is added. But as our example shows, other features of it may be relevant to the resulting size as well (namely, mass), even though there is a single determinable that applies both to the added component and to the whole. It does not follow, simply from the fact that the notion of a degree of F-ness applies both to a component and to a system, that only the degree of F-ness of the component can contribute to the degree of F-ness of the system. If there is something special about simplicity in this regard, it remains unclear what it would be, and it would require clarification of what notion is at issue prior to further argument.

Our main objection, however, is to premise 5, which is demonstratively false. This can be shown with a simple counterexample, illustrated in figure 3.1. In this model, elements are squares, and systems are combinations of squares. The simplicity (S) of an element or complex is measured by the number of sides it has. The fewer the number of sides, the simpler it is. In scenarios (A) and (B), the elements have the same degree of complexity, namely, 4. The system to which the element is added in scenario (A) has a degree of simplicity of 6 prior to the addition of the element to it, and only 4 afterward. In contrast, in scenario (B), while the element has the same degree of simplicity, the system does not decrease in complexity when the element is added to it, but increases in complexity. This is a function of both the number of sides of the elements and complexes and the way they are combined. This feature of the example may be thought of as analogous to whether a mental representation is tokened in the belief box, desire box, etc. More complicated dynamical models showing the same thing are possible. Yet this simple example is enough to show that even when the same degree concept applies to components and the system, the components need not contribute additively to the relevant property of the system. Premise 5 above, which is required to resurrect Fodor's argument along the lines suggested above, is false, and the argument is therefore unsound.

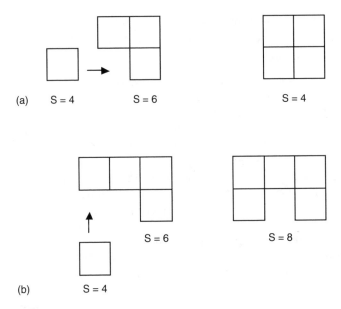

(a)    S = 4            S = 6                    S = 4

(b)         S = 4

**Figure 3.1**
Counterexample to premise 5.

## 4   Beyond Simplicity

Our discussion thus far has focused on the case of simplicity, as it is the example that Fodor develops throughout his own discussion. But there are other properties that are said to be global.[5] So are there reasons to think that any candidate for a cognitively relevant global property will turn out, on closer examination, to fare better than simplicity of belief? As a first step toward

5. Fodor briefly discusses "conservatism," which he characterizes as "how much it would cost to abandon a belief," saying that this feature of a mental representation depends on what theory it is embedded in (p. 34). Another example is the centrality of a given belief to a theory (p. 34).

answering this question, let's consider an example Fodor himself discusses of a putative global property that turns out not to be one. The example is the following:

Say that a text is 'globally odd' if it contains an odd number of words, 'globally even' otherwise; and consider the contribution that the sentence 'John loves Mary' makes to determining whether a text that contains it is globally odd. Query: is this contribution context dependent? Perhaps you're inclined to say, "sure it is; because if a given text has an odd number of words, then adding 'John loves Mary' makes the resulting text globally even; whereas, if the text has an even number of words, then adding 'John loves Mary' to it makes the resulting text globally odd" . . . but no. To be sure, the consideration just raised shows that its contributing what it does to the texts that you add it to is a relational property of 'John loves Mary' but it's a context-independent relational property for all that. The sentence makes the same contribution whether the text you add it to is globally odd or globally even; in either case it contributes the number of words it contains. And of course, containing the number of words that it does is a syntactic, hence an essential, property of a sentence, hence not context dependent. What is context dependent is not what a sentence contributes to determining the global oddity of a text, but rather the result of its contributing what it contributes in determining the global oddity of a text. In some contexts the result of adding three words is a text that's globally odd; in other contexts it's not.[6] (*MDW*, 27)

The distinction that Fodor draws here between the result of a contribution and the contribution itself is what we invoked above in showing why the simplicity of a belief (as originally defined by Fodor) is not context dependent and, hence, not, according to the official definition, a global property of it.[7] In

6. Fodor credits Paolo Casalegno with the example.
7. Fodor rejects any analogy between simplicity and word number (*MDW*, 28).

general, when it appears that some property of a belief must be a global property, we could plausibly expect to employ this distinction to show that a property is available that is not global and that explains why the result of a constant contribution varies from context to context. If there is some item that we are tracking from context to context, then it must have context-invariant properties, which enable us to see it as the same thing in different contexts. If it has different effects depending on different contexts, then the overwhelmingly likely story is that a context-invariant property of it (syntactic properties if CTM is right), together with the context-invariant properties of the other items in the system, explains why it has different effects in different conditions—for that is the way causation works throughout Nature, so far as we know.

It might be thought that we could get a stronger result. Consider the definition of simplicity above. It is introduced as the property of a belief that determines whatever its contributions are to the complexity of various sets it might be a member of. Can we not always introduce similarly a property that is guaranteed to be context invariant to explain the different effects in different contexts? Let the item in question be I, and let S be restricted to relevant types of systems, and E to relevant types of effects. Here, it might be said, is the context-invariant property we can appeal to:

the property P of I such that for any system S, and any effect E, if E is the effect of adding I to S, then that I has P determines that E is the effect of adding I to S.

The property P would be context invariant by definition. Unfortunately, it is not so easy to settle the matter, for this succeeds in picking out a property only if the matrix, "for any system S, and any effect E, if E is the effect of adding I to S, then

that I has x determines that E is the effect on adding I to S," is
uniquely satisfied. Unless there is an a priori reason to think that
it must be, we cannot be sure that we have secured a property
by this sort of introduction rule. Neither of the forms of argument we have considered above (in sections 3 and 4) succeed in
establishing that there is no such property, the first because it
presupposes that there is, and the second because it relies on an
a priori false assumption. But there also appears to be no a priori
reason to think that there must be such a property for arbitrary
I and E. That is to say, there does not appear to be any a priori
reason to think that CTM is true. CTM appears rather to be an
empirical hypothesis.

Whether CTM itself is correct, it seems more plausible on
balance to believe that context-invariant properties of mental
representations are responsible for the simplicity or complexity
of theories or plans containing them. To appreciate this, we can
reflect on what would have to be so for this to be false. There
would have to be properties of mental representations that were
genuine relational properties of them, properties that they had
only in the context of other mental representations, which figure in laws that are not deducible from the intrinsic properties
of the elements of the system, their arrangements, and the laws
governing them. It would be as if the relational property of being
a planet were to figure in a brute law. This is not conceptually
impossible. But the history of science provides inductive evidence for the overhypothesis that relational properties like this
do not figure in brute laws, namely, that we have not so far had
to countenance them in any area as ultimate laws. For example,
Kepler's laws of planetary motion appeal to the property of being
a planet but have been explained in terms of more fundamental
laws, which dispense with this higher-level relational property.

## 5   Conclusion

In the present chapter, we have argued that the globality argument of Fodor's *The Mind Doesn't Work That Way* is unsuccessful and, in fact, self-defeating. Fodor's central assumption is that if the simplicity of a belief is intrinsic, it must always contribute a constant increment or decrement to a theory to which it is added. However, this assumption cannot be true given the definition of "simplicity of a belief" and Fodor's observation, which is also used in the argument, that beliefs do not contribute to the complexity of theories by a constant increment or decrement. In addition, we considered whether an alternative argument for the same conclusion could be constructed from materials in the discussion, which avoided the pitfalls of the official argument. We suggested an argument that rested on the assumptions (i), that the only property of a belief that could contribute to the complexity of a theory would be a degree of simplicity in the same sense as that which applies to the theory as a whole, and (ii), that when there is a property of an element and a property of a system to which it is added that are determinants of the same determinable, the contribution of that property of the element to that property of a system to which it is added is additive. Then, we identified some reasons to think that the first of these assumptions is not true, and argued that any attempt to provide support would have to tackle the job of explaining in detail what notion of simplicity is at work in the argument. Further, we argued that the second assumption is false by presenting a simple counterexample to it. We briefly considered whether we are guaranteed to be able to find a context-invariant property of a mental representation that would explain its contribution to the properties of the whole of a system to which it is added by

way of an introduction rule of the sort employed in the definition in section 2 of "simplicity of belief." We argued that we
have no reason to think this can be ruled out a priori, but that
it is an empirical matter whether the relevant description has
a denotation. There are general grounds for optimism because
the alternative must treat higher-level relational properties as
appearing in brute laws, and the history of science provides
inductive evidence that there are no such brute laws.

Let us now take stock of what this book has attempted thus
far: these last few chapters have dismantled the two arguments
for pessimism about centrality that are, ironically, part of the
mainstream LOT program. In addition, chapter 2 began to integrate the LOT program with research on the central system in
cognitive science, outlining a computational account. This book
has thereby made good on its promise to offer a significant departure from the standard LOT program's position on centrality.

Now let us turn to the second major problem that the LOT
program faces: LOT desperately needs an account of symbolic
mental states. The following chapter explores the depth and significance of the problem of symbol natures and begins framing
its solution.

# 4   What LOT's Mental States Cannot Be: Ruling out Alternative Conceptions

Symbols are at the very heart of the LOT program. Given this, it is surprising that there has never been a single sustained account of the nature of LOT's mental symbols. These next two chapters shall provide the needed account: I shall argue that LOT and CTM must type symbols by the role they play in the algorithms of a completed cognitive science.[1] My dialectical strategy is twofold: negatively, I rule out the other theories of symbol individuation—they are ill suited to do the philosophical work that LOT requires of them. Such is the task of the present chapter. Positively, I provide three arguments for the algorithmic conception of symbols (chapter 5). Then I develop my proposal further in

1. As mentioned in the first chapter, both Jerry Fodor (1994) and Stephen Stich (1983) have occupied this position, although the view was not adequately developed. Stich appealed to individuation of syntax by computational role in his well-known defense of syntactic eliminativism, *From Folk Psychology to Cognitive Science: The Case Against Belief* (1983). Unfortunately, very little elaboration and defense of this manner of individuation was provided. And Fodor, in his first appendix to *The Elm and the Expert* (1994), had provided a two-page discussion in which he tried to individuate symbols by the role they played in computations of a Turing machine. For critical discussion, see Aydede (2000a).

the context of responding to critics (chapter 6). Although these chapters do not prove that the brain computes symbolically—this is at least partly an empirical issue to be addressed by future cognitive science research—they lay down the philosophical groundwork for investigating this issue, illustrating that the LOT program at least has a coherent theory of what symbols are.

As with the previous two chapters, I continue to develop a LOT and CTM that differs from the traditional conception. I will soon leave you with, among other things, a theory of symbolic modes of presentation (MOPs) that informs conceptual atomism in such a manner that it becomes a species of pragmatism, a position that LOT, as standardly conceived, has traditionally opposed.

The game plan of the present chapter is simple: section 1 outlines the philosophical roles that mental symbols are summoned to play for the LOT program, for one must bear in mind these roles to determine whether a candidate account of symbols is indeed suitable. Then, in section 2, I consider each of the accounts of symbol types that I know of, arguing that each one fails. Although some fail for other reasons, a recurring theme is that many of the theories do not deliver a notion of a symbol that can perform one or more nonnegotiable functions that symbols are supposed to play for the LOT program. This paves the way for the positive view I set forth in chapter 5.

## 1  Symbols and Their Roles

What of existing theories of symbol natures? Are they adequate? A first step toward answering this question involves considering the central and commonly agreed on philosophical functions that symbols are supposed to play. For when I consider the candidate theories of symbols in section 3, I shall ask whether any of the alternatives to my own theory do in fact fill these nonnegotiable roles. And the answer shall be: *none do.*

Before I begin, it is necessary to briefly explain a few terms that are employed in discussions of the nature of LOT symbols. Such symbols are often called *items in LOT syntax*, where *LOT syntax* is supposed to consist in both (i), the rules of composition of the language of thought, and (ii), the expressions in the language, both primitive and complex. As the present task is to individuate the primitive vocabulary items, a more precise term that encompasses only the vocabulary items would be helpful. So henceforth, I will mainly set "syntax" aside and speak of "symbols" in the language of thought. But it should be noted that "symbol" is sometimes used in a way that this project will ultimately not endorse. Symbols are sometimes taken as being entities that are both computational *and* semantic in the following strong sense: they are said to have their contents essentially. But how to individuate a symbol is precisely what is at stake in the present discussion. It is up for grabs whether the primitive "syntactic" items should be individuated by contents, or merely by computational features. Indeed, most proposals for individuating the primitive vocabulary items do not, in fact, take content as individuative.[2]

Fortunately, a nonsemantic use of "symbol" is appropriate, for one also hears talk of "uninterpreted symbols," and by and large, symbols are paradigmatically regarded as being narrow, and computational, having interpretations assigned to them. This is because meanings are, on the standard view, regarded as

2. Aydede (2000a); Pessin (1995) and Prinz (1999) have each discussed the different proposals.

being irrelevant to the formal workings of a computational system.[3] Herein, I use "symbol" in this purely computational sense: on my view, symbols are individuated by computational features alone; they also have semantic features, but such features are not essential. Thus, it is open that type-identical symbols can be assigned distinct interpretations—such might be, for example, the computationalist's interpretation of the Twin Earth case. I will also sometimes speak of "words" (i.e., symbols) in the language of thought. This being clarified, let us now consider in a bit more detail the philosophical roles that symbols, understood in the manner just outlined, are supposed to play.

### Roles for Symbols

(i) *Symbols are neo-Fregean MOPs.* The most crucial philosophical role that symbolic representations are supposed to play concerns their role as MOPs. Consider: there are different ways of representing the same entity. Despite differences in ways of representing things, diverse ways can pick out, or refer to, the same entity. Philosophers of language have called these ways of representing things *guises*, leaving it open what their precise nature is. Within philosophy of mind, theories of narrow content take themselves to be offering accounts of MOPs. Cognitive scientists have also taken computational entities, such as LOT symbols and activation patterns in connectionist networks, as providing a notion of a MOP that is purely narrow, being determined by the intrinsic properties of the system.

By construing symbols as MOPs, LOT importantly secures a notion of a mental state that is at a level of grain suitable for capturing our familiar way of conceiving the world; symbols are,

---

3. For a nice articulation of the standard view see Haugeland (1989).

in a sense, computational versions of what laypeople sometimes call one's inner "concept," or "notion."[4] In this vein, symbols must be finely grained enough to distinguish intuitively distinct thoughts that happen to co-refer (e.g., *Cicero/Tully*). As Frege's *Hesperus/Phosphorus* example emphasized, one's ways of conceiving of an entity are distinct from the entity referred to: one may grasp a referent by means of certain of its features and yet be ignorant of others. Now, Frege's insight often inspires one to appeal to a semantics in which co-referring thoughts differ in their meanings; but for others, it merely inspires a theory of thought in which thoughts only differ in their (nonsemantic) cognitive significance. Importantly, because proponents of LOT generally appeal to a referential semantics, they must occupy this latter position. For them, symbols *must* differentiate co-referring thoughts; meanings cannot do so.

(ii) *Symbols are causally efficacious.* Computational theories of MOPs, like the LOT approach, look to theories of cognitive processing in cognitive science to supply the basis for an account of the causal production of thought and behavior. In this vein, symbol tokenings are supposed to be causally efficacious, in the sense that they function causally to generate other mental states and behaviors. Relatedly, symbols function in causal explanations of thought and behavior, including, importantly, explanations of the aforementioned productive and systematic nature of thought.

It is worth emphasizing that (i) and (ii) make excellent bedfellows: LOT's neo-Fregean MOPs, unlike Fregean senses, are

4. *Concept* is a term of art within cognitive science, however. Proponents of LOT generally take a concept to be individuated by both its broad content and symbol type, as chapter 6 explains.

causally efficacious, as per (ii); at the same time, symbolic MOPs, like Fregean senses, capture one's way of conceiving of a referent, as per (i). Senses, taken by themselves, are not causally efficacious, and their relation to efficacious mental states is unclear; in contrast, LOT purports that the same entity, symbolic MOPs, deliver both (i) and (ii).

(iii) *Symbols facilitate naturalism.* Third, as discussed in the introduction, symbols are essential tools for any sort of answer to the problem of intentionality. It has long been suspected that thought is somehow categorically distinct from the physical world, being outside the realm that science investigates, for how is it that a thought (e.g., the belief that the cat is on the mat, the desire to drink a cappuccino), which, as we now know, arises from states of the brain, can be directed at, or about, entities in the world? This is the classic problem of the nature of intentional phenomena. In broad strokes, the LOT program answers the problem of intentionality by claiming that the intentionality of a thought is a matter of a causal, and ultimately, physical, relationship between symbols and entities in the world. As Barry Loewer and Georges Rey put it, symbols are "locked onto" properties or individuals in virtue of standing in a certain nomic or causal relationship specified by a theory of meaning or mental content (Loewer and Rey 1993).

These roles are clearly recognizable as being of central import to the LOT program. This is largely due to the work of Fodor, who, as we know, has developed a well-known philosophical program in which mental symbols are said to play each of the above philosophical roles. But is it even plausible to venture that each of these roles is *nonnegotiable*, being required for the philosophical success of the LOT program? I believe so. Turning to (i) and (ii), these roles are absolutely key: symbols are inner mental states that are supposed to explain how and why an individual thinks and behaves in the way that she does. And they are of enhanced significance given that proponents of LOT generally do not appeal to mental content to do the work of neo-Fregean MOPs, for on their view, content is broad. Turning to (iii), LOT/CTM is a naturalistic program that regards locating an answer to the problem of intentionality as being of primary import. Hence, I am inclined to say that each of these roles is nonnegotiable.

Does any single conception of a symbol satisfy all these roles? Initially, one might suspect so. The proponent of LOT finds this philosophical work to be well conceived and, given this, might assume that LOT has a clear conception of what a symbol is. However, identifying a philosophical role for a putative entity is not tantamount to giving its individuation conditions. For example, in his classic "New Work for a Theory of Universals," David Lewis identifies numerous roles for sparse properties, yet shies away from firmly deciding between Armstrongian universals or a form of class nominalism (1983). At least in principle, different conceptions—that is, entities having different individuation conditions—can play the same roles. In a similar vein, to understand the nature of symbols, one needs a conception of the individuation conditions for that which is supposed to play the roles just identified. For instance, should two symbol tokens be regarded as being of the same type when they have the same semantic content? Or should symbols instead be type individuated by their underlying neural properties?

However, the aforementioned roles do provide some insight into symbol natures in the following sense: given competing conceptions of symbols, it is reasonable to select the one that is best able to play the important philosophical roles that symbols are supposed to play, if any does. This is only fair. While debates over certain metaphysical categories (e.g., laws) feature discussions in which each side disagrees on what philosophical roles need to be satisfied by the category, this problem will not arise today, for while those interested in LOT may certainly debate whether symbols should play certain, more controversial roles, the roles that the different views fail to satisfy today are all ones that are clearly nonnegotiable to all.[5]

This being said, let us ask the question at hand: What are the conditions for a given LOT token to be of a particular symbol type? Or, put slightly differently, what are the conditions for determining symbol types?[6] I focus on answering these questions for simple term types—the nonsemantic correlates of concepts—rather than for complex expressions. Further, I assume that (for the language of thought, at least) complex expressions can be constructed from combinatorial operations on the

5. Another key role for symbols is the following: symbols are supposed to be the bearers of mental content, where the operative theory of content is generally externalist. But syntactic eliminativists would dispute this, because they do not believe in content (see Stich 1983).

6. These questions are closely related in the following sense: an answer to the former question requires an answer to the latter one, but not vice versa. The former requires the latter because in order to type LOT tokens, there must be a proposal on the individuation of the property types themselves. If one has a concrete proposal on the property types, then, given an antecedent manner of identifying the physical state tokens (provided by the relevant lower-level sciences), these tokens can be typed. But one may have an answer to the second condition in hand, knowing the criterion for individuation of syntactic properties, without a complete answer to the first question. For there may not yet be an account of how to determine when something is a token (e.g., when something is a brain state). I will assume that this issue is a matter for the lower-level sciences to determine; my task, herein, is to determine when a given physical state token is of a particular LOT type.

simples. I begin by ruling out three popular accounts of symbol natures, starting with the semantic proposal.

## 2  The Semantic Proposal

Symbols stand for things. But whether they do so essentially is another story. At one time, Fodor individuated symbols by their meanings (1989, 167). On the other hand, John Searle (1980) speaks of meaningless symbol manipulations in the context of his classic Chinese Room thought experiment, and Stevan Harnad worries about the symbol grounding problem in which meaningless symbols are manipulated (1990). Clearly, there is no consensus on whether symbols are to be individuated by meanings. But let us nonetheless determine if some sort of semantic proposal would work. In particular, since LOT is currently developed against the backdrop of a referential semantics, let us see whether a referential proposal is plausible.

According to the referential proposal, symbols should simply be classified by their broad contents:

(CD1) Two primitive symbol tokens are of the same symbol type if they have the same broad content.[7]

We can quickly see that (CD1) is very problematic. (1) It fails to deliver a notion of a symbol that facilitates naturalism (role iii), because a referential manner of typing LOT expressions would ruin the prospects for naturalism (Pessin 1995). We've observed that LOT aims to naturalize intentionality by taking the intentionality of thought to be a matter of symbols bearing some sort

7.  Again, theories of broad content take the basic semantic properties of thoughts to be reference and truth (e.g., the broad content of a name is the individual named).

of external relationship (e.g., causal, informational) to entities in the world. But if the intentionality of thought is supposed to reduce to a physical and nonintentional relation between symbols and the world, symbols themselves cannot be typed semantically. If symbols have semantic natures, the intentionality of thought wouldn't be explained using resources that are all naturalistically kosher, for the supervenience base would include semantic facts.

(2) Bearing in mind that proponents of LOT generally envision symbols as being at a level of grain suitable to explain one's way of conceiving the world (role i), referential individuation clearly will not suffice. For consider that co-referential symbol tokens (e.g., *Hesperus/Phosphorus*) will be regarded as being type identical while functioning very differently in one's cognitive economy. (3) Relatedly, treating co-referential but intuitively distinct symbols as type identical will lead to poor explanations of the causation of thought and behavior because the tokens can function very differently in bringing about subsequent thoughts and behaviors (role ii) (Fodor 1994; Schneider 2005; Braun 2001a and b; Richard 1990).

So a referential manner of typing symbols will fail to deliver a notion of a symbol that plays any of the aforementioned roles that symbols are supposed to play. Now, one might believe that the problems are all due to symbols being typed referentially, rather than merely semantically. For instance, would the individuation of symbols by narrow content avoid some of these problems? Assuming that one has a plausible theory of narrow content in hand, and that the narrow contents track one's way of conceiving the world, this would eliminate the second and third problems. However, the first problem extends to any kind of semantic proposal. And given the centrality of naturalism to the LOT program, this is a decisive reason to reject any semantic proposal. So let us turn to the next approach to symbol natures.

## 3  Orthographic or Type Identity Proposals

Proposals concerning the nature of symbols have been said to be *orthographic* when they appeal, in some rough sense, to the "shape" of a symbol in the language of thought (Millikan 1993). Unfortunately, although expressions like "shape" and "orthography" are employed in discussions of LOT symbols, these notions, when applied to thoughts, are extremely vague. Turing himself proposed that symbols are individuated topologically, by their arrangement of points (Turing 1936, 135, fn.), but it is unclear how to extend this proposal to the case of the brain.[8] Symbols are not literally inscribed in the brain as they are on a Turing machine table. There is no "brain writing"—there are only neurons, minicolumns, and the like. But the view is not entirely baseless: beneath these vague metaphors is a suspicion that symbols are to be type individuated by certain of their neural properties. This is not to be laughed at. For one thing, cognitive neuroscientists speak of concepts being located in particular assemblies of neurons, and, to an extreme, Christof Koch and others have defended the existence of *grandmother cells*: single cells that seem to fire only in the presence of certain familiar individuals (e.g., grandmother, Obama, etc.). Now, it is far from clear whether the presence of such cells motivates anything like a type-identity theory in philosophy of mind, but it is at least prima facie plausible that some sort of type-identity account will

8. I am grateful to Whit Schonbein for calling Turing's remark to my attention.

be borne out as neuroscience develops and refines accounts of higher cognitive functions. So let us consider the following:

(CD2) Two primitive symbol tokens are of the same symbol type if and only if they are tokens of the same brain state type.

Of course, this condition is just a version of the well-known type-identity theory of mental states, fashioned for symbol types.

Numerous problems emerge for (CD2). As Fodor has remarked to me in conversation, (CD2) pushes much of the problem of symbol individuation to the problem of how brain states are individuated, and it is by no means clear how to individuate brain states.[9] Fodor suggested that neuroscience sometimes appeals to the convention of typing brain states by certain of their neuroanatomical features. But here, two complications arise: first, important concepts (e.g., MOTHER, DOG) seem to

9. Fodor's *LOT 2* hints that he may now have a more optimistic view of CD2 for the case of individuating symbols within a given person, although he is pessimistic about employing resources in neuroscience to determine types in the cross-person case: "It seems entirely likely that distinct minds should turn out to be *more similar under PA* [propositional attitude] *description than they are under neural description*" (2008, 89). Unfortunately, aside from a quick remark, he doesn't develop the issue of a neuroscientific means of typing tokens intrapersonally, and at page 90, he seems to reject it entirely: "that would make it *a priori* that silicon Martians don't think." The discussion in the appendix of this chapter leaves me with the suspicion that he is currently typing tokens by sameness and difference in computational role, although he does not explicitly endorse this view (see pp. 92–100). For example, he writes, "If mental representations differ in their roles in mental processes, they must be formally distinct in ways that mental processes can distinguish" (92). Of course, if this is indeed his position, he will need to explore how this relates to CD2, assuming he is sympathetic to it. And he will need to address publicity worries.

survive hemispherectomy, commissurotomy, and various types of injuries. This indicates that familiar concepts may be duplicated throughout one's cortex. If the same concept is multiply realized in different parts of the cortex, then it is unclear how a neuroanatomical proposal would work. And it fails in the across-person case for a related reason, for it is now well-known that there are great interpersonal variations in the data structures of the cortex. So this would not yield a theory of symbols in which different individuals token symbols of the same type. In sum, these issues make the development of a neuroanatomical version of (CD2) very challenging indeed.[10] Another proposal that may come to mind involves an appeal to the semantic features of the brain states, but this sort of position will not help the symbolicist, for as noted, a semantic conception of a symbol will only muddle LOT's ambition to deliver a naturalistic theory of intentionality. As noted, facilitating naturalism is an important role that symbols are supposed to play.

In sum, both the semantic and type-identity approaches fail. Still, there is one more approach to consider (or rather, family

10. The proponent of (CD2) could point out that this book agrees with the view that different individuals may not have symbols of the same type. They could then employ my response to the publicity objections that I offer in chapter 6. Fair enough. But my concern with (CD2) is that what it amounts to is unclear, given that it doesn't say how brain states are individuated. In the context of intrapersonal individuation, I suspect that the only way that (CD2) would work is if it arrived at the same taxonomy of states as the condition I shall propose, being a kind of neuroscience-based computational-role account that tracks sameness and difference in the role the state plays in one's cognitive economy. In this case (CD2) and the condition I propose in the subsequent chapter would pick out the very same class of symbolic states. My arguments for a computational role condition are outlined in the following chapter.

of approaches). This popular approach types symbols by the role the symbol plays in computation.

## 4   Computational Role Approaches

Proponents of this approach include Fodor (1994) and Stich (1983), although, as noted, neither has developed this position in any detail. There are two basic types of computational-role accounts. The division concerns how the notion of computational role is to be understood by the theory. According to one view, the computational role of a symbol includes the entire role the symbol is capable of playing in one's cognitive economy. The symbol is individuated by *all* the generalizations that the symbol figures in, where such generalizations are not "folk" generalizations, but, in the spirit of a posteriori functionalism, are generalizations detailed by a completed cognitive science. Let us call such accounts *total computational-role* accounts. The second type of proposal has a more restrictive understanding of computational role in the sense that it singles out only some elements of the total role the state is capable of playing as being type individuative.[11]

Chapter 5 shall argue for the first approach, and chapter 6 shall provide a detailed response to critics' objections to it, so let us now consider the second type of proposal. This second approach is a sort of *molecularism* about LOT symbol types, designed in the spirit of molecularism about narrow content individuation. Molecularism about symbols singles out from the class of causal relations, and more specifically, the class of

11. Notice that both conceptions generally take the computational roles of a symbol to specify the *causal powers* of the symbol, rather than merely specifying the actual causal history of the symbol.

computational relations that the expression has, a certain privileged few as being type individuative. The causal connections appealed to are designed to get a common equivalence class of systems that, when tokening a given symbol and in common conditions, will, *ceteris paribus*, think or behave in similar ways. For instance, there might be a population of novices who all know the same small amount of information about a kind. Here, let us employ talk of *mental files*. In the mental file for a natural kind of concept, a novice may have only the most basic facts. For example, someone may know only that *brane* names a fundamental entity in M-theory. Other novices have only this very sparse grasp of this putative natural kind as well. So the proponent of molecularism about symbols can say that a mental word, like [brane], is shared between the novices; that is, those who also have this very skeletal idea of what a brane is. A similar scenario can apply to names; consider the contrast between an expert's knowledge of Einstein and a novice who may only know that Einstein is the person who devised relativity theory.

The strongest case for molecularism concerns mental words for logical and mathematical expressions: just as it is relatively easy to locate definitions for logical and mathematical expressions, it is also easy to isolate a computational role that all who have these kinds of MOPs share. In the context of discussions of the plausibility of conceptual role semantics, logico-mathematical concepts are generally the parade cases. However, the problem is that the case for MOP-type constituting computational relations is significantly weaker for other expression types. Critics charge that molecularist theories of narrow content have failed in a related attempt to identify certain conceptual or inferential roles as being constitutive of narrow contents. In broad strokes, the problem that arose for the related accounts of narrow content is that there seemed to be no principled way to distinguish between those elements of conceptual or inferential role that are meaning constitutive from those that are not (see Fodor and LePore 1992). Similar issues emerge for molecularism about symbol types, although the issues do not concern content individuation but symbol individuation. Indeed, Murat Aydede has posed the following dilemma for the molecularist: insofar as one singles out a select few symbol-constitutive computational relations, the analysis will fail to distinguish intuitively distinct symbol types. But if one builds more relations into the requirements for having a symbol, different individuals do not have symbols of the same type. For instance, suppose that the symbol [dog] is individuated by computational relations involving [canine] and [standardly four legged]. But alas, what if someone thinks dogs fly, or that they do not bark, or that they are not house pets? If they think any of these things, do they really have the same notion of a dog as you and I? If not, are we really prepared to say that they nonetheless share the same MOP or mental symbol? A natural reaction is to strengthen the requirement on having [dog] in various dimensions. But now, because [dog] is sensitive to many elements of the symbol's computational role, different individuals will not generally token it. Instead, they will each have their own idiosyncratic mental symbols for dogs. Conceptual role accounts of narrow content faced a similar dilemma (Aydede 1999).

The proponent of molecularism may suspect that one merely needs to develop a detailed argument for including certain computational relations and excluding others. But I will not attempt to devise such an argument, for I suspect that it would go nowhere. For as I shall now argue, insofar as there is *any* difference in computational role between tokens of identical symbol types within a given system, either LOT/CTM will be incomplete or there will be counterexamples to computational generalizations. The strategy behind the argument is the following: assume that P is some principle of individuation of LOT symbols and that P is *not* equivalent to individuation by total computational role. This is, for instance, the case with molecularist individuation conditions. Then, wouldn't there be cases in which two LOT expressions are type identical according to P while differing in their total computational roles? This must be the case, for if it is not, then P is just equivalent to a principle that types LOT primitives in terms of sameness and difference of total computational role. But as I will argue below, if there is a case in which two LOT tokens of the same type differ in any element of their total computational roles, as molecularist ones do, then either there will be missed predictions or there will be counterexamples to computational generalizations.

This being said, here's the argument: Let CR denote the causal role of a given LOT token, *a*. And let CR* denote an individuation condition for the type that *a* is a token of. CR* is a condition that employs individuation by computational role, where the computational role includes every computational-level causal relation that the token enters into with other primitives except for one relation, R*. So R* is not individuative of the type that *a* is a token of. But now suppose that *a* has R*.

Let us pause to note that the above assumptions are entirely in keeping with molecularism. Because molecularism holds that certain computational relations do not figure in a token's individuation, molecularism is required to say that there will be computational relations that do not individuate a given token.

Now, to continue the argument, I take it that the causal relations that specify the computational role of a given token are detailed by the computational laws. So there is a given computational law, L, which specifies R*. Now, let *b* be a token *within the very same system* that has only the causal role specified by CR*, and not CR, because *b* lacks R*. And let us suppose that like *a*, *b* is typed by CR*. Then, either (i), both *a* and *b* will not be subsumable in L, or (ii), they will both be subsumable in L. In the case of (i), the theory will have a missed prediction: it will miss that *a* has a causal relation that is specified by L. Now consider the second scenario (ii), in which they will both be subsumable in L. In this case, *b* does not have the causal relation detailed by L. So we wouldn't expect it to behave in accordance with L. Hence, *b* will be a counterexample to L. Hence, insofar as even one element of the total computational role is ignored by an individuation condition, as with molecularist conditions, there will be counterexamples or mixed predictions.

Further, the sort of counterexample will be a kind of Frege case. By a *Frege case*, I mean a certain sort of counterexample that arises for psychological laws that subsume states that are individuated in a manner that is too coarsely grained for the purpose of capturing important behavioral similarities. Frege cases are well known in the literature on broad content and intentional explanation.[12] It was in that context that they were raised in the introduction. But Frege cases can arise at the computational level as well. In general, Frege cases are situations in which an agent satisfies the antecedent of a psychological generalization but fails to satisfy the consequent because the theory treats mental representations as being type identical that are actually causally distinct in the way the mental representations function in the system's cognitive economy.

12. Such shall be the topic of chapter 8. See also Fodor (1994); Aryo (1996); Aydede and Robbins (2001).

It is crucial to note that Frege cases at the computational level cannot be solved in the way that I try to solve the intentional-level cases in a subsequent chapter of this book. In chapter 8, I urge that the Frege cases can be included in the *ceteris paribus* clauses of intentional laws because they are tolerable exceptions. In making such an argument, I need to explain that there was a difference in underlying LOT states, and that the person didn't realize that the states referred to the same individual. Without going into detail concerning the intentional-level cases, let me simply observe that even if this strategy works in the intentional case, the crucial thing to note is that unlike Frege cases arising at the intentional level, there is no relatively lower psychological level to appeal to that would allow LOT to distinguish the relevant states. For the proponent of LOT, the symbolic level is the level sensitive to MOPs; symbols are the psychological kind that is supposed to distinguish between the states. But we've just supposed that the symbol tokens are type-identical.

So it seems that molecularism falters as an explanation of the causal ancestry of thought and behavior (role ii), for on this conception of symbols, there will be either missed predictions or counterexamples to computational generalizations. Clearly, if molecularism is to be effective, it must respond to this problem. In addition, as discussed, it requires a plausible argument for regarding certain computational roles as essential to the symbol, while disregarding others.

## 5   Conclusion

This chapter sought to convince you that the competing accounts of symbol natures are deeply problematic. And in reflecting on all this, you have likely drawn the conclusion that the LOT program is in deep trouble should it fail to define symbols. For instance, we have observed that MOPs are needed to distinguish co-referring thoughts. If the identity conditions on symbolic MOPs are not specified, one clearly doesn't know whether differences in MOP will be finely grained enough to differentiate co-referring thoughts. After all, the referential conception of symbols doesn't achieve this. Further, without an individuation condition on symbols, how can the proponent of LOT be confident that symbols are ultimately part of the domain that science investigates? For what are they? Indeed, why would one want to claim that symbols exist at all if no individuation condition is forthcoming? *Ceteris paribus*, it is better to opt for a theory of mind with a well-defined notion of a mental state. For the proponent of LOT to uphold naturalism without making progress on symbol natures looks like a hidden appeal to the sort of mysterious mental entities that the naturalist aims to avoid.

The present chapter has been negative—*very negative*—but I would urge that in the face of the results, the proponent of LOT should consider the algorithmic conception. So let us now move forward. It is my hope that in the next two chapters, we shall arrive at a richer understanding of LOT's position on the nature of mental states.

# 5   Mental Symbols

What are symbolic mental states? The only viable answer to this question is that LOT's symbols have *algorithmic* natures, being individuated by the role they play in computation. In this chapter, I advance three arguments for this position. The first claims that LOT's classicist approach requires that symbols be typed in this manner. The second argument contends that without this kind of symbol individuation, there will be cognitive processes that fail to supervene on symbols, together with the rules (i.e., rules of composition and other computational algorithms). This situation is problematic for CTM, because CTM holds that cognitive processing just *is* the processing of mental symbols, according to rules. The third argument says that cognitive science needs a natural kind that is typed by its total computational role. Otherwise, either cognitive science will be incomplete, or its laws will have counterexamples. Once these arguments have been advanced, I explore the notion of computational role that is operative in these arguments so that the commitments of the algorithmic approach are clear. Then, my case for this approach continues into chapter 6, where I respond to the publicity argument and other pressing objections. Further, in responding to critics, I explore how symbols, so conceived, figure in cognitive explanations. Chapter 6 also illustrates how the theory of symbol natures informs conceptual atomism, and relatedly, how, once symbol natures are understood, LOT is, quite surprisingly, a pragmatist theory.

Let us now turn to the three arguments for the algorithmic approach.

## 1 Three Arguments

### The Argument from Classicism

The first draws from basic tenets of classicism. According to classicism, a mechanism computes when it produces outputs (or tokens) given certain input tokens, according to an algorithm. On the classical view, the nature of a token is stipulated to be such that:

(T1) any token can be substituted by another token of the same type in an operation without changing the computation.

This point is often taken to be trivial. Indeed, this is a basic feature of the classical view that is found in even elementary discussions of classicism.[1] For instance, John Haugeland introduces the concept of types by analogy with chess pieces. He underscores that pieces of the same type must function in the same way within the program; interchanging them makes no computational difference: "Formal tokens are freely interchangeable if and only if they are the same type. Thus it doesn't make any difference which white pawn goes on which white-pawn square; but switching a pawn with a rook or a white pawn with a black one could make a lot of difference" (1989, 52).

1. See, for example, John Haugeland's well-known introduction to classicism: *AI: The Very Idea* (1989).

Evidently, those working on the individuation of LOT's symbols have overlooked the significance of these rather platitudinous discussions, as they provide a decisive reason to accept a condition that types symbols by their total computational roles. For (T1) yields a condition that says that for two LOT tokens to be type-identical, it is necessary that they have the same total computational role. Put a bit differently, (T1) says:

(T2) Any token of the same type will generate the same (proximal) output and internal states of the machine, given that the same internal states of the machine are activated.

And this yields the following necessary condition on two symbol tokens being type identical:

(T3)  $\forall x \, \forall y$ (If $x$ and $y$ are type-identical LOT tokens, then $x$ and $y$ will have the same total computational role.)

Further, according to classicism, substituting token of type S1 for token of type S2 in a string results in a different computational process, which, assuming the process runs its course, will produce at least one different output or internal state (Haugeland 1989, 52). This yields the following:

(T4)  $\forall x \, \forall y$ (If $x$ and $y$ are type-distinct LOT tokens, then $x$ and $y$ have distinct total computational roles.)

By further logical operations, we have the following sufficient condition on type identity:

(T5)  $\forall x \, \forall y$ (If $x$ and $y$ have the same total computational role, then $x$ and $y$ are type-identical.)

So, by stating basic facts about how classicism views the nature of symbols, I have made explicit the commitments that classicism has to their type individuation. Those offering various theories on how primitive symbols in the language of thought should be typed have failed to note that there really is no room for negotiation. We have located both a necessary and a sufficient condition on being a LOT symbol that seems to be required by classicism. Being typed by sameness and difference of total computational role is just what it is to be a classical "token"!

A simple and clear elaboration of these points is found in Haugeland's well-known discussion of the classical theory of computation (1989). In the second chapter, he lays out the notion of a classical computation, which he identifies as a sort of formal system in which there is a "token manipulation game." Here, again, he explains the notion of a token by analogy with chess pieces.

Ultimately, the rules are what determine the types of the tokens. The rules specify what moves would be legal in what positions. If interchanging two particular tokens wouldn't make any difference to which moves were legal in any position, then it couldn't make any difference to the game at all; and those tokens would be of the same type. To see the significance of this, consider chess again. In some fancy chess sets, every piece is unique; each white pawn, for instance, is a little figurine, slightly different from the others. Why then are they all the same type? Because, in any position whatsoever, if you interchanged any two of them, exactly the same moves would be legal. That is, each of them contributes to an overall position in exactly the same way, namely, in the way that pawns do. And that's what makes them all pawns. (Haugeland 1989, 52)

The upshot: classicism requires a symbol to be typed by the role it plays in the program, that is, by sameness and difference of total computational role. How will any other notion of a symbol work with classicism? Individuation by total computational role seems to be axiomatic.

Admittedly, this argument is difficult to swallow, for it is hard to see how different individuals can have symbols of the same type. One reaction to this is to venture a two-tiered account of the nature of symbols. One could take the argument from classicism as specifying the correct way to type individuate vocabulary items in the language of thought *intrapersonally*. One could then seek a different way of typing vocabulary items to describe two systems as having the same "internal language." This would leave one with two sorts of classificatory schemes for vocabulary items in the language of thought: one scheme, which we could call the *intrapersonal LOT scheme*, taxonomizes intrapersonal LOT types; another scheme, the *interpersonal LOT scheme*, classifies interpersonal LOT types. Assuming that the argument from classicism is correct, and assuming different systems can token symbols of the same type, then one's internal computations are classified by two different classificatory schemes, one that is summoned for the purpose of explaining the detailed workings of a particular system, and one classificatory scheme that type individuates the vocabulary in what is supposed to be a shared mental language.

Such an approach is a non-starter, however. For in what sense are these shared mental words, when limited to being a special vocabulary for the interpersonal case only, really words in one's language of thought at all? The answer is: not much of a sense. Presumably, the rules that the mind employs operate on the intrapersonal types only—for the intrapersonal types are supposed to figure in the algorithms describing how the cognitive mind operates. Relatedly, LOT is supposed to explain the causal production of thought, including the compositionality, productivity, and systematicity of thought, but an explanation of these features would appeal to the mental processing in the language that the system actually computes in, not the interpersonal taxonomy. It is difficult to justify regarding any purely interpersonal notion of a mental state as being a conception of a symbol in the language of thought. It seems like a different sort of entity altogether.

Now let us turn to the supervenience argument.

## The Supervenience Argument

Consider the following *reductio* argument: assume that *within a given system*, two primitive symbol tokens, *a* and *b*, are of symbol type 1, but *a* has the following causal relation that *b* does not have:

(T) Causing a tokening of LOT sentence S1 under circumstances C

How can we explain the causal difference between *a* and *b*? (T) is obviously a phenomenon that is of interest to CTM because it involves cognitive and, moreover, symbolic processing. Now, according to CTM, computations are entirely determined by:

(i) the type identity of the primitive symbols in the language of thought.

(ii) the grammar of the language of thought—that is, the rules of composition that yield compound symbols in the language, including sentences.

(iii) the "rules," or algorithms, that are supposed to describe cognitive processes and predict behaviors.

The grammatical properties of the language, together with the totality of symbol types, are commonly referred to as the *LOT syntax*. Now, I've just supposed that there is a computational difference between tokens *a* and *b*, although they are type-identical symbols. But notice that this difference in causal powers clearly does not translate into a difference in either (i) or (ii), for I've assumed that the tokens are type-identical symbols, and the assumed difference in causal powers between *a* and *b* should not affect the grammatical properties of the language.

Turning to (iii), would this difference in causal powers perhaps be a matter of a difference in the rules? Since there is a difference in causal powers between $a$ and $b$, and since the causal powers in question involve mental processing, might there be some algorithm that token $a$ can figure in but token $b$ cannot? Unfortunately, the argument from classicism already ruled out this possibility: if $a$ and $b$ are type-identical, they must be capable of functioning the same way in the classical program. We can also state the issue in terms of laws, rather than algorithms. Since, *ex hypothesi*, $a$ and $b$ are type-identical symbols, and according to the proponent of LOT, the computational laws are supposed to be sensitive to symbol types, any computational law that subsumes $a$ will also subsume $b$. Thus, there will not be a "special computational law" that $a$ satisfies and $b$ does not, and that captures the causal difference between $a$ and $b$. Laws, like classical algorithms, are insensitive to causal differences between tokens of the same type. The upshot: it seems that we have mental processing that is not determined by LOT syntax together with the algorithms, contra CTM. Hence, to preserve CTM, we must regard $a$ and $b$ as being type-distinct symbols. The reductio leaves us with the following constraint on LOT property individuation:

(Principle P) $\forall x \, \forall y$ (It is not possible for $x$ and $y$ to be tokens in the same system, of the same type, and differ in their computational roles.)

This constraint just says that sameness in (total) computational role is a necessary condition on the type-identity of LOT symbols.[2]

2. Unlike the argument from classicism, the supervenience argument does not establish the sufficiency of any condition that proceeds by sameness or difference of total computational role. However, sufficiency is not really an issue, because the condition admittedly slices symbols extremely thinly.

This, then, is the supervenience argument. What is the significance of this failure to supervene? Recall that Fodor has observed in the context of his globality argument (2000) that if there is mental processing that does not supervene on syntax, CTM is incomplete, for it cannot characterize mental processing in the central system. Recall that in the present context, the feature of cognition which LOT cannot explain is (T):

(T) Causing a tokening of LOT sentence S1 under circumstances C

Ironically, what (T) is a case of, and which goes unexplained, is symbolic processing itself. Now, it would be unproblematic if LOT were merely incomplete in the sense that it needed to be supplemented by a nonsymbolic theory of sensory states. That computational processing of the sort carried out in, for example, early vision, is nonsymbolic is both plausible and unproblematic. But it is another matter entirely when the explananda are cognitive phenomena, and in particular, the reason one LOT sentence causes another. Relatedly, if LOT is incomplete as an account of symbolic processing, then how intentionality is to be naturalized is left unclear, because projects that attempt to naturalize intentionality that appeal to LOT clearly look to LOT for a complete account of symbolic processing. For intentional phenomena that defy explanation at the level of the computational theory would be mysterious and unnaturalizable.

Finally, let us consider the third argument.

## The (Computational-Level) Frege Cases Argument Revisited

My third argument is just the aforementioned computational-level Frege cases argument that the previous chapter advanced as an argument against molecularism. Upon reflection, the argument is both against molecularism and *for* the individuation of symbols by their total computational roles. Recall that the argument assumed that P is some principle of individuation of primitive LOT symbols and that P is not equivalent to an individuation condition that taxonomizes states by their total computational roles. It concludes that there would be either missed predictions or counterexamples; such were called *Frege cases*. Importantly, the Frege case argument is somewhat different from the previous two arguments, because it can be stated in a way that does not assume classicism or CTM. The gist of the argument is that without individuation of modes of presentation (MOPs) by total computational (or for noncomputational theories, narrow functional) role, then either there will be missed predictions, or there will be counterexamples to certain psychological laws. The argument should generalize to alternate conceptions of guises, or MOPs. Philosophy of mind has suggested a number of entities that might play the theoretical role of MOPs. (As noted, some well-known candidates are narrow contents, activation patterns in connectionist networks, and LOT symbols.) The basics of the argument seem to present a demand for a taxonomy of psychological states in terms of total functional or computational role, although it is up to the proprietary theory to say whether such MOPs are to be construed computationally, rather than merely functionally. The upshot is that unless one individuates psychological states in this extremely thin manner, either missed predictions or counterexamples will ensue.[3] Thus, my first two arguments, which suggest that symbols would be sliced very thinly, cannot be construed as yielding

3. This is not to say that *all* psychological kinds need to be individuated in this manner. Indeed, this picture is compatible with an appeal to a semantic, or intentional, level as well, which subsumes thoughts taxonomized by their broad contents. Indeed, this is the sort of view developed later in this book.

a psychological kind that is, from the vantage point of cognitive science, unnecessary and avoidable.

This concludes my discussion of the three arguments. In essence, I've argued that symbols should be typed by their total computational roles, where, to a first approximation, the total computational role of a symbol is the role it plays in the relevant "program." I would now like to make the notion of a total computational role more explicit, as it is doing a good deal of work in the three arguments. I will also identify a specific individuation condition based on the three arguments and respond to a number of imperative objections to it.

## 2   Total Computational Role

Let us assume that there are internal representations—patterns of energy and matter inside the head—that, according to the symbol manipulation view, fall into symbol types. According to the proponent of LOT, such patterns instantiate rules, such as production rules ("if preconditions, 1, 2, and 3 are met, do actions 1 and 2"). We can think of these rules as algorithms that describe cognitive processes. In light of this, the question of what computational role amounts to is really the following question: What rules (or algorithms) does the brain employ?

We can restrict our question a bit: LOT is intended to be a theory that describes cognitive processing—processing in LOT's central system. Recall that the central system is the subsystem in the brain that is the seat of higher cognitive function, and in which sensory information is integrated and conscious deliberation occurs. This being said, given that the central system is supposed to be the domain to which LOT applies, it is natural to look to ongoing and future research on the central system for the needed algorithms. The point is not which algorithms are sensible candidates—in chapter 2, I identified certain work as promising—but it is well known that cognitive science knows far, far more about modular, particularly sensory, processes than it does about higher cognitive function. An inventory of central algorithms is an undertaking of a future cognitive science. Nonetheless, we can figure out how to individuate symbols today:

**(CAUSAL):** A symbol is defined by the role it plays in the algorithm that describes the central system.

It is worth underscoring that (CAUSAL) individuates symbols by the algorithm that characterizes the central system and not by the actual causal profile of the given symbol. In general, in defining a mental state by its causal role, one can define it in terms of its actual causal history (what has been called the *actual causal profile*) or one can, more inclusively, define it by its dispositions or causal powers, some of which may not be manifest. If symbols are individuated only by the algorithms they happen to satisfy, they will be mischaracterized as being type-identical in cases in which the actual history of the system in question is too short.

Now let us consider objections to the proposed individuation condition. First, one might object to (CAUSAL) on the grounds that it is circular because it invokes in the righthand side of the analysis algorithms in which the very symbol types themselves figure. To deal with this problem, (CAUSAL) can be reframed by employing the method of Ramsification. According to this method, a given symbol is defined by the role that it plays in a Ramsey sentence. To construct the needed sentence, one begins with the conjunction of computational generalizations in which symbols figure; here, one would conjoin all the algorithms that a final cognitive science employs to describe the workings of the central system. The names of any symbol types are then replaced with variables. The definition of a given primitive symbol would then be like the following (put very simply and generically):

$x$ has #beer# = $df$ $\exists P \exists Q$ (input___ causes P, and P causes both Q and output____, and $x$ is in P)

Where P is the predicate variable replacing "has #beer#" in the theory, and Q refers to a different primitive symbolic state. (This, of course, is a gross oversimplification: in reality, there will be far more inputs, symbolic states, and outputs). Notice that there is no explicit mention of symbol types in the righthand side of the analysis. A well-known virtue of the method of Ramsification is that it banishes definitional circularity from functionalist proposals.[4]

Fodor has suggested to me in conversation that even if formal circularity is banished, my appeal to Ramsification is nonetheless *epistemologically* circular, for to grasp which laws figure in the Ramsification that serves to type individuate the LOT primitives, we must borrow from an antecedent knowledge of symbol types, one that we do not have prior to their definition, for we must already know what the property types are to know which laws figure in the Ramsification.

In response, consider that when scientists discover property types, they generally note that a given object of interest, including a microphysical object, such as a particle, behaves in particular ways in certain settings, as do similar objects. Quite naturally, they infer that there likely is a common property, or properties, that these similar objects share. As inquiry proceeds, properties that are identified to be of key interest to inquiry at

4. Readers seeking an overview of Ramsification and functionalism are encouraged to read chapters 5 and 6 of Kim (2006).

a given scientific level are taxonomized by what they do or are projected to do in certain circumstances. In light of this, it is difficult to see how the discovery of property types could proceed independently of the discovery of generalizations about their causal powers and hence be independent of the fashioning of law statements in which the property types figure.

Still, this phenomenon merely suggests that when it comes to the discovery of scientific properties, our epistemic access to property types is via what their tokens do and, hence, is tightly bound up with the laws in which the types figure. *But one's epistemological route into properties need not dictate one's metaphysics.* For instance, consider that the authors of two leading ontological schemes, David Lewis and D. M. Armstrong, while disagreeing on a good deal, concur with this basic story about the discovery of property types. They accept that in all the nomologically possible worlds, properties can be classified by the role they play in the laws; such is a reliable means of taxonomizing properties. Nevertheless, both Lewis and Armstrong believe that property natures are categorical; that is, properties have a nature that is self-contained, being distinct from their causal powers. (In contrast, properties are dispositional when their nature consists only in their causal powers or dispositions).[5] As categorialists, Lewis and Armstrong hold that a property's causal powers or dispositions are contingent: for instance, it is metaphysically possible that a given fundamental property may have tokens in

5. In addition to these positions, John Heil, C. B. Martin, and others hold a two-sided view. On this view properties are both dispositional and categorical. There is a fourth option as well: some properties have natures that are entirely dispositional, while other properties have natures that are entirely categorical. For discussion see (Armstrong 1997), (Heil 2003) and (Schneider, forthcoming).

other possible worlds that lack some or even all of the causal powers that tokens of the same type have in the actual world.

The point here is that although Lewis, Armstrong, and many others endorse a classificatory scheme that types properties by the role they play in laws, they both offer noncircular metaphysical accounts of the nature of properties. In fact, according to both of these ontologies, the order of metaphysical priority is *reverse* of the order of epistemic discovery: properties are categorical, and further, they are more basic than laws. (For Lewis, the laws supervene on the mosaic of properties across spacetime; for Armstrong, laws reduce to a necessitation relation between universals). Both views of laws and properties are available to my account, as are others; I am not presupposing a particular ontological scheme herein.[6] The upshot: the epistemic route into symbol types does not indicate that the ontological situation is such that properties have no noncircular definition.

In essence, Fodor's worry is that we must know the property types themselves to know which laws figure in the Ramsification. But this is just the usual epistemic problem of having to classify properties causally in order to determine their types. And my answer is: (1), this doesn't say anything about the underlying metaphysics, for there are all sorts of reductive metaphysical accounts available that are compatible with this epistemic situation; and (2), I've already shown that the definition of symbols isn't formally circular. So I believe that we can set aside the present objection.

6. Indeed, it is important to bear in mind that one adopting (CAUSAL), which is a functionalist proposal, need not hold, as many functionalists do, that property natures are dispositional. The properties that satisfy the functional roles may have categorical natures that are nomically correlated with their causal powers.

The critic has a second objection up her sleeve, however. She may urge that because cognitive scientists have not discovered the algorithms describing central processing, (CAUSAL) is an uninformative individuation condition, merely gesturing at work to be done by a completed cognitive science. To respond to this matter, even if one disagrees with the content of the current host of computational theories of the central system, it is sufficient to agree with my claim that the central system will eventually be computationally described—that is, there will eventually be algorithms available that can be summoned in an individuation condition in which symbols are typed by the role they play in the central system. (And, reader, if you accept LOT yet are not in agreement with the claim that algorithms will be found, it is reasonable to ask: why believe in LOT at all? For recall, if the central system isn't computational, how is LOT, which is a computational account of the mind, supposed to be correct? Isn't the primary domain of LOT supposed to be the central system?)

I can say a bit more about the content of (CAUSAL) at this point, however. (CAUSAL) includes at least the following two sorts of algorithms. First are those I have described as *symbol-neutral generalizations*: generalizations that quantify over LOT symbols in general, but not by their particular types (e.g., consider *modus ponens* or George Miller's generalization about the chunks of manageable information that working memory systems can contain). Second are the aforementioned generalizations that quantify over LOT expressions by their specific types (e.g., when system S has the mental sentence #x is in pain# then S has the mental sentence #assist x#). This latter sort of generalization plays a key role in symbol individuation, for if only the first sort of generalization typed symbols, as Murat Aydede has noted, it would not be sufficient to distinguish intuitively distinct LOT expressions, as many distinct symbol types with the same gram-matical role (e.g., #dog#, #cat#) can satisfy the same symbol-specific generalizations; such generalizations are quite generic.[7]

Now let us turn to an important matter concerning how to formulate (CAUSAL). It is important to ask: Does (CAUSAL) merely classify symbol types *within a given system,* or, in addition to this, does it license claims about the "across system" case? That is, does it allow that different tokens in distinct systems can be type-identical insofar as they play the same total com-putational role in each system? Throughout this chapter, I have presupposed an affirmative answer, but it is important to illus-trate why this is the case. To answer the question, we must ask whether the three aforementioned arguments merely suggest a "within system" (or *intra*personal) condition, or whether they speak to the "cross system" (or interpersonal) case as well. To appreciate the difference between them, consider the following theses:

7. Aydede 2000. As Aydede notes, it is the inclusion of these sorts of generalizations in algorithms that individuate symbols which leads to the failure of symbols to be shared. If only the former sorts of general-izations individuated symbol types, symbols would be shared all the time.

Because this latter sort of generalization contains types that aren't shared, some may suggest that such are not bona fide generalizations. However, they are generalizations in the following senses: (1) as with the first sort of generalization, they are rules the system uses to state abstract relationships between variables, allowing one to express gener-alizations compactly, learn, and represent relationships that hold for all members of a given class (Marcus 2001, 5); (2) they can be shared, at least in principle, by systems having all and only the same central algorithms.

P1. Within a given system, two tokens belong to the same type if and only if they play the same total computational role in that system.

P2. For any two systems, or within any given system, two tokens are the same type if and only if they have the same total computational role.

(Again, by "total computational role," I mean the role the symbol plays in the algorithms that cognitive science ultimately employs to characterize the central system.) Note that P1 is weaker than P2 in the sense that P1 is silent concerning the cross-system case. P1 is compatible with the denial that any cross-system condition exists; on the other hand, P1 is also compatible with the following:

P3. For any token $x$ in system S1 and any token $y$ in system S2, $x$ and $y$ can be of the same type yet play *different* computational roles.

In this case, there is a within-system condition, P1, that types tokens by the total computational role the symbol plays in the given system. But for the case of typing tokens across different systems, a different standard applies. (Perhaps, for instance, molecularism holds.)

Now, what principles do the three arguments support? Argument Two supports P1 only, for it was clearly limited to the within-system case (it began with, "Assume that *within a given system,* two primitive symbol tokens, *a* and *b*, are of symbol type T1, but *a* has the following causal relation that *b* does not have"). What about Argument One? Overall, the discussion in Argument One refers to individuation within the rules of a particular program. However, the argument could be construed as supporting P2, the view that tokens, even in distinct systems, must function the same way in the same program to be type-identical. Consider, for instance, the example of a game of chess, which Haugeland raised as an example of a symbol-manipulation game. It is very much in keeping with this view to say that different tokens on different boards are type-identical (e.g., tokens of the type *rook*) insofar as they function the same way in all and only the same rules.

I do not need to develop this issue further, however, for I find additional support for P2 from Argument Three. As discussed, there is at least a position in logical space in which P1, being silent about the cross-system case, is conjoined with a cross-system condition like P3. However, Argument Three can be viewed as both an argument against P3 as well as a further argument for P1 and P2. This argument says that psychology needs a natural kind that is individuated by its total computational role; otherwise there will be counterexamples or missed predictions. Recall that the argument involved stipulating that two tokens, *a* and *b*, be individuated by the same condition, CR, yet *a* have a computational relation, R*, that *b* lacks. As it happens, the argument can actually be presented in two ways: *a* and *b* could be within a given system or in distinct systems. So consider the distinct system case, and as before, assume that a token, *a,* has a computational relation, R*, that another token, *b,* does not, and that further, the individuation condition, CR, is insensitive to R*. On the common assumption that causal relations are backed by laws, there would then be a computational law, or at least a nomologically necessary generalization, L, which specifies R*. But then either (i), both *a* and *b* will *not* be subsumable in L, or (ii), they will both be subsumable in L. In the case of (i), the theory will have a missed prediction: it will miss that *a* has a causal relation that is specified by L, and in (ii), both will be subsumable in L. In this case *b* does not have the causal relation detailed by L. So we wouldn't expect it to behave in accordance with L. Hence, *b* will be a counterexample to L. This modified version of Argument Three thus provides reason to believe that across systems, tokens are type-identical only if they are characterized by all and only the same algorithms. And because it is uncontroversial that sameness of total computational role is sufficient for sameness of type, the condition can read "if and only if." So Argument Three yields, in its cross-system incarnation, an argument against P3 and for P2. (And in its within-system incarnation, it is an argument for P1).

A further problem with P3 arises as well. What would a cross-system symbol type really amount to? Unless one can refute the three arguments, one is committed to type individuating vocabulary items in the language of thought within a given system by total computational role. So if P3 is appealed to as well, this leaves one with two sorts of classificatory schemes for vocabulary items in the language of thought: one scheme for the within-system case and another for the cross-system case. We've already observed that such an approach is on the wrong track: it does not make sense to speak of a "language of thought" that is supposed to apply only to the cross-system case and yet be the language of *thought*. For a language to qualify as a language of thought, it should be the actual language that the system computes in, and that describes the system's underlying psychological processes.[8]

8. It could be that there is some incentive for the proponent of LOT to adopt an intrapersonal individuation condition for symbols *and* a cross-system MOP of a different sort (where such are not LOT symbols). While this chapter doesn't rule out such a project, I see no reason to appeal to such a kind. For even if individuation by total computational role is taken to be the only manner of individuation of MOPs (as I am happy to assume herein), psychology can, in fact, be public.

The upshot: the arguments of this chapter suggest that P1 and P2 hold but P3 is false—a cross-system condition is licensed only insofar as the systems in question are characterized by all and only the same central algorithms. And this brings us to the important issue of why, given that P2 holds, I need to argue that publicity obtains even if symbols aren't shared (that is, even if different systems do not token symbols of the same type). The reason is that, as noted, given that P2 is correct, for shared symbols to exist at all, different individuals' central systems must be characterized by all and only the same algorithms. Plausibly, this occurs in the Twin Earth case, because the "twins" are physical duplicates. (And indeed, this could be an explanatory advantage for LOT, if it adopts the present view of symbol individuation, for it allows for sameness in symbol/MOP type across twins, despite semantic differences.) The problem concerns the ordinary (nontwin) case. Research on the central system is only in its infancy; to say that different individuals' cognitive systems will be specified by the same algorithms strikes me as speculative, especially given individual variations in cognitive processing.[9] The plausibility of LOT's theory of symbols should not stand and fall with this issue. It is for this reason that I assume symbol types are not shared, and that I argue in the following chapter that the explanation can nonetheless be "public."

I have already considered two objections to (CAUSAL). Now let us turn to one that concerns the notion of computational

---

9. *Mutatis mutandis* for what is called the *intrapersonal diachronic case*, that is, the case of the individuation of mental states over time in a single person. For consider that not only are our neural connections continually reshaping themselves, but there are significant neuroanatomical changes in the brain of a single individual over the course of one's lifetime.

role that I appeal to. A natural objection is that my appeal to as yet undiscovered algorithms is problematic, because it is merely a promissory note to a future cognitive science. First, that the nature of the algorithms is largely unknown does not make the three arguments offered any less plausible, for these arguments would seem to apply whatever the relevant algorithms turn out to be. Second, such an objection would also rule out all forms of a posteriori functionalism, because all appeal to largely as yet undiscovered laws, but without any substantive argument as to why such a posteriori approaches are implausible. The present approach is merely an instance of the general approach of psychofunctionalism. This would leave us with purely armchair approaches to mental state individuation, yet without any real argument for the ineffectiveness of a posteriori functionalism. And third, rejecting (CAUSAL) for this reason is tantamount to ruling out all proposals that individuate an entity by its causal powers (e.g., Sydney Shoemaker's theory of properties), for presumably, such causal powers are ultimately a matter of scientific discovery.[10] Clearly, one can offer compelling arguments for an individuation condition, say, on the nature of properties, in absence of knowledge of the precise content of the laws (dispositions, causal powers, etc.) themselves.

Of course, Fodor himself would deny that the program can be specified. Stronger yet, he would deny that we have justification to believe that such a program exists. According to him, the central system is probably not computational. Indeed, this point raises a new dimension of the debate over symbol natures: if, as this book argues, symbols must be individuated by their

10. For a theory in which properties are individuated in this manner see (Shoemaker 1984.)

computational roles, and if Fodor is correct that the central system is probably not even computational to begin with, then one should reject LOT altogether. For in this case, one should conclude that the language of thought program will likely fail. After all, what computational roles would be available to individuate symbols if the central system is likely not computational to begin with? Note that this situation would apply to molecularist theories of symbols as well. Fodor's well-known concerns about the central system thereby seems to present yet another serious obstacle to the LOT program, ruling out computational role conceptions of symbols. This is particularly worrisome given the problems with type identity and semantic theories of symbol individuation that were raised in the previous chapter. Luckily, as I've argued, the central system is computational after all.

## 3   Conclusion

This brings to a close my initial case for the algorithmic account of symbol natures. In venturing a solution to Problem Two, the present chapter has covered a good deal of terrain, supplying three arguments for the individuation of symbols by total computational role and specifying the conception of computational role that is employed by the three arguments. The results of this chapter, when coupled with those of the previous one, suggest that the algorithmic conception is the *only* theory of symbols that the proponent of CTM can appeal to.

At this point in the dialectic, I suspect that you share my suspicion that the other theories of symbols face serious problems. Yet it is natural to ask: Does the proposed view of symbols really satisfy the important philosophical roles outlined in chapter 4? The critic will likely grant that (CAUSAL) satisfies the first role—that of identifying a mental kind that can serve as a neo-Fregean MOP—for individuation by computational role is finely grained enough to capture subtle differences in one's way of conceiving things. And being nonsemantic, (CAUSAL) should suffice for the purposes of naturalism (Role Three). Yet the critic will likely observe that (CAUSAL) fails to provide a sense in which different individuals share symbols, and this is highly problematic for explaining the causation of thought and behavior (Role Two). In particular, although the algorithmic conception allows for explanations of the thoughts and behaviors of single individuals, according to critics, it does not allow for explanations that cover groups of individuals or even the same individual over time, for that matter (Aydede 2000; Prinz 2002). Yet it seems that different people at least sometimes represent entities in the same way. For example, different individuals may consider Venus as the morning star rather than the evening star and behave accordingly. Critics charge that if symbols are individuated by the role they play in one's entire cognitive economy, because we commonly differ with respect to memories, personality traits, and so on, symbols will not be shared. As we shall see, this gives rise to several pressing objections.

In the following chapter, I turn to these important issues. In so doing, I explore the role symbols play in psychological explanation, especially how they function as neo-Fregean modes of presentation. Further, I extend the results of the present chapter to LOT's favored theory of concepts, conceptual atomism, illustrating why, given this understanding of symbols, the LOT program must embrace pragmatism.

# 6 Idiosyncratic Minds Think Alike: Modes of Presentation Reconsidered

Mental symbols have algorithmic natures. Or so I have argued. But to confess, there is a common retort to the argumentation of the previous chapter: *Your position on symbols may indeed be nonnegotiable, but its very nonnegotiability is just another nail in the coffin of the LOT program, for the algorithmic view introduces more problems than it solves.* The problems the critic alludes to all arise from the fact that symbolic modes of presentation (MOPs), so understood, are not shared between different individuals or even the same person at different times.[1] For consider the following objections:

1. *The publicity objection.* I have just claimed that primitive symbols are typed by their total computational roles. And this sort of view is notoriously fine grained, resulting in a situation in which few, if any, symbols are shared. This situation leads Jerry Fodor and Jesse Prinz to respond that, on my view, different individuals will apparently not fall under the same computational generalizations, for on the symbol-processing view of cognition, computational generalizations are supposed to be sensitive to

1. Recall that symbols or MOPs are not "shared" when a given theory holds that different individuals, or the same individual over different times, do not have tokens of the same type.

symbol types. At best, psychology would have system-specific laws, laws that cover the workings of a particular system at a given time. So psychology will not be public.

2. *The shared MOP objection.* Relatedly, Fodor and Prinz further object that even if one grants that explanation can be public, a competing theory of MOPs in which individuals have type-identical MOPs is superior from an explanatory standpoint, for importantly, different individuals can share the same way of conceiving of the world.

3. *The objection from concept nativism.* If symbols are not shared, it is natural to expect that LOT—ironically, given its origins—requires the truth of concept empiricism. For how can concepts be innate if symbols are not even shared?

Each problem is prima facie serious enough to warrant the suspicion that algorithmic typing would, in fact, bring about LOT's demise. So in this chapter I respond to them. But this chapter is not merely defensive; for in considering the critics' objections I further refine my positive account. In particular, we've seen that mental symbols play the role of neo-Fregean modes of presentation (MOPs) for the LOT program, being the ways that individuals represent the world. (To call your attention to this, I shall sometimes speak of symbols as *symbolic MOPs*). In responding to my critics, this chapter develops a more detailed picture of how MOPs figure in psychological explanations. So let me begin.

## 1   Responding to the Publicity Objection

Fodor has remarked to me in conversation that CAUSAL is a "gesture of despair" because it is holistic, but I must confess, I find it rather appealing. After all, if there are indeed symbols in the language of thought, they are a natural kind that figures in psychological explanations. Classifying natural kinds on the basis of sameness and difference in causal powers is a common scientific practice (where, mind you, the powers are not *all* the object's powers but those germane to the given level of inquiry). So it *should* be relatively natural to appeal to a manner of typing symbols that cuts them at the level of grain of sameness and difference of their computational-level causal powers. I am terribly curious if and how this observation about kinds can be denied.

In any case, I must come clean and admit that Fodor's reaction is quite common. Those who have discussed conditions like CAUSAL in the literature have discarded such conditions because they are said to be holistic, precluding the possibility of different people (or the same person at different times) having type-identical symbols (Pessin 1995; Prinz 2002; Aydede 2000).[2] Perhaps even worse, a revival of a computational-role condition may strike some as eternal recurrence of the same bad theory. For the complaints in the literature on LOT symbols roughly mirror the charges that Fodor (1998a) and Fodor and LePore (1992) leveled against conceptual-role semantics in the context of debating the plausibility of narrow content.

The publicity objection has the potential to be devastating. In light of this, I now provide a fourfold response to it.

### First Response: Publicity via Externalist Explanation

In response to the first objection, observe that insofar as there are semantic or intentional generalizations that subsume individuals

2. This is not a form of meaning holism, but a holism that involves symbol individuation, in which symbols are said to be individuated by the role they play in a larger network of symbols. And, because MOPs are symbols, this is a kind of holism infecting MOP individuation as well.

with respect to broad contents, individuals will be able to satisfy the same psychological generalizations despite the fact that technically, they do not share the same symbolic MOP types.

A natural question to ask is: Are such generalizations found within cognitive science? Or better yet: Will a completed cognitive science feature them? While it is still too early to project what the character of generalizations in a completed cognitive science will be, existing philosophical considerations suggest that the LOT program has a plausible case for an affirmative answer to the latter question. Ned Block, Jerry Fodor, Zenon Pylyshyn, and Georges Rey have argued that cognitive science needs laws that subsume agents by the broadly referential properties of their symbolic states (Block 1986; Fodor 1994, 51; Pylyshyn 1986; Rey 2009). They claim that such generalizations (which I'll call *referential generalizations*) are required to capture predictive uniformities among symbolic thoughts that represent the same state of affairs in different ways. This is because people live in the same general environment and have similar mental structures. People's behavior toward referents tends to converge despite small, and even large, differences in their ways of representing the world. For instance, one person may think of water as "the stuff that contains both hydrogen and oxygen"; another may think of it as "the liquid people like to drink." Nonetheless, both parties satisfy many of the same water-related generalizations. This observation is insightful: Different systems having distinct ways of representing the same entity will frequently behave in similar ways because they are embedded in similar environments and because they make similar demands on these environments. But how would this tendency toward similar thoughts and behaviors be captured by the generalizations of a psychology with only MOP-sensitive generalizations to appeal to?

Here, the critic could raise the concern that generalizations sensitive to broad contents are merely required insofar as MOPs fail to be public, and the publicity problem is just a relic of my own theory. Otherwise, cognitive science would not require referential generalizations at all. This is not the case, however, for we should distinguish a situation in which computational states (or contents) can be individuated in a way that is system specific, and thus not shared, from a situation in which they are shared, but in which what the critic would likely regard as "reasonable" cognitive or perceptual differences individuate the states. Even if there is a way to type computational states (or contents) across distinct systems, any plausible theory of typing will distinguish states with *very* different computational or conceptual roles. However, even when there are "reasonable differences" among the states, people's behavior toward the referent generally tends to converge. Such convergence can be captured by broad laws.

Turning to another tactic, the objector can point out that my entire first answer to the publicity argument pertains to the case of intentional explanation, rather than to explanation of the computational workings of a system. And the original publicity objection still applies in the context of computational explanation, even if shared intentional explanation is possible, for how is computational explanation feasible if individuals do not even share the same symbols?

To respond, I believe that explanation in computational psychology does not literally require shared LOT expressions. Indeed, it is commonly accepted that the main emphasis of computational explanation is not the subsumption of events under laws; instead, it is concerned with explanation in terms of functional analysis or decomposition (Block 1995; Hardcastle 1996;

Cummins 1983). But as my second reply asserts, even according to the present theory of symbols, such explanation can still be public.

## Second Response: Publicity in Terms of Functional Analysis

According to the method of functional analysis, a system is described in terms of the causal organization of its components and the way in which the components interrelate. Now, proponents of the publicity objection fail to note that functional analysis does not require that systems have symbols of the same type. Consider, for instance, one of the most familiar introductory-level discussions of functional decomposition, Ned Block's "The Mind as the Software of the Brain" (1995). Block provides two examples of functional decomposition; in both examples, the description of the machine's functional organization abstracts away from the actual symbols that the machine computes. Consider Block's first example:

Suppose one wants to explain how we understand language. Part of the system will recognize individual words. This word-recognizer might be composed of three components, one of which has the task of fetching each incoming word, one at a time, and passing it to a second component. The second component includes a dictionary, i.e., a list of all the words in the vocabulary, together with syntactic and semantic information about each word. This second component compares the target word with words in the vocabulary (perhaps executing many such comparisons simultaneously) until it gets a match. When it finds a match, it sends a signal to a third component whose job it is to retrieve the syntactic and semantic information stored in the dictionary. This speculation about how a model of language understanding works is supposed to illustrate how a cognitive competence can be explained by appeal to simpler cognitive competences, in this case, the simple mechanical operations of fetching and matching. (Block 1995)

This case is quite simple, but it is designed to be like actual cases of functional decomposition in cognitive science. Observe that all the mental operations are explained without appeal to the particular symbols in the device's memory. This is because different systems will process different words, and each system may have an entirely different vocabulary in its database. The explanation of fetching and matching tasks needs to abstract away from the particular words to unite similar phenomena into a shared explanatory framework.

This point can be further illustrated by reflecting on an actual case of functional decomposition, Alan Baddeley's influential explanation of working memory (Baddeley 1992; Baddeley 1986). His account does not require shared MOPs or symbols because it abstracts away from such details, focusing instead on the general processing of any contents of working memory. Baddeley conceives of working memory (WM) as a system that gives "temporary storage and manipulation of the information necessary for complex cognitive tasks as language comprehension, learning and reasoning" (Baddeley 1992, 556). His focus is not on the particular contents of memory but on providing a functional decomposition that begins with a tripartite division of the WM system. Working memory comprises a *central executive,* which is an attentional controlling system, and two slave systems: the *phonological loop,* which stores and rehearses speech-based information, and the *visuospatial sketchpad,* which holds and manipulates visuospatial information.[3] The workings of each slave system are described in a way that abstracts away from the particular items in one's database.

Of course, we cannot explore all the examples of functional decomposition in cognitive science, but it is fair to say that at this point, the burden is on the critic to show that functional decomposition would be ruined by a failure to arrive at a theory of shared symbols. Even if symbols aren't shared, computational psychology is still public in its most crucial explanatory dimension—that of functional decomposition.

I shall now outline yet another manner in which psychology can be public, even if symbols are not shared. My discussion begins with a criticism of this second response.

### Third Response: Symbol-Neutral Generalizations

The critic begins with an observation: although much of cognitive science is concerned with elucidating cognitive capacities, there is also much interest in discovering and confirming laws or effects.[4] And it is in the domain of laws, if not functional decomposition, that the predicament with symbol types infects the possibility of computational explanation, or at least a vital part of computational explanation. For if symbols are individuated algorithmically, computational laws do not cover distinct systems.

This is incorrect, however, for even if there are no shared symbols, there can still be computational laws that are sensitive to symbols. For computational psychology frequently appeals to generalizations that quantify over LOT symbols, but without quantification over particular symbol types. Such statements generalize over LOT expressions without actually specifying them. I shall call such generalizations *symbol-neutral generalizations*.

3. For discussion, see Baddeley (1992, 1986) and Gazzaniga, Mangun, and Ivry (2002).
4. For discussion of these issues, see Cummins (2000, 114–144).

To elaborate, in the context of related debates over the plausibility of narrow content, it was suggested that computational psychology has certain laws that quantify over MOPs in general without actually quantifying over particular types.[5] This suggestion is apt, although, as I will explain, symbol-neutral laws are not the only sorts of laws that computational psychology appeals to. But focusing for now on the symbol-neutral laws, a strong case can be made that such generalizations are present throughout cognitive science.

In the context of the narrow content debate, Block gives the following example:

For any goal g and action a, if one wants g and believes that doing a is required for g, then, *ceteris paribus*, one will try to do a. (Block 1998)

Notice that such generalizations do not require a theory of shared MOPs (i.e., narrow contents, LOT symbols, et cetera): all that is required is that there be a principle of individuation that distinguishes MOP types *within a given system*, that is, synchronically and intrapersonally.[6] Indeed, within fields that have generalizations that are sensitive to MOPs, an appeal to such neutral laws is commonplace. By way of illustration, consider generalizations about memory and attention, which abstract away from

5. Suggested by Fodor (1987). Ned Block also suggests this in his (1998). Block's suggestion concerns narrow contents, but in this paper, he suggests that narrow contents are individuated by their computational role in a symbolic system. In chapter 8 I argue that the states individuated in this manner are not really contents.
6. Here, I am trying to state the issue in a way that does not assume that researchers in such fields uniformly believe in LOT. Of course, the proponent of LOT will construe MOPs as being symbols. Others will construe MOPs as narrow contents, activation patterns in connectionist networks, etc.

the particular items being processed, focusing instead on general patterns that explain phenomena like storage capacity, encoding, and retrieval. An instance of this is George Miller's generalization about the upper limit on the number of items in working memory: the "magical number seven, plus or minus two" (Miller 1956). And MOP-neutral generalizations are rife throughout the literature on concepts. Consider, for example, the prototype effects discovered by Eleanor Rosch and her cohorts (Rosch 1976, 1978). MOP-neutral generalizations are also found throughout work on social cognition: for example, in generalizations that are concerned with patterns involving social stereotyping, which abstract away from the details of a particular case, and focus on general patterns of thinking and behavior.[7] And consider "syntactic" or proof theoretic versions of logical generalizations like *modus ponens* and conjunction elimination.

Now, I am not proposing that cognitive science *only* has such generalizations, or that a completed cognitive science will merely have such. Computational psychology currently clearly finds certain more specific generalizations to be of interest. For instance, consider:

(M) The moon looks larger on the horizon than it does in other parts of the sky.

The existence of such generalizations does not pose a problem for my account of symbols, for such generalizations are most suitably regarded as being referential. Intuitively, even if there are such things as shared narrow contents or shared symbols, if (M) were sensitive to such types, it would artificially exclude individuals who seem to satisfy this generalization, for individuals

7. Many such generalizations are laid out in Kunda (1999).

normally do have differences in their MOPs of the moon (or horizon, or sky), while still experiencing the moon illusion.[8]

## Response Four: Contexts in which Cognitive Science Needs to Quantify over Particular Symbol Types?

We are situated at the beginning of cognitive science, so let us be cautious about projecting the precise situations in which cognitive science would be interested in generalizations that quantify over particular symbol types. One thing that *is* sensible to maintain at this time, however, is that, assuming that the language of thought picture is correct, computational psychology needs to make use of such generalizations to explain the detailed workings of a particular system. If one seeks an account of the particular workings of a system—for example, to explain how a particular system satisfies a given cognitive function—the needed explanation would invoke particular LOT states. Such laws would quantify over particular symbol types, as they are intended to detail a system's transition from one symbolic state to another. Would this situation be problematic if symbols are not shared? I do not believe so, for why would one expect such laws to apply to distinct individuals in the first place? It is plausible that such explanations, by their very nature, are supposed to detail the idiosyncratic workings of a particular system.[9]

8. Some might find my referential interpretation of (M) to be unsatisfactory, as the domain of computational psychology seems to be narrow and syntactic. However, the law, while obviously being a prediction, is actually a statement that is to be explained by a particular computational account of the moon illusion. It is not itself intended to serve as the underlying computational account. For more discussion, see Cummins (2000).

9. It could be argued that such are not laws, because they have only one instance. This view strikes me as problematic, however. For one thing, almost any law that has a single instance could, in principle, have had more.

This concludes my fourfold response to the publicity argument. I've argued that even if individuals do not have symbols of the same type, psychological explanation can still be public. First, I argued that functional decomposition does not demand that two systems have any of the same symbols in their database. Second, I observed that according to the LOT program, explanation that is sensitive to broad content plays a crucial role in cognitive science, but as with functional decomposition, explanation covering different systems can occur without the systems having the same internal states. Third, I argued that generalizations involving LOT symbols do not, by and large, quantify over particular symbol types; rather, they quantify over symbols only in general. So different individuals frequently do fall under the same generalizations by virtue of having symbolic states. And finally, I noted that the only situations in which LOT symbols need to be subsumed by laws with respect to their particular symbol types (as opposed to being subsumed by virtue of simply having some LOT symbol or other) involve explanation that, by its very nature, requires the detailed workings of a particular system. And in such situations, it is inappropriate to call for symbol types that are shared across distinct sorts of systems. Thus, as far as I can tell, Fodor and Prinz's charge of "publicity violation" is entirely benign: the publicity failure pertains to the states; it doesn't extend to the actual cognitive explanations themselves.

Let us now turn to the second objection, which also concerns the role that symbolic MOPs play in psychological explanations. This objection can be offered in the face of my response to the publicity objection, because it suggests that there is in fact an explanatory demand for laws that are sensitive to shared symbols. But it also stands alone as an independent reply to my theory of symbol individuation.

## 2  The Interpersonal MOP Objection

Consider:

(Principle P) *Ceteris paribus*, a competing theory of MOPs in which MOPs are shared will have a clear advantage over the view of MOPs defended herein.

Principle P seems fair: even if one grants that explanation can be public, a competing theory of MOPs in which individuals have MOPs of the same type appears to be superior from an explanatory standpoint, because it captures the sense in which different individuals can share the same way of conceiving a referent.

There are considerations that deflate the force of Principle P, however. First, as noted, even if symbols are not shared, individuals can still have thoughts that are type-identical at the intentional level because individuals with different inner symbols may nonetheless have symbols with the same broad content. Second, although Principle P is reasonable, for it to speak against my account, shared MOPs must be a genuine theoretical option, and the burden of proof is on the critic to illustrate that it is. The Frege case argument claims that without the individuation of symbols by their total computational roles, either there will be counterexamples to certain psychological laws, or psychology will be incomplete. As noted, the basics of the argument present a demand for a taxonomy of psychological states in terms of total functional or computational role. The upshot is that unless one individuates psychological states in this extremely thin manner, either missed predictions or counterexamples will ensue. If one accepts this argument, then why not reject shared MOPs altogether?

Those interested in connectionism may look to activation patterns in connectionist networks for a theory of shared modes of presentation. But here, one finds that modes of presentation are individuated by the role they play in the larger network, giving rise to a well-known criticism that such entities are not shared (Churchland 1998; Fodor and LePore 1992). Many have suspected that shared MOPs can be provided by a theory of narrow content, but there is no general consensus on such a theory, and criticisms of the leading views abound (Prinz 2002; Fodor and LePore 1992; Segal 2000). Although I respond to some leading theories of narrow content in chapter 8, I will not attempt to provide an exhaustive discussion of competing theories of MOPs—doing so would require a book of its own. But it is reasonable to suggest that if the critic wishes Principle P to have dialectical force, she must first illustrate that an independently plausible conception of shared MOPs is even available.

Third, Principle P is not as compelling as it initially sounds. For consider that the main reasons for appealing to LOT symbols still hold, even if symbols are not shared. Previously, we discussed how symbols nonetheless figure in psychological explanations. Additionally, it is crucial to bear in mind the motivations raised in the last few chapters for advancing a criterion for individuating symbols:

(i) to enable CTM, as a computational theory, to provide a well-defined notion of a symbol;

(ii) to allow LOT to specify the nature of MOPs, which are supposed to be the inner vehicle of thought and figure in a naturalistic explanation of intentionality;

(iii) to express the intuitive sense in which twins share the same internal psychological states;

(iv) to supply a kind that enables psychology to specify the computational configuration of a particular system, and to explain the narrow causation of thought and behavior.

These motivations are all satisfied by the present view. And, I would add, given our discussion of symbol-neutral laws, the following motivation:

(v) to offer a theory of symbols that provides a kind which a certain class of interpersonal laws are sensitive to, namely, MOP-neutral laws.

Of course, proponents of LOT maintain that LOT best explains the systematicity, compositionality, and productivity of thought. Doing so is surely essential to LOT's ability to satisfy (iv). Notice that LOT still can account for such features even if symbols are not shared, for a combinatorial language can involve primitive expressions that differ from person to person. You could, in fact, coin a language right now, employing rules of combination that operate on your own, invented, stock of primitive expressions.

In sum, the algorithmic theory of symbols serves a variety of vital functions. And as I've argued, even if it turns out that symbols aren't shared, there is, unexpectedly, no violation of publicity. So why are common MOPs even required?

In response to all of this, Jesse Prinz has remarked to me in conversation that there is a class of examples that may suggest that at least some psychological laws *must* be sensitive to shared MOPs. Consider the following tinker toy generalization:

(S) If people see Superman, and they believe danger is near, then ceteris paribus, they will run to Superman.

Suppose that Superman is not in costume. Now consider those who know that Kent is also Superman and, believing danger is nearby, run to him. Now, in the solution to the problem of Frege cases that is advanced in chapter 8, I illustrate that instances of individuals *not* realizing that Kent is also Superman can be included in the ceteris paribus clause of the relevant intentional law. Fodor has employed a similar tactic (Fodor 1994). As a result, the correct equivalence class can be demarcated. But Prinz's concern is somewhat different: he worries that referential generalizations cannot capture the reason these individuals all satisfy (S), while those who only know of Kent in a "Kent way" do not. Intuitively, the reason is that they all seem to have MOPs that represent Superman in a "Superman way." So it would seem that Principle P is indeed apt; certain laws must be sensitive to particular MOP types.

There are four tactics that can be employed to satisfy Prinz, however. First, one can appeal to similarities in behavior, including utterances, and sameness of other broad beliefs to indicate that the underlying MOPs of these people are similar in important ways. For instance, in the present case, all of these people would assent to "Kent is Superman," all have the broad belief that the man who wears a red and blue uniform is standing nearby, and so on. Second, one may also appeal to a law statement that is worded along the lines of (S), employing the expression "Superman" rather than "Kent" to call to attention the salient phenomenon. (By analogy, within the literature on belief ascription, the neo-Russellian recognizes that certain expressions are selected in conversation for pragmatic reasons, to call attention to a salient phenomenon.) And third, as I explore in chapter 8, certain requirements about MOPs will figure in the ceteris paribus clauses of intentional laws; namely, as we shall see, the agent must represent the relevant referents in "matching ways." This calls attention to the phenomenon that certain of those who represent something in one sort of way, and not in the other, behave in a particular way cited by the generalization. And again, even if there are no shared LOT expressions, these ways can be described, for they can be distinguished metalinguistically and by appeal to other broad beliefs that the person has. This is precisely the same phenomenon that the proponent of the narrow theory is interested in making salient in her generalizations. It is just that in the case of the broad way of doing things, it is made salient in both the generalization itself—that is, by appeal to the particular sort of wording—and by appeal to the computational-level details, other broad contents, and behaviors (including "Superman" and "Kent" utterances). In a sense, by employing these tactics, broad psychology is able to mimic a narrow theory.

A further tactic is available as well. The broad psychologist may modify the generalization by selecting a certain description that expresses the reason for the action and embedding it in the antecedent. An illustration will help. In the case at hand, (S) could be altered in the following manner:

(S') If people see Superman and believe that danger is near, and believe that that this man who they see is the superhero who protects people, then ceteris paribus, they will run to Superman.

(S') will now express the reason why each individual runs to Superman; each person believes that he is a superhero who will protect them. Note that this added material is construed referentially: (S') has not been converted into a MOP-sensitive generalization. This is illustrative of a general strategy that would be available in other cases as well.

The critic is likely to say that these ways of doing things are ad hoc. I'm not so sure; after all, it is not really ad hoc to include the above description in (S') because it makes the reason for action more obvious. Similarly, the above attempts at alluding to differences between MOPs, without offering an actual condition providing for shared MOPs, are designed to call attention to the phenomenon that those who represent something in one sort of way, and not the other, behave in the way cited by the generalization. Again, this is the same phenomenon that the proponent of the narrow theory is interested in making salient in her generalizations.

Considering this objection, as well as the previous one, has been useful to one larger aim of this chapter: the aim of arriving at a better understanding of LOT's neo-Fregean MOPs. For in responding to these criticisms I have in effect outlined how symbolic MOPs function in psychological generalizations. This is a matter I return to, and further refine, when I attempt to solve the problem of Frege cases in chapter 8. I now turn to the timely topic of the nature of concepts, responding to the objection from concept nativism. My treatment of concepts continues into chapter 7, where I develop a new version of conceptual atomism.

## 3   The Objection from Concept Nativism

Ordinary people—that is, those not in the grip of an academic theory—consider concepts to be inner ideas: the ways we grasp the world around us. But within the walls of academe, "concept" is a term of art. According to conceptual atomism, the content of a primitive concept is determined by the information it carries about its environment, or what it refers to. Conceptual atomism says little about the role concepts play in our mental lives; its approach to concepts is referentialist. This sort of approach flies in the face of our ordinary understanding of a concept, which is psychological through and through. In the next chapter I develop a form of conceptual atomism that is psychological, yet still referentialist. But let us now consider conceptual atomism in the context of the objection from nativism.

Few individuals, if any, adhere to radical nativism. Yet the question of whether certain concepts are innate is of great import to cognitive science, and it is not implausible to suspect that there will be some innate concepts (e.g., FACE and OBJECT). Surely LOT should be open to any empirically plausible position on the origin of concepts, and given its nativist roots, it is vital that it be compatible with concept nativism. But here's the rub: if individuals do not share the same symbolic vocabulary, then symbols are not shared. So how can concepts be innate? After all, we generally think of innate concepts as being shared from person to person.

We can begin to make progress on this problem by distinguishing symbols from concepts. Again, *concept* is a term of art, there being multiple theories of concepts that figure in contemporary discussions. Notice that the only way in which the failure to find shared *symbols* results in a failure of *concepts* to be shared is if symbols individuate concepts, and on most views of concepts, symbols are *not* individuative. It is only when concepts are individuated by their symbol types that concept nativism is threatened. As it turns out, the only theory of concepts that currently holds that symbols individuate concepts is conceptual atomism, which claims that concepts are individuated by both their broad contents and their symbol types. So let us ask: does conceptual atomism allow concepts to be innate on the assumption that different individuals fail to have type-identical symbols?

It will prove useful to have a richer understanding of conceptual atomism in hand. According to the conceptual atomist, lexical concepts are primitive, being semantically unstructured: that is, they are not comprised of further concepts.[10] For instance, it is not the case that BACHELOR is a construct of the more basic concepts UNMARRIED and MALE. Concepts are, in this sense, *atomic,* and hence the position earns its title, *conceptual atomism.* Conceptual atomism further holds that concepts are individuated, at least in part, by the information that the symbol carries about the world (Fodor 1998a; Margolis and Laurence 1999, 62; Prinz 2002). Further, conceptual atomism defines primitive concepts in the following manner:

Conceptual Atomism (CA)

**Existence condition**    A primitive concept exists if and only if a primitive symbol in the language of thought (LOT) has a broad content.

**Identity condition**    Primitive concepts are identical if and only if they are of the same symbol type and have the same broad content (Fodor 1998a, 37).

(Complex concepts, in turn, are defined in terms of combinatorial operations on the primitives.) A concept is thereby individuated by two components: its broad content, where such is understood as, roughly, the information that the concept carries about its environment, and its symbol type (Fodor 1998a). Although Fodor has emphasized, "concepts are . . . formulae in Mentalese" (2008), conceptual atomism is not normally associated with this view. In fact, many portray conceptual atomism as claiming, simply, that a concept is a broad content. Equating concepts with broad contents is a common error; one which

10. Lexical concepts are concepts like BEER, BOSON, and CAFFEINE— concepts that correspond to lexical items in natural language.

Fodor has done little to correct. I take up this matter in the subsequent chapter. For now, it suffices to bear in mind that conceptual atomism is mainly known for the following claims about the semantics of mental representation: a concept's meaning is just its broad content, lexical concepts lack semantic structure, and concept "pragmatism" is a misleading philosophical enterprise (Fodor 1998a, 2008; Laurence and Margolis 1999; Rives 2008). I shall discuss this third claim in detail shortly; for the moment, simply note that in light of LOT's neglect of symbol natures, it is unsurprising that conceptual atomism is largely known for its semantic claims.

Yet glancing at (CA), notice that the conceptual atomist can actually distinguish concepts along two dimensions, a symbolic dimension and a referential one, because both features are individuative. Consider that, on the one hand, for the purposes of intentional explanation, the LOT program can speak of a concept "referentially" by typing it in terms of its broad content and abstracting away from its computational role. In the case of intentional explanation, any two co-referring concepts having the same grammatical form are regarded as being type-identical. On the other hand, in contexts in which one is explaining modes of presentation, including the proximal causation of thought and behavior, as in the contexts discussed in answering the first objection, the LOT program may find it useful to single out concepts by their symbolic, that is, computational-role, dimension only. (Given that the conceptual atomist's primary focus is semantic, some may be surprised that I claim that the standard conceptual atomism individuates concepts by their symbol types, as well as their broad contents. The subsequent chapter will illustrate that this is indeed the case by exploring Fodor's remarks on this matter.)

Bearing all of this in mind, let me return to the question of whether the atomist's view is truly compatible with concept nativism, insofar as symbols are understood algorithmically. An example will prove useful, so let us consider the concept of a human face, one of the more plausible examples of an innate concept. The conceptual atomist who accepts CAUSAL can say exactly what a proponent of the standard LOT program would likely say: if the concept of a face is innate, then it is biologically determined that any normal human infant will have an innate symbol, and by extension, concept, in her language of thought that refers to faces. Biology and neuroscience will provide an account according to which the concept has such and such biological basis, is triggered at such and such developmental point, and so on. What is distinctive about the atomist's approach to innate concepts is that they are singled out by their referential properties for the purpose of providing intentional generalizations across different individuals. The intentional generalizations are insensitive to differences at the level of computational role; the computational-role dimension drops out of the explanation. For instance, consider the following tinker toy generalization: *When infants are born, they immediately show interest in human faces.* The conceptual atomist can appeal to a version of this generalization that subsumes each individual's LOT expression by its broad content.

This is not to suggest that the conceptual atomist holds that innate concepts can *only* be explained intentionally or psychologically. Quite the contrary, the atomist acknowledges that explaining the biological underpinnings of innate concepts is primarily an issue for biology and neuroscience, not psychology. The point is that even Fodor's conceptual atomism takes a referential approach to innate concepts, for, as we've seen, Fodorian conceptual atomism is mainly a semantic doctrine, leaving the details to biology and neuroscience. No additional disadvantage is introduced by my approach to symbols. What is offered is a stance similar to the orthodox view: a referential strategy. More specifically, if symbols are not shared, then the LOT program simply cannot generalize over concepts with respect to particular symbol types—that is, insofar as it allows symbols to individuate concepts. Other explanatory strategies are available, however, even if symbols are individuative of concepts: the atomist can appeal to intentional generalizations, MOP-neutral generalizations, and explanation by functional decomposition. Hence, even if symbols individuate concepts, concept nativism is compatible with any failure to locate an interpersonal type-identity condition on primitive LOT expressions.

I would also add that LOT can also express a different kind of nativist commitment. LOT can be regarded as an innate cognitive capacity, because any sophisticated languagelike computational system requires an internal language with primitive vocabulary items that obey rules enabling the language to be systematic, productive, and compositional. This sense in which LOT is innate strikes me as being quite sensible. It has been developed by Gary Marcus in a chapter of his book *The Algebraic Mind* (Marcus 2001).[11]

## 4  Conclusion

This completes my response to the three objections. These objections all arose from the fact that symbolic modes of presentation,

11. It may surprise some that it is not the main aim of Marcus's chapter to develop concept nativism. But he has other fish to fry: "The suggestion that I consider in this chapter is that the machinery of symbol-manipulation is included in the set of things that are initially available to the child, prior to experience with the external world. According to this, there is an innately given representational format that allows for

when understood algorithmically, are not shared between different individuals or even the same person at different points in time. I believe that I have now clarified how explanation of thought and behavior is nevertheless possible. I hope that in considering each of these responses, you now have a deeper understanding of how symbolic MOPs, construed algorithmically, figure in psychological explanations. This chapter also completes my answer to the second of the three problems that this book aims to solve, the problem of the nature of symbols.

Now that symbols are individuated, the philosophical roles that symbols are summoned to play for the LOT program can be satisfied. Further, symbolic types can figure in laws, whether they be symbol-neutral or system-specific ones, for there can be a clear conception of what event sequences would constitute an instance of the law. Relatedly, there can be testable predictions. Other results of the present theory of symbols will likely be more controversial. First, as we've noted, if the algorithmic account is correct, the central system *must* be computational. This is because symbols themselves are individuated by central algorithms. *So the success of LOT requires resisting Fodor's injunction that research in cognitive science rest at the modules.* Second, and perhaps even more controversially, the algorithmic account of symbols transforms conceptual atomism into a pragmatist theory. For in the next chapter I will argue that conceptual atomism should be, and ironically, has always been, a pragmatist theory. So let us now rethink conceptual atomism.

the possibility of operations over variables, an innately given set of operations that can be computed over those variables, an innately given apparatus for combining these operations, an innately given format that accommodates structured combinations, and an innately given representational format that accommodates representing individuals distinct from kinds" (2001, 144).

# 7 Concepts: A Pragmatist Theory

Concepts are the fabric out of which thought is woven. We've noted that in the eyes of laypersons, concepts are patently psychological entities. Theories of concepts in psychology agree. Conceptual atomism, in stark contrast, is well known for rejecting this approach to concepts. It is largely for this reason that conceptual atomism has few followers. It is too emaciated, missing out on the central, psychological, functions that concepts play in our mental lives. In this chapter, I develop an alternative form of conceptual atomism that draws from LOT's referential semantics *and* features a psychological element: *Pragmatic atomism*. To do so I draw from LOT's traditional enemy, concept pragmatism. I begin by clarifying what the doctrine of concept pragmatism is (section 1). I then argue that a conceptual atomism featuring a pragmatist component is superior to conceptual atomism as it is standardly construed, for it satisfies more of the desiderata that many in the concepts literature believe any plausible notion of a concept must satisfy (section 2). Indeed, Fodorian conceptual atomism actually has a pragmatist component that is frequently missed (section 3). One caveat: *pragmatism* is an expression referring to an immense and diffuse spectrum of ideas; here, I align the new LOT with what Fodor identifies as *concept pragmatism*, the form of pragmatism which he attacks. I claim that LOT is pragmatist in *this* sense. This will all be nice and controversial—one should never shy away from a philosophical bloodbath.

## 1   Appreciating LOT's Pragmatist Dimension

Fodor's attack on pragmatism has become part and parcel of the mainstream LOT. For example, recall Fodor's comment in *LOT 2* that "one of the ways *LOT 2* differs from LOT 1 is in the single-mindedness with which it identifies pragmatism as the enemy *par excellence* of Cartesian realism about mental states" (2008, 12). But what does this opposition to pragmatism really amount to? Fodor is not engaging in an all-out attack on the pragmatist tradition; rather, his interest lies in theories of concepts (or content) that define concepts (or content) with respect to the manner in which they are used. Indeed, because Fodor's use of the expression "pragmatism" is so idiosyncratic, it is worth emphasizing what his real target is. In an illuminating description of the positions under attack, he writes (or rather, rants):

I do think that concept pragmatism is practically all of what the last hundred years of Anglophone philosophy of mind (/language) has been about. For example, concept pragmatism is what crude behaviorists (like Quine and Skinner) have in common with sophisticated behaviorists (like Ryle, Wittgenstein and Davidson). Both kinds of behaviorists take for granted that concept possession is a kind of knowing how. . . . Likewise, philosophers who stress the social, interpersonal character of thought (Dewey, Quine, Wittgenstein, Davidson, etc.) take it for granted that *behavior is prior to thought* in the order of analysis; their point is just that it's in the nature of the relevant kind of behavior to be accessible to public appraisal. (Discriminative responses are the traditional paradigms.) In fact, it's hard to think of more than a handful of important twentieth century philosophers who weren't concept pragmatists about the mental and/or the semantic according to my criteria (excepting, of course, those who were eliminativists). I'm told even Continental icons like Heidegger hold some or other version of concept pragmatism. Maybe one day I'll read them and find out. Or maybe not. (2004, 30)

Fodor then remarks in a footnote to this passage:

It's not just philosophers of course. Cognitive psychologists routinely assume without comment that the test for a creature's possession of the concept C is whether it can discriminate things that fall under C from things that don't. Thus Paul Bloom summarizing the cog sci consensus in his recent book: "These accounts all share the assumption that knowing the meaning of x involves being able to tell the differences between those things that are x and those things that are not" (Bloom 2000, p. 18). (2004, 30, fn 2)

Many of the thinkers and positions mentioned in the above passages are not normally regarded as being within the pragmatist tradition. This makes the use of "pragmatism" in the concepts literature somewhat unfortunate. In any case, in its present context, *concept pragmatism* is simply intended to designate a motley lot of views that maintain that concepts' natures are determined by one's conceptual abilities (e.g., recognitional, classificatory, or inferential capacities) (Fodor 1998a, 2004; Crane 2004). Fodor's discussion in the above passages aptly calls our attention to a general approach to concepts that spans an otherwise diverse array of positions, for importantly, all of the views that Fodor identifies in the above passage hold the following:

(C) "To have [concept] C is to have C involving capacities" (Fodor 2008, 26).

Contemporary cognitive psychology shares a pragmatist tendency with its behaviorist foe—in the former case, a concept is taken to be defined by one's discriminatory capacities, and as with behaviorists, concept possession amounts to a sort of know-how. Similarly, Heideggarians conceive of our mental states as being determined by our know-how, which, for them, is more basic than propositional knowledge (Heidegger 1972; Dreyfus 1992). And in contemporary Anglo-American philosophy of mind, theories of concepts descended from conceptual, functional, or inferential role-based accounts of meaning individuate concepts by these roles (Fodor 2004, 34).

Fodor's antipathy to concept pragmatism runs deep: recall, for instance, his remark that this sort of "pragmatism" is a "catastrophe of analytic philosophy of language and philosophy of mind in the last half of the Twentieth Century" (2003). As an alternative to concept pragmatism, Fodor advances a position that he calls "Cartesianism":

What's important about Cartesianism, for my purposes, is that it understands concept possession non-epistemically; Cartesians hold that concept possession is an intentional state *but not an epistemic one. In particular, it's not what you know (-how or -that) that determines what concepts you have; it's what you are able to think about.* To have the concept DOG is to be able to think about dogs as such; and conversely, to be able to think about dogs as such is to have the concept DOG. That's all there is to concept possession, according to (my kind of) Cartesian. (2004; 31, italics mine)

In essence, Fodor presents us with two options: one can be a pragmatist, individuating concepts via the role the concept plays in thought and/or action, or one can be a Cartesian, individuating concepts by their aboutness, particularly their broad contents. As the italicized sentence indicates, he advances Cartesianism as a view that rejects pragmatism.

Yet if this book is correct about symbol natures, LOT cannot reject concept pragmatism—instead, *LOT is a pragmatist theory.* Here is why:  conceptual atomism has said next to nothing about the nature of symbols, which leaves the theory dreadfully incomplete. Leaning on its semantic dimension, Fodor has provided a referential theory of concepts that he opposes to a broad class of theories of concepts that type concepts by the role they play in one's cognitive economy. But consider that conceptual atomism, when viewed in light of my results concerning the nature of symbols, becomes pragmatist. *For symbols must be individuated by what they do, that is, by the role they play in one's cognitive economy, where such is specified by the total computational role of the symbol.* Of course, maybe concepts shouldn't be individuated by symbol types; however, the present point is that the proponent of LOT will likely say they are, and to this extent, she is thereby committed to concept pragmatism. (And even if concepts are not individuated thus, LOT itself must be pragmatist because it must define symbols by what they do.)

What about the conceptual atomist's well-known commitment to Cartesianism about concepts? Because Fodor frames Cartesianism as a view that rejects pragmatism, strictly speaking, conceptual atomism is not even a Cartesian position. Still, it strikes me that in a sense, even a pragmatist-inspired atomism can embrace the spirit of Cartesianism, if not the letter. For the gist of Fodor's Cartesianism is the following:

(WC) How one gets to think about Xs is by having a symbol that is nomologically locked to Xs.

Let us call a position that adopts (WC) *weak Cartesianism*. Notice that weak Cartesianism is compatible with concept pragmatism. On the one hand, a concept has a MOP or symbolic component, but remember, this component is nonsemantic; on the other hand, a concept's aboutness is determined by its "locking relation," which is a semantic issue. Although Fodor regards Cartesianism and pragmatism as being mutually exclusive and defines them as such, the view of concepts developed herein accepts (WC). It thereby aims to combine insights from both the pragmatist and the Cartesian.

Bearing this in mind, I shall now argue that this view of concepts is superior to mainstream conceptual atomism. To begin with, let me observe that although conceptual atomism is commonly regarded as being well suited to satisfy certain key requirements that many believe any theory of concepts should satisfy, it is generally discarded because it fails to satisfy other key requirements. I will now illustrate why people generally draw this conclusion about conceptual atomism, and more significantly, I will show that a pragmatic atomism satisfies all the requirements that the standard view fails to satisfy as well as continuing to satisfy the ones the standard view finesses. By way of illustration, I shall employ a list of requirements compiled from two influential books on concepts (Prinz 2002 and Fodor 1998a). Some of the requirements Prinz and Fodor raise will obviously be more controversial than others, but being overly inclusive will do no harm. I will include any desiderata that either author lists, although I will modify a given requirement when appropriate, explaining my rationale for my modification. For instance, Prinz demands that a theory of concepts satisfy an acquisition desiderata, but not surprisingly given his empiricist agenda, he does not include the requirement that a theory be compatible with nativism.

Now, consider that it is widely agreed that conceptual atomism satisfies the following three desiderata: (1) it can explain how concepts come to represent or refer to things other than themselves by appealing to a theory of reference that currently has popular appeal (such is called the *intentionality requirement*); (2) it satisfies the *publicity requirement*, that is, the demand that different people or the same person over time can have the same kind of concept (Fodor 1998; Prinz 2002; Laurence and Margolis 1999); and (3) conceptual atomism meets the *compositionality requirement*, the requirement that the mental content of complex expressions be determined by the mental content of the primitive expressions, together with the grammar.

Yet conceptual atomism has been criticized extensively for failing to satisfy two requirements that concern the psychological role concepts play in our mental lives. First, it fails to satisfy the *MOP requirement*, the requirement that concepts be well suited to play the role of neo-Fregean MOPs.[1] Prima facie, any theory of concepts should meet this demand: we've noted that pretheoretically, when we speak of one's "concept," we mean something like one's inner understanding or notion. This commonsense understanding is an essential component of psychological theories of concepts as well. Embracing a theory of concepts that fails to satisfy the MOP requirement would call for a radical revision of both our ordinary and our scientific understandings of what concepts are.

I am of course open to conceptual revisions, especially ones that involve the modification of an ordinary concept for philosophical purposes—straightforward conceptual analyses *never* work, after all—but such must be well motivated. Yet here, a motivation is lacking. In chapter 4, I underscored that MOPs play several key philosophical roles for the LOT program, such as facilitating naturalism, explaining the causation of thought and behavior, distinguishing between co-referring concepts,

---

1. Prinz calls the MOP requirement the "cognitive content requirement" (Prinz 2002). Recalling that neo-Russellians regard MOPs as nonsemantic, I speak more neutrally of the desideratum as "the MOP requirement."

and more generally, accounting for our ways of conceiving the world. The LOT program highlights the import of MOPs; so why is a conceptual revision needed? I suspect it is needed because, although symbols are supposed to deliver the goods, providing atomism with a MOP component, no conception of a symbol happens to do so. As Prinz notes, the standard conceptual atomism is generally thought to fall short of the MOP requirement because it lacks a plausible account of the nature of symbols, for such are supposed to play the philosophical role of MOPs for the LOT program (Prinz 2002, 95–97). This is no rationale for a revision: it is an admission of defeat. Indeed, the failure of conceptual atomism to accommodate the MOP desideratum has led many to reject it altogether.

Second, conceptual atomism says little about the role that concepts play in categorization. But psychologists view the categorization requirement as the overarching motivation for postulating concepts in the first place, viewing concepts as being the mechanisms by which one categorizes (Prinz 2002, 99).

I will not provide a full-fledged defense of a theory of concepts herein, for I suspect that doing so would require a book of its own. Yet I offer a suggestion: if one allows that symbols are individuated by their total computational roles, one arrives at a superior version of conceptual atomism. To keep the old and the new versions of atomism distinct, I have called this modified form of conceptual atomism *pragmatic atomism.*

Pragmatic atomism meets the MOP requirement, for symbols, being individuative of concepts, capture one's ways of conceiving the world. Pragmatic atomism satisfies the categorization requirement as well: symbols have computational roles that characterize the role the concept plays in categorization, determining whether, and how rapidly, a person can verbally identify a visually presented object, confirm a categorization judgment, identify features an object possesses if it is indeed a member of a given category, and so on. These roles are built into the concept's nature, in the sense that they determine the nature of symbolic MOPs, which, in turn, individuate the concept.

Now let us turn to the publicity requirement—the requirement that concepts be capable of being shared across different individuals and at different points throughout an individual's lifetime. Recalling the discussion of publicity objections in the previous chapter, observe that while symbols are highly idiosyncratic, not being shared across different minds, concepts are shared in their semantic dimension all the time. (As the title of the previous chapter reads, "idiosyncratic minds think alike"). This satisfies the publicity requirement on concepts to the same degree as the standard conceptual atomism does: publicity is delivered in terms of sameness of broad content. Further, this does not bar psychological explanation from being public, for I have explored several ways in which psychological explanation is possible, even if symbols are not shared.

Let us further reflect on the categorization requirement in the context of an additional advantage that pragmatic atomism brings to the table. I have merely considered pragmatic atomism in relation to the standard version of conceptual atomism, but the following advantage may allow it to outshine its competitors in cognitive psychology as well. Pragmatic atomism is highly general: it can subsume the psychological accounts. That is, to the extent that a particular theory of concepts appeals to insightful research about the structure of concepts, the atomist can regard the research as detailing the computational roles of the atomist's concepts. Consider, for example, the prototype theory, which was developed in opposition to the classical theory of concepts, i.e., the theory that holds that concepts have necessary and sufficient defining conditions known to competent users, (e.g., one has the concept BACHELOR if and only if one has the concepts UNMARRIED and MALE). According to the prototype theory, the classical view fails to explain important features of how we categorize, such as the fact that categorization is easiest at the "basic level," that is, at the intermediate level of abstraction (e.g., at the level of DOG and CHAIR, as opposed to a lower level, such as BEAGLE and MORRIS CHAIR or a higher one, such as ANIMAL and FURNITURE). Nor can it explain why certain statistically typical and perceptually salient features, including ones that are not necessary, are used more readily for categorization. Drawing from Wittgenstein's observation that things covered by an expression often share a family resemblance, the prototype theory contends that concepts are not definitions but *prototypes*: representations of clusters of properties that good examples of a category tend to share (Rosch and Mervis 1975; Rosch 1978).

That we categorize more readily at the basic level, and that we identify more typical category members more rapidly, stems from reliable data that has now withstood several decades of scientific scrutiny. As Fodor himself notes, Rosch and her colleagues "have provided striking demonstrations that the prototype structure of a concept determines much of the variance in a wide variety of experimental tasks, chronometric and otherwise" (1981, 293). Yet critics question whether prototypes are well suited to serve as the basis for a theory of concepts. They claim that prototypes fail to yield a satisfactory theory of reference determination (Laurence and Margolis 1999) and that prototypes do not compose; one cannot derive the prototypical pet fish from combining the prototypes for PET and FISH (Fodor 1998a; Fodor and LePore 1992). Critics further maintain that not all concepts are prototypes; for instance, as we learn, we often override superficial characteristics of a kind for underlying features that are not sensory based (Keil 1989).

But consider: in the eyes of a (pragmatically inclined) atomist, the experimental results in the literature on prototypes are indications of features of the relevant symbols' underlying computational roles. These features, being individuative of the symbols, in turn individuate the concept. Yet, to recur to the philosophers' criticisms of the prototype view, the atomist need not say that prototypes figure in a theory of meaning, for the computational role of a symbol does not determine reference but instead determines the concept's cognitive significance (or MOP type), where such is nonsemantic. Nor do all kinds of concepts need to behave as prototypes do; perhaps, for instance, some behave as definitions or theories. And further, even if the atomist acknowledges that some concepts have computational roles that are in keeping with the research on prototypes, pragmatic atomism is compositional, for broad contents compose.

To underscore the generality of the approach, let us now briefly consider the competing *theory theory*, which suggests that concepts are in fact mini-theories of the categories that they represent, encompassing our beliefs about hidden features, underlying causal mechanisms, and ontological divisions (Keil 1989; Carey 1985; Murphy and Medin 1985; Gopnick and Meltzoff 1996). Advocates of the theory theory suggest that it captures explanatory relations between features while the prototype theory does not do so (Smith and Medin 1981). In a well-known criticism of the prototype view, children appear to use beliefs about a creature or thing's underlying essence to override categorization judgments based on superficial sensory features (Keil 1989). The theory theory suggests that a key element of conceptual development is the "characteristic to defining shift": a developmental shift from superficial sensory characteristics to beliefs about essences (Keil 1989). Now, the pragmatic atomist need not take sides in the debate between the prototype theorist and the theory theorist—indeed, perhaps some concepts behave as theories, while others behave as prototypes.[2] The debates provide insights regarding concepts' underlying computational roles, but no matter how the debates play out, a concept's nature is determined by its broad content and symbol type.

Thus far, pragmatic atomism looks promising, but we still need to discuss two desiderata. So let us now turn to the *scope requirement*, that is, the requirement that a theory of concepts be able to account for all of the different kinds of concepts that we have: perceptually based concepts (e.g., RED), abstract concepts (e.g., INTERNET), natural kind concepts (e.g., DOG), and so on (Prinz 2002). Prinz believes that mainstream conceptual atomism satisfies the scope desideratum because symbols are generic enough to represent various kinds of entities:

Some concepts cannot be imaged, some concepts cannot be defined, some concepts have no exemplars or prototypes, and, perhaps, some have no correlated theories. In contrast, any concept can be represented by a single unstructured symbol. The expressive breadth of unstructured symbols is nowhere more evident than in languages. Words can represent any number of things. (2002, 94)

However, it strikes me that the standard view does not really satisfy this requirement, because for symbols to be generic enough to represent various kinds of entities, LOT needs a theory of symbols to begin with. While mainstream atomism lacks an account

---

2. Mutatis mutandis for other psychological theories of concepts (e.g., the exemplar view). Conceptual atomism can even acknowledge that some concepts are sensory based, but the proponent of LOT would maintain, contra Prinz and Barsalou, that the cognitive processing of such is in an amodal code, not a modality-specific one. (See Prinz 2002; Barsalou 1999; Machery 2009 for discussion).

of symbol natures, pragmatic atomism has a theory of symbols in hand. It thereby outperforms the standard view on this front.

Finally, any theory of concepts should be compatible with plausible accounts of the phenomena of innateness and learning.[3] The previous section responded to the surprising worry that the new LOT cannot accommodate innate concepts. Conversely, mainstream conceptual atomism has been faulted for being unable to accommodate concept learning. If this is correct, then a similar problem would emerge for the pragmatist version. While this would not leave my account any worse off than the standard view, given my interest in developing a LOT that does not entail radical concept nativism, this matter warrants a brief discussion.

Because Fodor's *The Language of Thought* developed LOT within the context of radical concept nativism, radical nativism has become tightly intertwined with the LOT program. Indeed, many assume that if there's a LOT, then vocabulary items in the language of thought must be innate. But notice that nativism is not entailed by the hypothesis that there is a language of thought, nor is it required to uphold CTM. And it is not invoked by the characteristic motivations for LOT involving the combinatorial nature of thought (systematicity, etc.). Indeed, even Fodor has repudiated radical concept nativism, while, of course, continuing to develop LOT (Fodor 1998a). Nowadays, "nativism" and "LOT" need not be uttered in a single breath.

Yet Fodor has offered an influential argument for nativism in his (1975) that raises a serious puzzle about how concepts can be acquired, especially given an atomist framework. His argument

3. Prinz frames this desideratum in terms of acquisition, leaving innateness out of the picture. This is because he rejects nativism (Prinz 2002).

is roughly the following: Since concept learning is a form of hypothesis formation and confirmation, it requires a system of mental representations in which the formation and confirmation of hypotheses is carried out. But if this is the case, one must already possess the concepts in one's language of thought in which the hypotheses are couched. So one must already have the innate symbolic resources to express the concepts being learned (Fodor 1975, 79–97; Fodor 1981; Margolis 1998; Laurence and Margolis 2002).

The above line of reasoning, as it stands, is open to the possibility that many lexical concepts are constructed from more basic, unstructured ones. These lexical concepts can be learned because they have internal structure, being assembled from basic, innate concepts. These lexical concepts are thereby not innate. So, strictly speaking, the above argument does not entail the extreme concept nativism that is associated with Fodor's project. However, Fodor rejects the view that lexical concepts are structured, for he holds that the leading theories of conceptual structure are highly problematic. If Fodor is correct, we are left with a huge stock of lexical primitives. And, according to Fodor, primitive concepts are innate (Fodor 1981).

Critics and proponents of LOT alike uniformly reject radical concept nativism. After all, it is hard to see how concepts that our evolutionary ancestors had no need for, such as [carburetor] and [photon], can be innate. Of course, proponents of LOT generally believe that LOT will turn out to have some empirically motivated nativist commitments invoking both certain innate modules and primitive symbols. However, it is important that LOT be able to accommodate any well-grounded empirically based view of the nature of concepts that cognitive science develops, even one in which few or no concepts are innate.

Nonetheless, Fodor's argument and concerns about conceptual structure are intriguing, for they raise some very important questions: What is wrong with the above line of reasoning? Can primitive (unstructured) concepts be learned? Are many lexical concepts structured?

Reflecting on the second of the above questions, Stephen Laurence and Eric Margolis have developed an account of concept acquisition for conceptual atomism (Margolis 1998; Laurence and Margolis 2002). Focusing on natural kind terms, they observe that primitive natural kind concepts are learned by acquiring "sustaining mechanisms": mechanisms supporting mind-world-dependency relations that lock symbols to broad contents. They propose various kinds of mechanisms, such as ones based on a scientific understanding of the kind (*theory-based mechanisms*) and ones for cases in which little information is known by the individual except how to locate an expert (*deference-based sustaining mechanisms*). They explain:

The idea is that although specific inferences implicating a concept aren't constitutive of the concept's content, they nonetheless contribute to the explanation of why the concept is tokened in a variety of contexts. Since having a concept involves having an appropriate sustaining mechanism, a psychological model of concept acquisition is to be directed at the question of how various sustaining mechanisms are acquired (1999, 63).

To illustrate their point, they explain that concept learning for natural kind concepts typically occurs when one accumulates contingent and mainly perceptual information—the kind of information one ordinarily gets from encountering a kind, such as shape and color—which one couples with a more general disposition to treat items as being instances of the category when they have the same essential property as clear cases of the category (Margolis 1998; Laurence and Margolis 2002). This establishes a mechanism causing an individual to token a concept under the conditions that constitute content, roughly, situations that exhibit the aforementioned "locking" relationship between symbols and referents.

Their account strikes me as promising, providing a means by which the atomist can account for concepts that are learned, despite their lacking semantic structure. Luckily, this strategy is available to the pragmatist as well. In sum: a pragmatic atomism does as well as the standard view concerning concept learning, being able to draw from Laurence and Margolis's work, and, as the previous chapter discussed, it fares just as well as the standard view in its ability to accommodate concept nativism.

I have now canvassed all the desiderata. While my discussion was by no means comprehensive—I do not offer criticisms of the various psychological theories of concepts, for instance—I have urged that pragmatic atomism is superior to the standard atomist view. It satisfies all the desiderata that the standard view fails to satisfy, and it doesn't fare worse with respect to any. Stronger yet, it appears to satisfy *all* the desiderata. So I leave you with this: if you are interested in theories of concepts, pragmatic atomism is worth your further consideration. Indeed, such a "two factor" view of concepts may be helpful to those outside the LOT tradition as well. One who rejects computationalism, for instance, could regard concepts' natures as determined by their functional—as opposed to computational—roles and their broad contents. And the connectionist may adopt pragmatic atomism as well, believe it or not, individuating a concept by its role in a connectionist network and its broad content. This rough framework brings together two features that many find attractive: a functional-role approach to the inner vehicle of thought and a referential approach to mental content. This general framework is, in a sense, a descendant of two factor views of content, although, as I emphasize in chapter 4, the symbolic/computational-role factor is not a form of meaning or content.[4] Yet surprisingly, although two factor theories of *content* have been around some time, two factor theories of *concepts* have received little or no development in the concepts literature.

It seems that Fodorian conceptual atomism is no longer the only atomist game in town: pragmatic atomism is more promising, at least if you ask me. And this is all well and good, for as I shall now explain, the standard LOT was pragmatist all along.

## 2  Was LOT a Pragmatist Theory All Along?

Recall that I have claimed that even mainstream conceptual atomism defines a primitive concept in a twofold manner, with respect to both its broad content and its symbolic type. You may have found this puzzling, as discussions of conceptual atomism tend to assume that primitive concepts are individuated exclusively by broad content. More explicitly, it is often assumed the atomist defines concepts thus:

**Existence condition:**   A primitive concept exists if and only if a primitive LOT symbol has a broad content.

**Identity condition:**   Primitive concepts are identical if and only if they have the same broad content.

For instance, in describing conceptual atomism, Georges Rey writes, "The identity conditions for a concept are (to a first approximation) provided not by some condition internal to a

4. I discuss this matter in chapter 8 as well, in the context of a discussion of Ned Block's two factor theory.

thinker, but by relations the thinker bears to phenomena in the external world" (Rey 2009). Conceptual atomism is generally framed in this manner, and to the best of my knowledge, Fodor has not expressed the concern that this commonplace description of atomism is erroneous.

Yet I've taken conceptual atomism as endorsing the above existence condition and a different identity condition:

**Identity condition:**   Primitive concepts are identical if and only if *they are of the same symbol type* and have the same broad content (Fodor 1998a, 37).

(Where the departure from the earlier identity condition is italicized).

Why am I suggesting that a concept's symbol type is individuative? Fodor himself acknowledges that broad content alone is inadequate for the purpose of individuating primitive concepts because it fails to distinguish co-referring primitive concepts (e.g., *Cicero/Tully*) (Fodor 1998a, 2008). In both his *Concepts* and his *LOT 2*, he explains that it is for this reason that he distinguishes concepts in terms of their MOP types, as well as their broad contents (1998a, chs. 1 and 2; 2008, ch. 3, especially p. 70). Consider, for instance, his reaction to the Paderewski case, a case introduced by Saul Kripke that involves Peter, who hears a piano performance by Paderewski and believes that Paderewski has musical talent. Peter later goes to a political rally and hears Paderewski campaigning. Not realizing that the two experiences concern the very same person, Peter thinks: *no politician has musical talent*. And later, he forms the belief that Paderewski lacks musical talent. Also believing that Paderewski has musical talent, it would appear that Peter is irrational. But, of course, he is not (Kripke 1979). Conceptual atomism will get the wrong result if a concept is only distinguishable by its grammatical form and its broad content. To deal with this case, Fodor also individuates concepts by their symbolic types: "Paderewski needs two different Mentalese names even though there is only one of him" (2008, 92; see also p. 72). And he appeals to the same type of solution to solve Frege's problem, the problem of what accounts for the fact that identity statements like "Cicero = Cicero" and "Tully = Cicero" can differ in their cognitive significance. Here, Fodor distinguishes the concepts because they involve different types of symbols; in so doing, he takes the neo-Russellian line that the differences between the concepts are nonsemantic (2008, 70). Hence, even working within Fodor's original framework, the conceptual atomist has the resources to distinguish concepts along two dimensions: a symbolic dimension and a referential one. Yet, as noted, conceptual atomism's symbolic dimension is largely ignored.

But this does not fully establish that mainstream atomism appeals to pragmatism. To do this, not only do I need to establish that symbols determine concepts' natures, together with broad contents, I also need to show that Fodor holds that symbols are individuated by the roles they play in our mental lives. Turning to this, notice that Fodor himself has expressed sympathy for this view, writing that MOPs are functionally individuated: "If MOPs are both in the head and functionally individuated, then a MOP's identity can be constituted by what happens when you entertain it" (1998a, 20). And he writes: "If mental representations differ in their roles in mental processes, they must be formally distinct in ways that mental processes can distinguish"

5. In his 2008 discussion, Fodor indicates skepticism about arriving at a means of typing symbols across different individuals, however (2008, 90). So it is best to take this statement as pertaining to the within-person (and synchronic) case only.

(2008, p. 92).[5] By "formal" distinctness Fodor means that the representations are distinct symbolically. These remarks suggest that symbols (and MOPs) are individuated by their role in mental processes.

Piecing all this together, since symbols individuate concepts, and symbols are defined by the role they play in thought, believe it or not, Fodor is embracing the pragmatist. Given his antipathy toward pragmatism, including his objections to my theory of symbols, these remarks are astonishing. Perhaps he hasn't conceived that because symbols individuate his concepts, his own view is akin to the pragmatism he attacks?

In any case, those familiar with his *LOT 2* (2008) will suggest that he is no longer sympathetic to the view that symbols are individuated by their psychological roles. Turning to Fodor's brief discussion of symbol individuation in this book, he stops short of explicitly offering an individuation condition on symbols, although at one point, he gestures at something like a condition that taxonomizes symbols via their neurological properties for the intrapersonal case, while rejecting such a criterion for the across-person case (2008, 89). Still, I suspect that his chapter implicitly appeals to individuation by the role the symbol plays in one's cognitive economy, at least intrapersonally, for in order to respond to Frege's problem, Fodor distinguishes co-referring MOPs like [Cicero] and [Tully], as well as [Paderewski1] and [Paderewski2] (2008).[6] Such finely grained individuation suggests that a MOP must be individuated in a manner that tracks sameness and difference in its psychological role. Why then does he speak of neural properties in this context? Upon reflection, this is compatible with a classificatory

6. I am using brackets to indicate that the enclosed expression is a MOP.

scheme that tracks the computational role of the symbol. For suppose he did single out a certain neural property P as individuative (he does not, but let us suppose so): intuitively, P must be such that it tracks sameness and difference in psychological role.[7] For remember: in this chapter Fodor aims to distinguish both [Paderewski1] and [Paderewski2] and [Cicero] and [Tully], for instance. And it is in this chapter that he makes the aforementioned remark that, "if mental representations differ in their roles in mental processes, they must be formally distinct in ways that mental processes can distinguish" (2008, 92). So it appears that this discussion is implicitly classifying concepts by the mental processes they figure in.[8]

In any case, you may be tiring of the exegetical turn that our discussion has taken. In defense of this thread, I delve into the details of Fodor's texts because it is important to grasp how natural concept pragmatism is to the LOT program—it was, surprisingly, there all along. Yet this pragmatist strain is not normally taken to be part of Fodor's Cartesian-inspired conceptual

7. A neurophysiological property figuring in an individuation condition on symbols need not track computational role, however. For instance, it could individuate symbols with respect to their neuroanatomical features.

8. In a footnote in his 2008, Fodor writes: "Two people have the same primitive concept iff they have coextensive primitive concepts" (p. 88). I suspect that Fodor is separating the case of intrapersonal symbol individuation from the across-system case, being unable to deliver a means of typing symbols across systems (see, e.g., p. 90). He merely observes that symbols are multiply realized by different neural properties and that it is mysterious why this is the case, so concerning the problem of interpersonal typing, he will "pretend it isn't there" (pp. 91–92). In any case, Fodor's discussion clearly distinguishes co-referring concepts intrapersonally by their symbol types.

atomism. After all, attacking the pragmatist is a major pastime of the mainstream LOT program. Of course, here, it is important to press for the import of the result: After all, what is in a name? Does the fact that conceptual atomism is pragmatist have any relevance to the debate over concepts, aside from correcting an error in the literature? I believe that it does—remember, I have urged that pragmatic atomism is, overall, a solid upgrade over the original version, or at least what is commonly regarded as being the original version.

The upshot of all this is that LOT must end its futile war with pragmatism. Concept pragmatism can *enrich* LOT, after all. So why can't we all just be friends? Of course some of us prefer to have an intellectual target; if you ask me to supply one, pessimism about computationalism is the true enemy.

## 3   Conclusion

Pragmatic atomism grew out of the algorithmic conception of mental symbols. It is initially surprising that a theory of symbols yields such a radical transformation of conceptual atomism. But upon reflection, given that LOT had ignored symbols—the most crucial element of its program—such transformations are to be expected. Symbols are, after all, LOT's very kernel. Further, we see the roots of pragmatism in Fodor's own thinking about concepts.

It is now time to turn to the book's third problem, the problem of Frege Cases. And as we shift gears, we will see the algorithmic account of symbols perform more feats for the LOT Program. Given that symbols' natures are finally specified, those working on attitude ascription can appeal to symbols to play the philosophical role of MOPs. As I observed in the first chapter, MOPs play an important role in such theories, yet MOPs are radically underdeveloped, with discussions crudely gesturing at inner representations in belief boxes, mental blackboards, and the like. So, in the next chapter I illustrate how symbolic MOPs can figure in a neo-Russellian account of attitude ascription. Symbols, understood algorithmically, will be summoned to play the role of guises in the context of my solution to the Frege cases. This conception of symbols, together with my larger justification for including Frege cases in the *ceteris paribus* clauses of intentional laws, shall eliminate the notorious problem of Frege cases. So let us turn to this matter.

# 8  Solving the Frege Cases

The standard LOT holds that it can get away with a referential semantics. It does much of its psychological work at the computational level, after all. But can it really get off so easy? Neo-Russellianism has well-known costs—for instance, due to it, the LOT program must reject the commonplace view that intentional laws are supposed to be sensitive to an agent's mode of presentation or way of conceiving of things. For according to neo-Russellianism, the proposition expressed by the sentence "Cicero is Tully" is an entity that consists in the relation of identity, the man, Cicero, and the man, Tully. Further, the sentence "Tully is Tully" also expresses the same proposition. Such propositions are called *Russellian propositions*. An important feature of Russellian propositions is that they are more coarse-grained than MOPs, or the ways of entertaining them. Neo-Russellians hold that "believing" expresses a binary relation between agents and Russellian propositions. So neo-Russellians hold the surprising view that anyone who believes that Tully is Tully also believes that Cicero is Tully. As a consequence of this, a proponent of LOT who accepts neo-Russellianism adopts the following claim about psychological explanation:

(PE), Sentences in one's language of thought which differ only in containing distinct primitive co-referring symbols (e.g., #Cicero#/#Tully#) are to be treated by intentional psychology as being type-identical and are thereby subsumable under all the same intentional laws (Fodor 1994).

You may be familiar with related discussions in the philosophy of language literature involving Frege's puzzle. One version of this puzzle concerns the cognitive significance of *simple* sentences. It asks: How do we account for the difference in cognitive significance between sentences like "Cicero = Tully" and "Cicero = Cicero"? Another version of the puzzle concerns seeming differences in truth-value of belief ascriptions that differ only in containing different co-referring names. Relatedly, due to (PE), a LOT that appeals to neo-Russellianism faces the problem of Frege cases. Consider a colorful example that is frequently raised in the literature on Frege cases, that of Sophocles's Oedipus, who didn't realize that a woman he wanted to marry, named Jocasta, is actually his mother. As a result of this, Oedipus has two very distinct ways of representing the same woman and doesn't realize that they co-refer. This situation creates problems if psychological laws are based on neo-Russellianism, for the laws are indifferent to these distinct ways. Oedipus thereby threatens to be a counterexample to the broad generalization:

(M) *Ceteris paribus*, if people believe that they shouldn't marry Mother and they desire not to marry Mother, they will try to avoid marrying Mother.

Oedipus satisfies the antecedent of (M). However, Oedipus fails to satisfy the consequent since, in virtue of his trying to marry

Jocasta, it is true, according to broad psychology, that he tries to marry Mother.[1]

To put the matter very generally, Frege cases involve individuals who are unaware that certain expressions co-refer, where such knowledge is relevant to the success of their behaviors, leading to cases in which they fail to behave as the broad intentional laws predict. Frege cases are regarded as being a major problem for the LOT program, suggesting that its neo-Russellian semantics is at odds with its view that thinking is symbolic. And many find that the standard LOT is not faring well with respect to this problem; indeed, the literature has been quite negative in its assessment of the capacity of LOT's neo-Russellianism to surmount the Frege cases (Arjo 1996; Aydede 1998; Aydede and Robbins 2001).[2] If these critics are correct, then any theory of psychological explanation that is based on neo-Russellianism is on poor footing indeed.

1. The Oedipus example may strike the reader as odd because "mother" is not clearly a name. But this colorful example is widely used in the philosophy of mind literature on Frege cases, so I'll follow the literature and employ it in my discussions. To underscore that I have in mind a referential reading of "mother," I will write "Mother" (capitalized) throughout. Other examples of Frege cases can be provided (e.g., Cicero/Tully).

2. Fodor would surely disagree because he has attempted to provide two different solutions to the Frege cases (1994; 2008). As we shall see, the literature on Frege cases has been critical of his 1994 approach (Arjo 1996; Aydede 1998; Aydede and Robbins 2001). Fodor's 2008 discussion unfortunately does not do more than merely assert that the MOPs are distinguishable.

Criticisms of neo-Russellianism and Frege cases have also appeared in the philosophy of language literature on belief ascription (e.g., Crimmons 1992, 32–34; Richard 1990, 219).

In this chapter, I attempt to overcome these criticisms, arguing that Frege cases are not genuine counterexamples to intentional laws because they can be included in the *ceteris paribus* clauses of the relevant laws. It is well known that special science laws have *ceteris paribus* clauses. The presence of *ceteris paribus* clauses means that a case in which the antecedent of a special science law is satisfied, while the consequent is not, need not be a counterexample. Instead, the case may simply be a "tolerable exception"—a situation in which the *ceteris paribus* conditions fail to hold. Consider, for example, the generalization in economic theory that given a decrease in supply of an item and given no change in demand, the price of the item will go up. This generalization is *ceteris paribus*, having certain exceptions (e.g., it will not hold if there is price fixing, if the only supermarket that sells the item happens to close, etc.). Such situations are not taken to be counterexamples to the generalization but are regarded as exceptions that are to be tolerated. For a case to be a counterexample, the antecedent must obtain, and the *ceteris paribus* condition must be met.

But a justification must be provided if a Frege case is to be included in a *ceteris paribus* clause. Although Fodor had attempted to outline the kind of justification that would be appropriate to Frege cases in his *The Elm and the Expert* (1994), critics responded with numerous challenges to the general approach (Arjo 1996; Aydede 1998; Aydede and Robbins 2001). The critics' charges were never addressed. Nonetheless, I believe that Fodor's general idea of including the Frege cases in the *ceteris paribus* clauses promising; what is needed is a plausible justification for including the Frege cases in the clauses that takes into account the critics' objections.

So herein I attempt to provide the needed justification, and in so doing, I aim to respond to the third problem that this book aims to solve. I argue that including the Frege cases in the *ceteris paribus* clauses is justified by a larger theoretical decision for intentional laws having a broad canonical form. Intentional laws have a broad canonical form when they are sensitive to mental states that are typed by their broad contents.[3] Any decision to include the Frege cases in the *ceteris paribus* clauses is the result of an overall assessment of the debate about which canonical form intentional laws should take, broad or narrow. While such a decision is a global affair, I will focus on the part of this theoretical decision that is internal to Frege cases—the element that involves the issue of whether nonintentional explanation of the psychological difference between co-referring thoughts will suffice.

The literature on Frege cases has been very negative on this matter. Three main lines of criticism have emerged. First, critics have argued that there are no grounds for treating Frege cases as tolerable exceptions (Arjo 1996; Aydede 1998; Aydede and Robbins 2001). Second, they have urged that even if the Frege cases can be treated as tolerable exceptions, doing so leads to missed intentional-level predictions of certain thoughts and behaviors (Aydede 1998; Aydede and Robbins 2001). And third, they have claimed that even assuming that the Frege cases are tolerable

3. Recall that proponents of LOT/CTM are generally *externalists* about mental content, holding that content depends on states and individuals in the world as well. Further, they have a specific sort of externalist mental content in mind, called *broad content*, in which content is basically referential. So, for instance, the broad content of both "Cicero" and "Tully" is simply the man, Cicero, despite the fact that the different expressions routinely differ in their cognitive significance.

exceptions and that there are no missed predictions, a broad theory will have to locate a means of predicting and explaining Oedipus's behaviors that is not intentional. And explanation of one's thoughts and behaviors must be intentional (Arjo 1996; Aydede 1998; Aydede and Robbins 2001). After exploring these criticisms in more detail, I argue, contra these critics, that Frege cases can be treated as tolerable exceptions. Further, there is no missed prediction of Frege cases: a broad psychology does not fail to explain events in its laws that narrow psychology, on the other hand, captures (under narrow description). Finally, I contend that there is no justification for believing that explanation of Frege cases must be intentional in nature, as opposed to computational.

This chapter proceeds in the following fashion: first, since Frege cases arise for a very particular sort of theoretical apparatus, namely, a neo-Russellian theory applied to the domain of psychological explanation, it will be useful to some readers if I further explain this general approach (sections 1 and 2). In particular, section 1 explores the motivation for neo-Russellianism. Section 2 then outlines an approach to psychological explanation that is based on a LOT that adopts neo-Russellianism and the algorithmic conception of symbols that I defended earlier. Then, in the remainder of this chapter, I develop and defend my solution to the Frege cases (sections 3–5).

## 1  Neo-Russellianism

I've followed the standard LOT in appealing to neo-Russellianism. It is now time to appreciate its controversial nature and explore why one might appeal to it in the first place. I've already noted one startling fact—neo-Russellians hold that individuals (e.g., Cicero, Mont Blanc) are literally constituents of propositions. A further unintuitive element of neo-Russellianism is the following. Suppose that Maria thinks that Mark Twain is a very clever writer, but she doesn't know that Twain is also named Clemens. Notice that it is quite natural to say that

(1) Maria believes that Twain is clever

is true, while

(2) Maria believes that Clemens is clever

is false. Yet the neo-Russellian must deny (1) is true while (2) is false.

Now, the bare fact that we have such intuitions about differences in truth-value is uncontroversial. What is controversial is what to do with such intuitions: Should a theory of attitude ascription take the intuitions at their face value, saying, as Fregeans and neo-Fregeans do, that the propositions expressed by the respective ascriptions differ? Alternately, perhaps one's point of departure should be to claim, with the neo-Russellians, that the intuitions really do not indicate anything about the semantics of attitude ascriptions; ordinary speakers are mistaken that there are differences in truth-value between the statements. Such differences, for example, might be regarded as being merely pragmatic differences that do not contribute to the propositions semantically expressed by the utterances.

Reactions taking the intuitions at face value actually come in two basic varieties. The neo-Russellian believes that both varieties are mistaken. One reaction to the intuitions about differences in truth-value is to say that the *that* clauses refer to different propositions: such propositions are to be individuated by some sort of cognitive component (e.g., a conceptual role or sense). Such views are commonly called "Fregean" if they appeal to senses, and "neo-Fregean" insofar as they depart from Frege by appealing to mental representations that are individuated by their conceptual roles.[4] Nuances aside, both entities are to play the philosophical role of MOPs—such roles were highlighted in chapter 4, recall. Unlike LOT symbols, these senses and conceptual roles are taken to be semantic in nature, entering into the proposition expressed by a thought or utterance.

It is generally agreed that the Fregean and neo-Fregean-based views fail for several reasons. First, those in the broadly Fregean tradition hold that when we attribute beliefs to others the *that* clause names the believer's way of conceiving of the referent. However, a common, and most would say decisive, criticism of Fregean-inspired views is that when we attribute beliefs to others, we do not generally know the believer's mode of presentation or way of conceiving of the referent. Nor is it the case that when we attribute the same belief to multiple individuals the different believers all have the same mode of presentation (Richard 1990).

Second, a wave of externalist arguments developed by Saul Kripke, Hilary Putnam, Tyler Burge, and others suggest that Fregeanism is flawed, for sense (and *mutatis mutandis*, conceptual role) does not determine reference as the Fregean tradition contends (Burge 1979; Putnam 1965; Kripke 1980). Because these issues have been treated extensively elsewhere, I will keep my discussion of this matter brief, focusing on a few criticisms that were offered by Kripke and Putnam.

4. Some of these views claim that propositions contain *both* neo-Russellian elements (individuals and attributes) *and* MOPs, while others claim that propositions contain only MOPs, which are sufficient to determine individuals and attributes, or at least extensions. These differences will not matter for our purposes.

(i) Consider the descriptivist position commonly associated with Frege and Russell. (To avoid confusion, remember that *neo-Russellianism* does not refer to descriptivism; neo-Russellianism is a different, referentialist view). According to descriptivism, the meaning of a proper name is determined by an individual's associating a certain definite description with the name. So, for example, speakers may associate the following description with Aristotle: "the pupil of Plato and the teacher of Alexander the Great." This "sense" is supposed to determine reference (Frege 1892). Now, in *Naming and Necessity*, Saul Kripke argues that the meaning of a proper name is not in fact determined by a description that an individual associates with an individual, for it would seem that if Aristotle happened to not be the pupil of Plato and the teacher of Alexander, an individual could nonetheless refer to Aristotle with the expression "Aristotle" (Kripke 1980).[5] Indeed, individuals seem capable of referring even when they know nothing of the person whatsoever. Further, users can misdescribe someone. For example, Kripke raises the example of Albert Einstein; apparently, many people believe Einstein was the inventor of the atomic bomb, and in such cases, this is the description they often associate with the name "Einstein." Of course, they are not using "Einstein" to refer to Oppenheimer just because they associate this description with the name (Kripke 1980). Although Kripke's discussion was directed at descriptivism, similar considerations apply to neo-Fregean positions that take content to be determined by conceptual or functional role. There is no singular mental representation type that individuals routinely associate with an individual, the having of which is required to refer to that person.

5. See also Kaplan for a similar point in the context of indexicals and demonstratives (1977).

(ii) In addition to Kripke's influential criticisms, Hilary Putnam's Twin Earth thought experiment led many to discard the Fregean-based views. According to his thought experiment, we are to consider two individuals who are physical duplicates of each other. They reside on planets that differ only in that one has $H_2O$ in its lakes, oceans, wells, and so on, and the other has a substance that looks, smells, and tastes like water but that, in fact, has a different chemical composition. We are then asked whether the meaning of the duplicates' respective "water" utterances differs. In response to this question, many people agreed with Putnam's observation that the meanings seem to differ because the relevant kinds differ. And many held that the twins' psychological states differed, with these differences in meaning. According to them, mental content is *wide*, being determined, at least in part, by features in the environment that are external to the individual (Putnam 1975). No purely "narrow," or internal, condition (sense, conceptual role, etc.) can determine reference. This position is often called externalism, with the view under attack being referred to as *internalism*.

In essence, Fregean-inspired theories of belief ascription simply seem to require too much of the ascriber: we don't always know the sense or the internal representation that the agent associates with a name. And such theories fall prey to the influential stream of externalist arguments that contend that meaning (or content) is not narrow or "in the head." These considerations have led many to regard neo-Russellianism as being a superior option, despite its aforementioned counterintuitiveness.

But there is a more serious alternative to neo-Russellianism, one that accepts important elements of the neo-Russellian position, including the externalist arguments outlined in the paragraphs above. According to "hidden indexical theories" (1) and

(2) express distinct propositions because, although they have the same *that* clause contents, the entire ascriptions differ. The predicate "believes" is said to be a three-place predicate holding among an agent, a neo-Russellian proposition, and a mode of presentation (or MOP). Two of the arguments (for the agent and the proposition) are explicitly mentioned by the belief ascription. The third argument is a mode of presentation, and, depending on the details of the particular view, either it is not mentioned at all by the ascription, being an *unarticulated constituent* of the proposition, or it is mentioned by some unpronounced word in the ascription. In any case, the propositions expressed by sentences (1) and (2) have, as constituents, different third arguments for this ternary relation. The covert reference to MOPs is said to be contextually determined: different MOP types may be referred to by different instances of utterance (Crimmins and Perry 1989; Crimmins 1992; Schiffer 1992).

Although existing hidden indexical views face technical problems, many suspect that something along these lines may prove to be correct. But now consider the LOT program in the eyes of the proponent of the hidden indexical view: apparently, those sympathetic to hidden indexical theories would object to broad intentional laws, for such theories would say that the canonical form of intentional explanation must not be as the neo-Russellians propose. For instance, consider the following broad intentional generalization:

If S believes that Clemens/Twain is insightful, and S wants to hear an insightful orator speak, then, *ceteris paribus*, S will try to attend Clemens/Twain's speech.

As we know, from the standpoint of this broad intentional generalization, whenever it is true that one believes that Twain is clever, it is also true that one believes that Clemens is clever. However, according to the hidden indexical views, while co-referring names have the same *that* clause content (for the hidden indexical theory agrees with the neo-Russellian that the *that* clauses express the same neo-Russellian proposition), the total belief ascriptions would still differ. So it is not the case that when it is true that one believes that Twain is clever, it must also be true that one believes that Clemens is clever. Crucially, the meaning of "believes" differs in each case, because distinct MOP types are involved.

In light of this book's appeal to neo-Russellianism, permit me to indicate why I find neo-Russellianism to be more attractive than the hidden indexical views: first, if intentional generalizations are sensitive to MOPs, different individuals will fail to satisfy the same generalizations, even if one assumes that a theory of MOPs is employed in which MOPs are shared. Different ways of conceiving of a referent can give rise to similar behaviors, and such regularities can be of interest to cognitive science, especially insofar as they demarcate phenomena that an underlying computational theory is to explain. We shall return to this matter in the following section. Relatedly, neo-Russellian generalizations are well suited to capture similarities in behavior between intelligent creatures with different sorts of cognitive or perceptual structures (e.g., artificial minds and human minds; human minds and the minds of great apes).

Second, I've argued that the proponent of LOT must individuate symbols algorithmically. And I've observed that if this is so, MOPs will likely be idiosyncratic to thinkers. In light of this, the hidden indexical theory would saddle LOT with intentional generalizations that are not public, instead of yielding ones that abstract away from idiosyncratic differences between thinkers. In essence, the advantages of referentialism would be lost.

Third, the reason that most people reject neo-Russellianism can be discarded. By and large, neo-Russellianism is rejected because it says, counterintuitively, that (1) and (2) have the same truth-values. Naturally, if one is to stomach such counterintuitiveness, the neo-Russellian must effectively explain away our intuitions about substitutivity failures. And the general view is that the commonplace way of explaining away these intuitions (via an appeal to a pragmatics-semantics distinction) is controversial. However, the neo-Russellian need not defend the controversial attempt to prove that our intuitions about substitutivity can be explained away in terms of pragmatics. As David Braun noted, one can appeal to knowing the proposition under a MOP (without even mentioning the issue of pragmatics) to explain away the counterintuitiveness (Braun 2000, 2001a, b). Most neo-Russellians and even some who reject the neo-Russellian view hold that a rational person could believe a proposition in one way, while not believing it, or even believing its negation, in some other way. This is supposed to explain how one could rationally think that two utterances of simple sentences expressing the same proposition can differ in their truth-values. According to Braun, this phenomenon also explains the situation involving belief sentences. This explanation is independent of any appeal to pragmatics to explain away intuitions about substitutivity. Braun's simple, insightful point has gained a good deal of traction in the attitude ascription literature over the last several years.

These, then, are some of the issues arising for the neo-Russellian position that I've appealed to, and this is why I find neo-Russellianism to still be viable, despite its unintuitiveness.

## 2  Broad Psychology

Now that you have a better sense of neo-Russellianism, let us return to the problem of Frege cases. I will now suggest a general framework by which a neo-Russellian–based LOT theory might deal with this problem. Here is the problem of Frege cases again, this time in very general terms. We've observed that the LOT program views intentional generalizations as being broadly referential in nature; they are sensitive to the broadly referential properties of a mental state, and are indifferent to the state's conceptual, functional, or computational role (that is, the particular role that the mental state plays in one's mental life). As a result of this framework, thoughts treated as intentionally type-identical may nonetheless function very differently in one's thinking, causing very different thoughts and behaviors. There is a tension between the causal functioning of these states, on the one hand, and the representational nature of the states on the other. Intentionally or referentially, the states are type-identical; yet causally, they are very different in ways that are clearly of interest to any psychology. This tension between the representational and the causal is the fundamental problem regarding psychological explanation for a neo-Russellian–based LOT theory.

I suggest the following general strategy to deal with this tension: while a neo-Russellian LOT cannot accommodate any causal differences between intentionally type-identical thoughts by appealing to *semantic* differences, there are other theoretical wares available for doing so. In the context of providing a solution to Frege's puzzle about belief ascription, the neo-Russellian often appeals to a guise, or MOP, of a thought, a mental particular (or property of mental particulars) that thinkers are said to have when they entertain a neo-Russellian proposition.[6] While theories of belief ascription have not provided any detailed elaboration concerning the nature of guises, it is fair to say that such entities are intended to capture the psychological role of the thought. I have previously noted that one popular way of cashing out guises, or MOPs, is to say that they are expressions in one's language of thought. And the last several chapters have developed a theory of symbols that can play the role of guises for theories of belief ascription, should the given philosopher of language wish it to do so, because symbols, on my conception, are sensitive to the functional, and more specifically computational, role of the thought. A similar appeal to LOT could be made by the neo-Russellian in the context of the Frege cases. Indeed, because CAUSAL types symbols with respect to their computational roles, we are assured that any bona fide Frege case will involve agents with co-referring MOPs that are indeed distinguishable by the LOT theory. More coarsely grained means of individuating symbols are simply unable to fit the bill, as they would conflate MOPs with different psychological roles.

Allow me to make this general framework for approaching psychological explanation more explicit. Let *broad psychology* refer to an approach to psychological explanation that appeals to two different levels of explanation, the computational and the intentional.[7] More specifically, broad psychology is a two-tiered psychological theory in which there are two levels of explanation:

6. A classic neo-Russellian appeal to guises is found in Salmon (1986).

7. Of course the expression "broad" in the name *broad psychology* refers to the intentional element of the theory. A more precise name for the theory would perhaps be something like *broad intentional/narrow computational psychology*, but alas, this name is too long.

Broad Psychology

(i) An intentional level of explanation that subsumes mental states by their broad contents and is indifferent to the functional, conceptual, or computational role of the mental state.

(ii) A relatively lower level of computational laws that is indifferent to the broad content of the mental state but is sensitive to a mental state's symbol type, or computational role.[8]

Now recall our discussion of the influential Twin Earth thought experiment, which, remember, was taken by many to suggest that mental content is *wide*, not merely being a matter of what is going on in the mind of the individual. Instead, content determination involves the world as well. In particular, specifying the nature of content requires understanding how the individual is related to particular kinds in the environment (e.g., whether one is related to $H_2O$ versus XYZ). But now consider broad psychology in light of the Twin Earth case: due to its two-tiered nature, there is a sense in which the traditional wide/narrow dichotomy fails to characterize broad psychology: such a psychology is wide, drawing from extrinsic states of the individual. But it is also narrow, since the computational level appeals only to a system's intrinsic states.

This is an explanatory advantage, I believe. For although many found the externalist intuitions about mental content individuation attractive, the externalist position was also viewed as facing a serious difficulty: it conflicts with certain explanatory demands on content. Reasoning involves the processing of representations that succeed one another in virtue of their internal, causal connections. And theories of mental processing

8. This two-tiered framework is inspired by Jerry Fodor's *The Elm and the Expert* (1994).

in cognitive science seem to abstract away from relations to the environment, focusing on internal computations (see Egan 1995). Such considerations have led many philosophers to observe that there is an important sense in which the twins' concepts and attitudes are the same—their internal, narrow psychological states are the same. However, at least at first blush, this observation runs contrary to the popular externalist reaction to the Twin Earth thought experiment. What is needed is a theory of psychological kind individuation that can accommodate these two, seemingly opposing, observations, or at least provide an effective refutation of one of them.

In appealing to a broad psychology, LOT can accommodate the gist of both observations. More specifically:

• Broad psychology can accommodate the intuition that the twins' thoughts play the same role in their respective psychological economies. For it can regard their symbolic states as type-identical, and subsume the twins in the same predictions at the computational level.

• Because content is taken to be broad, broad psychology aims to accommodate the externalist intuition that their thoughts have different meanings or contents.

By employing this dual framework the LOT program can provide both a wide and a narrow taxonomy of thoughts. Suppose that I utter, "I need a bucket of strong coffee just about now." When I do so, I have a thought to this effect; there is a particular state in my brain that is characterizable, at least in broad strokes, by my public language utterance. Notice that there are two explanatory levels at which the broad psychologist can subsume this quite accurate thought. First, there is the intentional or representational level of explanation, according to which the thought is merely singled out at a very coarse level of grain, so that any thought tokens having the same grammatical form that refer to the same state of affairs are type-identical. Let us call this mental kind the *broad thought*. In addition, there is another explanatory level at which the theory subsumes the very same mental state. This level is insensitive to content but instead subsumes the thought token with respect to its symbol type. The mental kind demarcated in this way is the *narrow thought*. On this view, narrow thoughts don't have their contents essentially.

Returning to the view of concepts developed in the previous chapter, observe that the pragmatic atomist's concepts can be situated within this two-tiered framework as well. Remember that conceptual atomism holds that a concept is individuated by its symbol type and its broad content. Given this, we can identify a broad and narrow notion of a concept, where primitive concepts are taken as mental particulars that, together with grammatical operations and other primitives, form token thoughts. As the previous chapter illustrated, if symbols are individuated algorithmically, then the conceptual atomist's concepts have a narrow, computational-role dimension, as well as a referential one.

It is worth underscoring the openness of this dual framework. The framework can be adopted by the connectionist, as computational states individuated by their role in a connectionist network can differentiate #Cicero# and #Tully# thoughts as well.[9] Further, the intentional level can be fleshed out by whatever

9. Connectionism is commonly regarded as a theory that invokes mental representations—indeed, even Paul Churchland talks of mappings between referents and (certain) computational states that are individuated in terms of their role in a connectionist network (Churchland 1995). But for a dissenting opinion see Ramsey, Stich, and Garon (1990).

broad theory of reference that, at the end of the philosophical day, seems most plausible. At this point in the game, any openness is a virtue.

I will now turn to a defense of the two-tiered structure. First, one can question the motivation for a broad level, over and above a narrow one. Indeed, even the semantic externalist may do so. Suppose that semantic externalism is true, and the semantic contents differ between the twins. Still, one could hold that a semantic theory should stay out of a theory of psychological explanation. For example, one could dispense with the semantic level altogether and just appeal to LOT symbols, or one could appeal to something along the lines of Brian Loar's notion of psychological content to do the needed work (Loar 1996). Prima facie, psychological content and LOT syntax are the sort of entities that seem to have a suitable level of grain for the purpose of explaining the causation of (narrowly described) thought and proximal behavior. Since they are candidates for filling this role, and broad contents are not, why not dispense with a broad level altogether? Because this question can be asked by a semantic externalist, the broad psychologist must provide an independent motivation for a broad level; that is, she must give a motivation over and above the intuition that the twins' semantic contents differ. For even if semantic externalism is correct, there is still the further question: Why should semantic properties individuate psychological kinds?

The needed motivation for a broad level arises from two sources. An appeal to a purely broad intentional level provides a dimension in which concepts are shared. In fact, to recur to the previous section, for similar reasons broad laws are superior to generalizations inspired by Fregean and hidden indexical theories of attitude ascription. First, it is well known that people can represent the same state of affairs in different ways from each other. Such ways of representing things are notoriously idiosyncratic, and many are skeptical that philosophy will provide a plausible theory of narrow content that succeeds in abstracting away from idiosyncratic differences, arriving at a sense in which different people share the same concept. The last several chapters have in fact argued that LOT itself requires a theory of MOPs in which MOPs are not shared.

Second, broad laws capture predictive uniformities between mental states that are distinct ways of representing the same referent. Given that people live in the same environment and have similar mental structures, people's behavior toward the referent tends to converge despite idiosyncratic differences in their ways of representing the world. On the other hand, if the intentional laws are sensitive to narrow content or LOT symbols, then any predictive uniformity in their referent-directed behaviors is lost.[10] As Ned Block explains:

Wide meaning may be more useful [than conceptual role] in one respect: to the extent that there are nomological relations between the world and what people think and do, wide meaning will allow predicting what they think and without information about how they see things. Suppose, for example, that people tend to avoid wide open spaces, no matter how they describe these spaces to themselves. Then knowing that Fred is choosing whether to go via an open space or a city street, one would be in a position to predict Fred's choice, even though one does not know whether Fred describes the open space to himself as "that" or "Copley Square." (Block 1994)

Now, I don't know that people really aim to avoid wide open spaces; nonetheless, Block's general observation is apt. Other

10. The motivations stated in this paragraph have been noted by Block (1994); Fodor (1994, 51); Pylyshyn (1986).

generalizations making the same point are available: for example, one may think of gold as "the stuff with the atomic number seventy-nine"; another may think of it as "the sort of jewelry Jane likes to wear." Nonetheless, both parties satisfy many of the same gold-related generalizations. In general, it seems uncontroversial that systems having different ways of representing the same entity will frequently behave in similar ways because they are in like environments and because they make similar demands on their environments. But it remains unclear how this tendency toward similar thoughts and behaviors can be captured by the generalizations of a purely narrow psychology.[11]

The usual criticism of this point is that co-referentiality does not ensure that the thoughts will always be behaviorally equivalent; for example, one can represent the man Cicero under the mode of presentation [Tully] and be unaware that he is also Cicero. As noted, people unaware of co-referentialities relevant to their behaviors threaten to be counterexamples to putative broad generalizations because they satisfy the antecedents of

11. One may offer the following objection to my case for broad laws: scientific psychology is not in the business of explaining behavior in terms of laws of any kind, much less laws about beliefs and desires. However, scientific psychology *is* concerned with laws. Although much of scientific psychology is concerned with explaining cognitive capacities, there is also much interest in discovering and confirming laws or effects. (For discussion see Cummins 2000). Further, many of these laws or effects concern beliefs, desires, and other attitudes. Such generalizations are employed throughout the field of social cognition, for example. And they are employed in computational psychology because they specify what the computational explanations are supposed to explain. Consider, e.g., computational explanations of the moon illusion, which seek to explain the generalization "people believe the moon looks larger when it's on the horizon."

the generalizations but fail to behave as those who know the relevant identity would behave. This brings us full circle to the problem that I'm hoping to solve. So let us turn to my solution to the Frege cases.

## 3   The Frege Cases: A Solution

As a point of departure, note that any broad theorist who would like to solve the Frege cases *must* include the Frege cases in the *ceteris paribus* clauses of broad intentional laws. There is no way around this dialectical burden. To see this, first notice that if content is narrow, then there is no need to include the Frege cases in the *ceteris paribus* clauses because the canonical form of the intentional laws is such that thoughts are subsumed by properties that are sensitive to differences between co-referring concepts. On the other hand, if the laws are broad, then the canonical form of intentional laws glosses over differences between co-referring concepts. In this case, the laws face putative counterexamples, so the broad psychologist must say that the Frege cases are tolerable exceptions and should be included in the *ceteris paribus* clauses (otherwise the Frege cases would be counterexamples, and the theory would be false). So including Frege cases in the *ceteris paribus* clauses is a consequence of a larger theoretical decision for a broad canonical form.

It is not well known that Frege cases arise for two-factor views as well. If one endorses a level at which thoughts are subsumed by their broad contents only, as many two-factor theorists do, there will be Frege cases. As I argue below, if Frege cases indeed arise for a theory, then the theory *must* include the cases in the *ceteris paribus* clauses. The solution that this chapter advances is available to the two-factor theorist, although certain details will differ, for contents, rather than symbols, are employed to distinguish the co-referring expressions.

Given that including Frege cases in the *ceteris paribus* clauses is an inevitable result of the choice of a broad canonical form, to decide whether the cases are to be included in the *ceteris paribus* clauses, one should ask: What determines which canonical form is the correct one? As far as I can tell, one's choice of a canonical form depends on the following issues: the plausibility of the competing theories of narrow content; the feasibility of two-factor theories; and finally, whether broad psychology can give a satisfactory account of the computational difference between co-referring concepts. Of course, the litmus test for whether broad psychology can accomplish this latter task is whether there is a viable computational account of the Frege cases.

So it seems that justifying including Frege cases in the *ceteris paribus* clauses is a global affair: if the best psychology should have a broad form, then we have motivation to include Frege cases in the *ceteris paribus* clauses. While I cannot delve into all the issues that determine the larger theoretical decision of which canonical form to choose, what I would like to do is focus on the part of the decision that involves the issue of whether computational explanation of Frege cases will suffice.[12] In so doing, I hope to persuade you of the following conditional thesis: assuming that the other issues listed above go in the direction of broad psychology (call this the *almost all-things-considered judgment*), then, because computational explanation of Frege cases adequately explains Frege cases, the phenomenon of Frege cases is unproblematic for the theory, and it is justifiable to include them in the *ceteris paribus* clauses.

12. However, I do offer a critical discussion of a few leading theories of narrow content later in this chapter.

If I am correct, then any failed justification for including the Frege cases in the *ceteris paribus* clauses would not emerge from problems internal to Frege cases but from external issues involving one's choice of a canonical or proper form for intentional explanations. Hence, I hope to put the Frege cases on the theoretical back burner. Although limited, this is a significant result: to the best of my knowledge, no one has attempted to respond to the variety of recent criticisms that computational explanation of Frege cases will not suffice. Since Frege cases are considered to be a major problem for the LOT program, if not the major problem, proving that they don't speak against it eliminates a significant problem indeed.

This being said, let us turn to the details of my defense of computational explanation of Frege cases. First, let us note that in order for the neo-Russellian to respond to the Frege cases, she must defend the following claims:

(1) Frege cases are tolerable exceptions, rather than counterexamples, to broad intentional *ceteris paribus* generalizations.

(2) Including Frege cases in the *ceteris paribus* clauses does not result in broad psychology failing to predict Frege cases. That is, Frege cases can be predicted somewhere within the total theory (but not necessarily at the intentional level).

(3) There is no compelling philosophical argument that differences between co-referring concepts must have intentional (as opposed to computational) explanation.

Intuitively, (1)–(3) are key components of any defense of the Frege cases. (1) is crucial because it is generally agreed by those who believe in *ceteris paribus* laws that for a putative counterexample to be included in the *ceteris paribus* clause, it must be shown to be a tolerable exception. But (1) is not sufficient to justify including Frege cases in the clauses, even assuming that the almost-all-things-considered judgment is for broad psychology, for the following reason. If including Frege cases in the *ceteris paribus* clauses leads broad psychology to fail to predict Oedipus's behavior, since greater scope is an advantage to a theory, then *ceteris paribus*, we have reason to take differences between co-referring names as being intentional, rather than computational. In this case the canonical form will not be one that includes the Frege cases in the *ceteris paribus* clauses. So (1) must be supplemented with (2).

But (2) addresses only the issue of predictive adequacy. Even if the theory is adequate in this respect, it may nonetheless fail to give satisfactory explanation of Frege cases. For critics charge that Oedipus's behavior can only be rationalized or explained by giving intentional explanation. In the eyes of many philosophers, the locus of doubt about the prospects of giving computational explanation of Frege cases centers around (3).

I shall now proceed to argue for (1). I will briefly outline why Oedipus is a tolerable exception. To avoid confusion, observe that Frege cases involve rational agents who generally are aware of co-referentialities relevant to the success of their actions, but who, in certain cases, fail to be aware of a co-referentiality. Frege cases are "abnormal" only in the watered-down sense that they are a breakdown in the normal course of events: normally, they do not occur because agents tend to be aware that two expressions co-refer when it is important to the success of their behavior.

Further, in virtue of their failure to be aware that certain expressions co-refer, agents having Frege cases fail to grasp the relevant propositions in matching ways. To see what is meant by "matching ways," consider, again, the case in which Oedipus is

a putative counterexample to (M). Oedipus satisfies the antecedent in virtue of having beliefs and desires that employ the mode
of presentation #Mother#. But, as a result of his ignorance of
the co-referentiality, he represents Jocasta differently when he
grasps the proposition figuring in the consequent; in this case,
he represents her under the mode of presentation #Jocasta#. So
he represents Jocasta in ways that do not match. As David Bruan
has insightfully suggested, this failure to represent Jocasta in
matching ways is grounds for regarding Oedipus as a tolerable
exception, rather than a counterexample, to (M) (Braun 2000;
2001a, b). All other things were not equal: although in general,
people seek to avoid marrying their mothers, Oedipus was atypi-
cal in the sense that he was ignorant of a co-referentiality, and in
virtue of his ignorance, he represents her in mismatching ways.
Including Oedipus in the *ceteris paribus* clause doesn't seem to
take away from the usefulness of (M); after all, (M) embodies a
generally accepted principle about human behavior and a large
population bears it out.

At this juncture, the critic may ask if treating Frege cases as
tolerable exceptions doesn't result in an intentional theory that
is a *notational variant* of saying that the mental states covered
by intentional laws have fine-grained propositional contents. To
see why this doesn't occur, consider:

(D) If people believe danger should be avoided, and believe
they are in danger, then *ceteris paribus*, they will try to avoid
danger.

On the standard construal of narrow intentional laws, if (D) is
a narrow intentional law, then the proposition expressed by the
relevant *that* clauses is individuated by the cognitive content of
the thought, where such has been construed in various ways,

most notably as a Fregean sense. When propositional contents are taxonomized in these ways, all those who satisfy a given law must conceive of the state of affairs referred to by the relevant *that* clauses in the same way. For instance, in the context of (D), all individuals must think of danger, avoidance, and so on under the same mode of presentation. This is clearly not a notational variant of laws having a broad canonical form. If (D) is a broad intentional law, then mental events are subsumed in the law by their referential properties, not their cognitive contents. So one person who satisfies (D) is free to conceive of danger (avoidance, etc.) under a different MOP from another person who satisfies (D). Perhaps the confusion arises from the matching ways requirement in the *ceteris paribus* clauses of broad laws; I suppose that it may sound Fregean in spirit, as it requires that the MOPs match up. It should be underscored, however, that the matching ways requirement merely requires that *within* a system that satisfies a given intentional law, the system must conceive of the relevant referents in ways that match up. It does not require a match in MOPs *across* systems the way that the Fregean or neo-Fregean positions do. Further, the required matchup is not one of propositional content, but one of computational state type.

(2) Now let us turn to the issue of whether broad psychology can predict Frege cases somewhere within the total theory. I will identify a number of reasons one may suspect that broad psychology cannot do so. Murat Aydede and Philip Robbins have argued that

a narrow psychology . . . can cover the occasional unsuccessful behavior, or accidentally successful behavior, to which Frege patients are prone. So a narrow psychology would have a wider scope, hence—*ceteris paribus*—greater explanatory and predictive power. And that surely suggests its superiority to the broad alternative. (Aydede and Robbins 2001)

To restate their claim in terms of the Oedipus example, they claim that narrow psychology, but not a broad psychology, can cover Oedipus's unsuccessful attempt to not marry Mother. As I've already noted, Oedipus fails to satisfy the following prediction:

(M) *Ceteris paribus*, if Oedipus desires that he not marry Mother/Jocasta, and Oedipus believes that not marrying Mother/Jocasta is the only way to bring this about, then he will try not to marry Mother/Jocasta.

(I write "Mother/Jocasta" rather than simply "Mother" to indicate that I have in mind a referential reading of "Mother.") And here we seem to arrive at a problem for the broad theory: when the theory includes Oedipus's thought *try not to marry Mother/Jocasta* in the *ceteris paribus* clause, according to the critics, it will not cover Oedipus's unsuccessful behavior that is narrowly described as his trying not to marry Mother. The theory will fail to do so because the intentional level is insensitive to this thought. However, the critics continue, there is still a sense in which Oedipus tries not to marry Mother, even though he fails. But a broad theory fails to predict that Oedipus will try not to marry Mother. Hence, it seems that narrow psychology can predict behavior that the neo-Russellian view cannot.

Of course, I agree with Aydede and Robbins that the following principle is true: *ceteris paribus*, greater scope is an advantage to a theory. But it is simply not true that broad psychology fails to cover "the occasional unsuccessful behavior, or accidentally successful behavior, to which Frege patients are prone." On the contrary, I will argue that including Frege cases in the clauses does *not* result in missed psychological explanation of Frege cases. This claim may seem surprising; after all, it is uncontroversial that broad psychology includes certain of Oedipus's thoughts in the *ceteris paribus* clauses. To prove my claim, I begin by distinguishing the following points:

(i) Frege cases are included in the *ceteris paribus* clauses of broad intentional laws.

(ii) Broad psychology fails to explain thoughts and behaviors that narrow psychology, on the other hand, does explain (when the events are described narrowly): namely, broad psychology fails to explain the events that are included in the *ceteris paribus* clauses.

Of course, if (ii) is correct then chalk one up for narrow psychology. I believe that many are assuming that (i), together with some reasonable premises, entails that (ii) is true. But such an argument is not valid: (i) is true while (ii) is false. Consider again the putative law (M): the critics urge that certain explanation of behavior is missed that narrow psychology does not miss, in not subsuming Oedipus under (M). Their concern is that at time *t*, before Oedipus meets Jocasta, Oedipus instances (M). After he tries to marry Jocasta, he fails to do so. So after *t*, explanation is unavailable, leading to a missed intentional generalization that narrow content does not miss since there is a sense in which Oedipus still tries not to marry Mother.

But this line of reasoning is flawed. Oedipus still instances (M) after *t*. Intuitively, when Oedipus believes that he should try not to marry Mother, he does so because he holds, like the rest of us, the moral prescription that one shouldn't marry Mother. The fact that he tries to marry Jocasta does not imply that he stops having this belief. Broad psychology can reflect this intuitive picture in the following way. When Oedipus believes the moral prescription, he has the mode of presentation #try not to marry Mother#, and this belief is intentionally described as a *try not to marry Mother/Jocasta* thought. So at least until he meets Jocasta, he satisfies the broad version of (M) like the rest of us do.

But what about after *t*? Certainly the broad theory does not require that after *t*, Oedipus drop his belief in the prescription simply because he now has a *try to marry Jocasta/Mother* thought as well. Oedipus satisfies (M) in virtue of believing the moral prescription, while in another situation, he is a putative counterexample to (M) when he thinks *try to marry Jocasta/Mother* (under the mode of presentation #try to marry Jocasta#). So a broad theory can cover Oedipus's unsuccessful attempt to not marry Mother.[13] I conclude that broad psychology does not fail to explain events in laws like (M) that narrow psychology, on the other hand, captures (under narrow description) in the narrow version of those laws. So while (i) is true, (ii) is false. Hence, including Frege cases in the clauses does not result in missed intentional-level explanation of Frege cases.

At this point in the dialectic, let us consider an important refinement to the solution to the Frege cases.

13. One might also suspect that because Oedipus's *try to marry Jocasta/ Mother* belief is included in the *ceteris paribus* clause of (M), broad psychology glosses over the fact that he tried to marry Jocasta. However, no missed intentional explanation arises from including the *try to marry Jocasta/Mother* thought in the *ceteris paribus* clause. Notice that the narrow thought, *try to marry Jocasta*, would obviously not have been subsumed by a narrow version of (M) either because the narrow version of (M) is about Mother, not Jocasta. Of course, the *try to marry Jocasta* thought would have satisfied the narrow prediction: "(N), If Oedipus wants to marry Jocasta and believes that he can try to marry Jocasta then he will try to marry Jocasta." But because Oedipus has a *try to marry Mother/Jocasta* thought (which he has when he has #try to marry Jocasta#), he satisfies the broad version of (N).

## 4   Refinement: Frege Phenomenon Explanation

Recall that I introduced this issue as a challenge to (2):

(2) (a) Including Frege cases in the *ceteris paribus* clauses does not result in broad psychology failing to predict Frege cases. (b) Frege cases can be predicted somewhere within the total theory (but not necessarily at the intentional level).

(I am dividing (2) into parts (a) and (b) for reasons that will soon become apparent.) My discussion thus far is intended only to serve as a defense of (2a). As we shall see, settling (2a) goes only partway toward a defense of (2b). For even bearing in mind the previous discussion, there seems to be the following gap in the neo-Russellian's prediction of Frege cases. Broad psychology can predict the following:

(1)  Oedipus will try not to marry Mother/Jocasta,

(2)  Oedipus will try to marry Mother/Jocasta.

But (1) and (2) do not tell us that Oedipus will have a Frege case: they merely suggest that he is in deep trouble. Intuitively, a defining feature of a Frege case is that the agent fails to be aware of a co-referentiality essential to the success of her behavior. A madman may know of the co-reference and try to do both actions in any case. Intuitively, the madman is not having a Frege case; what gets him into trouble isn't any ignorance about co-reference but his failure to act rationally. Simply knowing that (1) and (2) characterize Oedipus is insufficient for us to tell whether he is a Frege case or is simply being irrational. The proponent of narrow content will point out that to distinguish these scenarios we need a manner of belief individuation that is sensitive to narrow content or the MOP of the thought. For we need to know if Oedipus narrowly believes that Mother =

Jocasta. Let us call this notion of belief "belief*" to distinguish it from the neo-Russellian notion of belief. According to the neo-Russellian, anyone who believes that Jocasta = Jocasta or Mother = Mother believes that Mother = Jocasta. In contrast, whether one believes* that Mother = Jocasta, as opposed to simply believing* that Jocasta = Jocasta, depends upon belief individuation that is sensitive to MOPs, or alternately, to narrow contents.[14] So at least at first blush, broad psychology cannot predict that Oedipus will have a Frege case. It would seem that this is a fairly serious omission: knowledge that someone is having a Frege case explains his rationality despite the apparent irrationality of his actions. So it would seem that any psychological theory that fails to predict Frege cases would be incomplete.

The problem with this objection, in broad strokes, is that the information about the agent's ignorance of the co-reference *is* in fact available to a broad theory. This information may be unavailable intentionally, but it is available at the computational level. So the total theory can distinguish Oedipus from the madman. Indeed, the total theory can inform us about Frege cases in an even richer way. To illustrate this point, I need to examine, in more detail, what it is to predict Frege cases. Consider, again, the prediction:

(M) *Ceteris paribus*, if Oedipus desires that he not marry Mother/Jocasta, and Oedipus believes that not marrying mother/Jocasta is the only way to bring this about, then he will try not to marry Mother/Jocasta.

14. The problem is that the broad theory would consider anyone as instancing the thought that Mother = Jocasta who believes that Jocasta = Jocasta or Mother = Mother. This is because, according to broad psychology, Jocasta = Jocasta is intentionally identical to Mother = Jocasta.

Notice that this statement does not predict that Oedipus will have a Frege case; it merely predicts that Oedipus will try not to marry Jocasta/Mother. It pays to keep in mind that the intentional laws in which Frege cases are included in the *ceteris paribus* clauses are not about Frege cases per se; (M), for instance, is about people trying not to marry Mother. After all, would (M) constitute an explanation for the phenomenon that when an agent fails to be aware of a co-reference relevant to his behavioral success he will appear to act irrationally in his action(s)? Intuitively, only a generalization concerning this phenomenon could predict Frege cases, and not, in contrast, a generalization concerning people trying not to marry Mother.

With this in mind, let us ask: where might a failure to predict Frege cases arise from? Intuitively, it arises when a statement like the following is false according to the psychological theory:

(FP) *Ceteris paribus*, if system S has distinct MOPs that represent entity a, but the MOPs are not linked in the system's database as being co-referential, and S's behavioral success depends on the system's linking this data, then S will appear to act irrationally in her a directed action.

I shall call explanation of the phenomenon behind Frege cases *Frege phenomenon explanation*. You may notice that (FP) is not a broad intentional generalization because it is sensitive to MOPs; more on this shortly. Before delving into this issue, I should like to clarify (FP) and then explain why it is significant. First, we can observe that in speaking of MOPs that are "linked in the system's database," I mean that there is some level of computational processing in which the subject's way of conceiving of Cicero and his way of conceiving of Tully are encoded as being about the same object.

This being said, (FP) is introduced to illustrate that there are actually two ways that Frege cases could figure as objects of explanation in psychological laws. In the case of laws like (M), the object of explanation is not Frege cases qua Frege cases, but some other phenomenon entirely—in this case, the phenomenon that one tries not to marry Mother. In contrast, Frege phenomenon explanation has Frege cases as the object of explanation. With this distinction in mind, we can now see that (2a) and (2b) are not equivalent: even if my previous argumentation succeeds in showing that including Frege cases in the clauses does not lead to missed prediction, the broad theory may nonetheless fail to predict Frege cases because it fails to include a generalization about Frege cases along the lines of (FP).

At this point, it is natural to ask: can broad psychology incorporate a generalization along the lines of (FP)? After all, (FP) does not subsume agents by the neo-Russellian propositions that their thoughts express, because it requires differentiating thoughts by their MOPs. Still, it can be regarded as a computational-level generalization, because this is a theoretical level that is sensitive to MOPs. In this way, broad psychology can employ this generalization to predict that Oedipus will have a Frege case. To recur to the case of the madman, (FP) can be summoned to distinguish irrational individuals who are having conflicting goals from rational agents who are experiencing Frege cases. Those who are aware that the expressions co-refer will fail to satisfy the antecedent of (FP).

It is likely that the critic will object to these suggestions, claiming that it is inappropriate to take (FP) as a computational generalization, because (FP), and explanation of Frege cases more generally, should be intentional. Notice that this charge is not really about the ability of broad psychology to predict

Frege cases; the present worry is that even if all the psychologically relevant events are covered by broad psychology, certain phenomena are explained at the wrong level of analysis. This is really an objection to (3), a claim that, at the outset of the section, I argued needs to be substantiated by any answer to the Frege cases.

## 5 Must Distinct Co-referring Names Differ in Their Contents?

Recall that (3) was:

(3) There is no compelling philosophical argument that differences between coreferring concepts must have intentional, as opposed to computational, explanation.

Why would only intentional explanation do the job? Indeed, it is a common suspicion that only intentional explanation can rationalize, or make sense of, thoughts and behaviors. Dennis Arjo voices a variant of the common concern that co-referring concepts must have intentional, as opposed to computational, explanation:

Given Oedipus' beliefs and desires—i.e. given the facts about how he believes the world to be and the way he wishes it to be—he acts exactly how we would expect him to behave, despite the utter unlikelihood of the results. . . . And this, it seems, requires a way of individuating the content of mental states which is sensitive to different ways the same thing in the world might be represented. (Arjo 1996, 244)

Arjo does not explain why narrow content, rather than MOPs, are needed to make sense of Oedipus's thoughts and behaviors. But I do not see why this should be the case—is there supposed to be some a priori reason why explanation of Oedipus's behavior must be intentional, as opposed to computational? While it is correct that rationalizations of one's thoughts and behaviors seem to be sensitive to ways of conceiving referents, MOPs, as well as narrow contents, can capture one's way of conceiving the world.

To be fair to Arjo, his point was just an aside—a pronouncement of skepticism in the conclusion of a critical paper on the problem of Frege cases. We should ask, What fuels such suspicions? It is likely that they are motivated by one or more of the following considerations:

(I) Co-referential expressions must differ in their contents, rather than merely in their LOT expression type/MOP, because a certain theory of narrow content or two-factor theory is correct (e.g., the mapping theory).

(II) Co-referential expressions must differ in their contents because it is counterintuitive to take differences between MOPs as sources of exceptions to intentional laws, for MOPs are precisely what intentional laws are supposed to be sensitive to.

(III) Psychological generalizations must be purely intentional (and narrow) because computational explanation faces problems with MOP individuation.

I will discuss each of these considerations in turn.

(I) Two influential theories of narrow content are Ned Block's version of conceptual role semantics and the mapping theory of narrow content (developed by Jerry Fodor, John Perry, and others). Given that narrow content has been treated extensively elsewhere, and given that an exhaustive survey of the various theories of narrow content is well beyond the scope of this chapter, what I propose to do is comment on why these leading theories fail to give us reason to regard the differences between co-referring names as being, in fact, differences in their content.[15]

Let us first turn to the mapping, or character-based, views of narrow content (Fodor 1987; Kaplan 1990; Perry 1977). Examples like the following are frequently given to motivate such views: Steve thinks, "I am about to be run over by a train," and Mitsuko thinks of Steve, "He is about to be run over by a train"; although the same singular proposition is expressed, the agent's behavior differs. On the other hand, if they both think, "I am about to be run over by a train," they will, *ceteris paribus*, engage in the same behavior. This contrast is supposed to motivate the view that the narrow content of a thought is its character; a function from the context of thoughts to extensions.[16]

The crucial problem with such views of narrow content, in very broad strokes, is that states that function very differently within the subject's cognitive economy can satisfy the same mapping from contexts to extensions. To borrow an example from Howard Wettstein, consider Sally, who sees Jose from outside a window of a building; and suppose that Jose is outfitted

15. I shall not discuss versions of narrow content based on descriptivism (including cluster versions), as they have been widely regarded as problematic given the aforementioned arguments of Saul Kripke, Hilary Putnam, and others. For problems with Gilbert Harman's long-arm conceptual role theory and other two-factor views see Segal (2000) and Block (1994).

16. Such theories of narrow content take inspiration from the case of indexicals, but they are intended to extend to other expressions as well. To keep things brief, I shall not delve into Kaplan's theory of indexicals and the related controversy surrounding whether, in fact, such a theory can serve as a basis for the content of nonindexical expressions more generally. This would take us too far afield; even assuming an extension is plausible, the problems that I mention below apply.

so that she cannot tell from looking at his right profile and from looking at his left profile that it is the same person. Suppose that Sally sees one side of Jose from the window (outside the building) and then walks to a doorway and sees Jose's other side and assumes that he is an entirely different person. Sally, upon learning of the identity, may say, "Ah, he is the same man that he is." Here, both tokens of "he" have the same linguistic meaning, but, intuitively, the states have different roles in the individual's cognitive economy (Wettstein 1991, 191). Objections along (roughly) the same lines can also be provided in the cases of proper names and kind terms; in general, two systems may have computational states that satisfy the same mapping function but play very distinct computational roles. Indeed, the mapping theory does not even treat Oedipus's #Jocasta# and #Mother# tokens as differing in their narrow contents; thus, the theory will face Frege cases.

In contrast to the mapping theory of narrow content, Ned Block's version of conceptual-role semantics provides a notion of narrow content that is designed to track sameness and difference of computationally relevant causal powers. Block, as noted, accepts referential generalizations and aims to provide another sort of content as well. He explains, "The internal factor, conceptual role, is a matter of the causal role of the expression in reasoning and deliberation, and in general, in the way the expression combines and interacts with other expressions so as to mediate between sensory inputs and behavioral outputs" (Block 1994, 93). Indeed, Block intends the specification of the causal roles to be in terms of internal computations in one's language of thought (Block 1994, 97–99). As it happens, conceptual roles seem to be individuated by the very same features that type the LOT states that serve as MOPs on my own view. So I obviously think Block is on the right track. But for Block's theory of narrow content to genuinely challenge (3), he must provide reason to believe that these entities individuated by their conceptual roles are really narrow contents, rather than merely being computational states (MOPs) that are nonsemantic.

So what reason is there to regard these narrow computational states as being narrow contents rather than merely items in LOT syntax? We might think that because, according to conceptual role theories, entities that individuate narrow contents are called *conceptual* or *inferential*, since such entities are standardly thought to be semantic, the narrow states get to be contents. But, as Block himself underscores, one cannot maintain that that which individuates the conceptual roles is itself semantic, for if one is concerned with reducing (or more aptly, naturalizing) intentionality in terms of computational states, one cannot explain semantic properties in terms of properties that are themselves semantic. He writes:

Calling the causal roles CRS [conceptual role semantics] appeals to "conceptual" or "inferential" shouldn't mislead anyone into supposing that the theory's description of them can appeal to their meanings—that would defeat the point of reductionist theories. The project of giving a nonsemantic (and nonintentional) description of these roles is certainly daunting, but the reader would do well to note that it is no more daunting than the programs of various popular philosophical theories. (Block 1994, 97)

In sum, naturalistic or reductive CRS programs must regard the features that individuate the narrow contents as being nonsemantic. So we have no rationale for rejecting (3) here.

Block's reason for regarding the narrow states as being contents is that narrow meaning "determines the nature of the referential factor." More specifically, "What theory of reference is true is a fact about how referring terms function in our thought process. This is an aspect of conceptual role. So it is the conceptual role of referring expressions that determines what theory of reference is true. Conclusion, the conceptual role factor determines the nature of the referential factor" (Block 1994, 109).[17] Block's remarks are unsatisfying: the fact that we are agents who have referring terms functioning in a particular way in our thought process does not suggest that our narrow states are, in fact, contents. For there is an alternate story that could be told: such conceptual roles are merely computational states that, only when supplemented with a reference relation linking the internal states to the world, have contents. And these contents are broad. On this alternate account, narrow contents drop out of the picture.

Perhaps the proponent of narrow content would say that the states are contents because they are ways of representing the world. However, computationally individuated states, without a reference relation that links the states to referents, are not themselves ways of representing the world. They are uninterpreted symbols. I suppose that one could simply stipulate that the computational states are contents, but this would not really answer the charge that these entities seem to be just syntax, and it would surely not provide the needed argument that differences between distinct co-referring names *must* be differences in content.

Now consider the second attempt to justify the view that differences between co-referring names must be differences in

17. Block hedges his bets on whether narrow contents are really contents: "Nothing in my position requires me to regard narrow meaning and narrow content as (respectively) kinds of meaning and content. As mentioned earlier, I regard them as aspects of or as determinants of meaning and content" (Block 1994, 92).

content. Rather than appealing to a particular theory of narrow content, in (II), the critic simply claims that my view is counter-intuitive. For on the standard view of intentional laws, intentional laws are supposed to be sensitive to MOPs, and it seems absurd, in light of this, to suggest that differences between MOPs are supposed to be treated as sources of exceptions to intentional laws. For intentional laws, by their very nature, are supposed to be sensitive to MOPs.

There are several problems with this objection. First, the objector is assuming that intentional laws track MOPs, and this is precisely what is up for debate, for the broad psychologist denies this. Now, I am happy to grant that the standard intuition about intentional laws supports the view that the laws are sensitive to MOPs. But here I would ask: How far should these intuitions go? That is, how extensively should they influence the dialectical status of the broad versus narrow content debate? I assume that both sides would agree that it is not built into the very concept of mental content that content must be narrow. Theories of broad content may strike a proponent of narrow content as being flawed, but certainly, they do not seem conceptually incoherent, like talk of round squares. But if it is not a conceptual truth that content is narrow, then it seems fair to say that a selection of a theory of content is an all-things-considered judgment, covering a variety of issues.

Admittedly, philosophical intuitions should weigh into this judgment. However, while I'm happy to admit that there's an intuitive pull behind the neo-Fregean picture, I venture that there is also reason to regard as intuitive a theory that glosses over intentional differences between co-referring thoughts. For, to return to Block's observation, there is a clear sense in which different individuals, no matter how they represent things, satisfy the same intentional generalization. (For example, no matter how people conceive of fire, they satisfy the generalization that people want to leave a crowded theater when they believe there is fire.) A purely narrow theory loses this sense and thus is susceptible to a counterintuitiveness charge as well.

One could respond that it is open to the proponent of narrow content to claim that there are a number of broad intentional laws as well. (This would amount to occupying a two-factor theory.) However, if this move is made, it is very difficult for the critic to maintain the original objection. For the original objection was that intentional laws just *are* the sort of entities that should be sensitive to ways of conceiving of things; intentional laws should not take differences between co-referring thoughts as the source of exceptions. But broad laws will require such exceptions, and this new response grants that some intentional laws are broad.

(III) Now let us entertain a third, entirely different, motivation for rejecting (3). One may claim that explanation of differences between co-referring names must be intentional, and narrow, because computational explanation faces problems with MOP individuation. It is the main thesis of a thought-provoking paper by Murat Aydede that an appeal to MOPs in a "solution to the Frege cases succumbs to the problem of providing interpersonally applicable functional roles for MOPs" (Aydede 1998). Here is the problem, in a nutshell: in order to include Frege cases in the *ceteris paribus* clauses, there must be some way to take the co-referring concepts as being of distinct MOP types. According to Aydede, any plausible theory of MOP state typing must cut states at the level of grain of sameness and difference of computationally relevant causal powers. But as I've noted in the previous chapters, this rather innocent demand cuts computational states extremely thinly. As a consequence, symbols will likely not be shared. Aydede believes that this lack of shared LOT expressions ruins the prospects for including Frege cases in the clauses.

I am obviously in sympathy with Aydede's suspicion that symbolic MOPs must be individuated by computational role. But his further claim is problematic, because it is not the case that a solution to the Frege cases will fail because MOPs are individuated by computational or functional role. Instead, all that is needed to include Frege cases in the clauses is a means of distinguishing symbol types *within a given system*. For instance, to include Oedipus in the *ceteris paribus* clause of (M), all that is needed is to distinguish Oedipus's #Jocasta# and #Mother# thoughts at a given time, but it is uncontroversial that a functionalist (and holistic) individuation condition can distinguish thoughts synchronically within the same system.

Here, the critic could provide an *interpersonal* Frege case. For instance, Aydede gives a hypothetical case of a psychological generalization about people running in the direction of Superman when danger is near. He asks us to consider the hypothetical generalization:

(P) When people feel threatened by perceived danger, and they think Superman will help them, they will run in the direction of Superman.

Now consider Lois Lane, who does not realize that the man she calls "Kent" is also called "Superman" and, because Superman/Kent is not in costume, fails to run to Superman/Kent when danger is near. As discussed, Lois is an exception to the generalization and will need to be included in the *ceteris paribus* clause. Now suppose that Sam is standing next to Lois when danger is near. Sam, on the other hand, is aware of the co-referentiality and, while Lois stands still, darts in Superman/Kent's direction. This "interpersonal Frege case" is supposed to raise the following problem for broad psychology: lacking a manner of typing LOT tokens interpersonally, how is broad psychology to explain the differences in behavior between Sam and Lois?[18]

Like the previous problem, this problem is not genuine: intrapersonal typing is all that is needed to solve interpersonal Frege cases. We can say that as Sam stands with Lois, sensing danger, he has an MOP that corresponds to the English name "Superman" and one that corresponds to "Kent," and that he knows that the same individual has these two English names. And Lois has an MOP that corresponds to the English name "Superman" and a distinct one that corresponds to "Kent," and she does not believe that the two English names pick out the same individual. Now, lacking a manner of interpersonal typing, we do not know whether Lois and Sam have thought tokens that are of the same LOT type (after all, many modes of presentation may correspond to one English expression), although we do know that the thought tokens refer to the same entity. However, despite this lack of knowledge, the "interpersonal" Frege case can easily

18. Notice that the version of the problem considered here asks how, given that Lois's case is included in the *ceteris paribus* clause of the law, while Sam (in contrast) instances the law, broad psychology can explain the difference in their behaviors, on the assumption that LOT has no means of distinguishing their respective LOT vocabularies. Sometimes discussions of "interpersonal Frege cases" raise a different problem as well, asking whether LOT has the resources to explain why two or more individuals satisfy an intentional generalization, or fail to satisfy it. The concern is that there will be cases in which they do so in virtue of having the same type of MOPs. I do not discuss this version here because I already responded to it in section 2 of chapter 6.

be solved. I have already established that we can handle a Frege case for Lois via inclusion in the *ceteris paribus* clauses. All that is needed to do so is intrapersonal typing. And intrapersonal typing is all that is needed to subsume Sam's thoughts in the generalization. He is subsumed in the same generalization that Lois is an exception to because their tokens share the same broad contents.[19] Hence, such objections can be set aside.

## 6   Conclusion

In this chapter I developed a solution to the third, and final, problem that this book aimed to solve. The Frege cases had generated a conflict between LOT's favored theory of mental content and its position that thinking is symbolic. If there were genuine counterexamples to intentional generalizations, LOT would be unable to explain thought and behavior intentionally, and it would be incapable of offering a comprehensive account of the nature of mentality. In light of the argumentation of this chapter, I believe that we now have reason to reject the bleak view in the literature concerning the prospects for the LOT program to manage the Frege cases. For I've urged that including the cases in the *ceteris paribus* clauses is justified by a larger theoretical decision for intentional laws with a canonical form that is broad. Any decision to include the Frege cases in the *ceteris paribus* clauses is the result of an overall assessment of the debate about which canonical form intentional laws should take, broad or narrow. While such a decision is a global affair, I have focused on the part of this theoretical decision that is internal to Frege

19. Mutatis mutandis, different systems may satisfy (FP), despite the holism of computational state individuation, insofar as each system has two (intrapersonally distinct) MOPs that represent the same entity.

cases: that which involves the issue of whether computational explanation of co-referring thoughts will suffice.

As noted, the literature on Frege cases has been quite negative on this score. Against these critics, I've argued the following: first, broad psychology can treat Frege cases as tolerable exceptions, rather than counterexamples, to broad intentional laws. Second, there is no missed prediction of Frege cases: broad psychology does not fail to explain events in its laws that narrow psychology, on the other hand, captures (under narrow description). Third, although broad psychology must include Frege cases in the clauses, it can nevertheless offer generalizations along the lines of (FP) to predict Frege cases. And finally, I've responded to various arguments that explanation of Frege cases must be intentional that are based on suspicions that a competing account of narrow content is correct, on commonly held intuitions about the nature of intentional laws, and last, on the view that shared MOPs are unavailable.

# 9 Conclusion

We have thus arrived at the end of today's project. At the very outset, I observed that at the core of philosophy of mind is the enterprise to grasp the nature of minds and their states. Nowadays, naturalistic approaches to the nature of thought and mind are all the philosophical rage, and those philosophers who aim to integrate mentality into the world that science investigates quite naturally turn their gaze to computational approaches in cognitive science, such as the (classical) computational theory of mind. But as important as computational approaches to the nature of mentality are, and as central as the symbol-processing approach is to information-processing psychology, the presence of three problems led me to suspect that LOT was ill conceived as both a theory of mind and its states. These problems were:

1. *The problem of the computational nature of the central system.* I observed that LOT urgently needed to orient itself with respect to current work on higher cognitive function in cognitive science rather than insisting that research on it grind to a halt. Otherwise LOT would lack a coherent and naturalistically kosher account of the nature of mind.

2. *The problem of mental state individuation.* LOT and CTM purport to be theories of the nature of thought, but their notion of

a mental state—in LOT's jargon, a "mental symbol"—had for years been a locus of criticism and remained massively underdeveloped. Yet, as this book has observed, symbols are at the heart of practically every philosophical and scientific enterprise that the LOT program engages in.

3. *The problem of the relation between meaning and symbolic mental states (i.e., the Frege cases).* LOT's favored theory of mental content seemed to conflict with its claim that thinking is symbolic. And this conflict gave rise to counterexamples to intentional generalizations, threatening the LOT program's ability to explain thought and behavior.

Here is what I have accomplished. As it is still fresh in our minds, consider first the previous chapter's solution to the third problem—the problem of Frege cases. There, I developed an extensive solution to the Frege cases, arguing that LOT's neo-Russellian, broad-content-based theory of meaning does in fact mesh with its position that thinking is symbolic.

While much of this solution is available to the standard LOT, the remainder of this book advanced solutions to other problems that would be repudiated by the mainstream LOT, for it is wrongly committed to both a pure Cartesianism about the nature of thought and a pessimism about the central system. Turning to the first problem, recall the efforts of chapters 2 and 3. At a time when research on higher cognitive function is finally emerging, LOT's leading philosophical proponent simply took LOT off the table as a computational approach. So this book serves a corrective function, arguing that pessimism about centrality is ill conceived. I have also sought to bring LOT forward, situating it within a larger computational account of the central systems. To be sure, our understanding of the central system will grow in sophistication, but I suspect the general shape of my account is apt, for the global workspace approach draws from the current understanding of the central system in cognitive science. Indeed, although the GW account surely awaits further refinements, considering it serves a larger purpose. For my aim has also been methodological—LOT simply cannot oppose itself to computationalism; it must integrate itself into the larger scientific framework of cognitive and computational neuroscience, in particular. Otherwise, symbols would lack a connection to the world that science investigates, and LOT's naturalism would fail. So I put it to you: this is how LOT *should* proceed.

No fewer than three chapters have been devoted to sculpting a viable response to the problem of the nature of symbolic mental states. After exploring the different philosophical functions that LOT requires of symbols, I illustrated that competing theories of symbols come up short in one or more key dimensions; instead, symbols must be individuated algorithmically. Further, this position does not preclude explanation across distinct individuals, or the same individual over time, as critics have argued. Much of this book has been devoted to putting our newly discovered understanding of symbols to work: employing it to help solve the Frege cases, summoning it to rethink LOT's conception of MOPs, and mining it to rework LOT's favored theory of concepts, conceptual atomism. In this latter domain, I've introduced a needed psychological component into the atomist's theory: a concept's nature is both what it does, as per pragmatism, and what it is about, as per weak Cartesianism.

In essence, the philosophical LOT had been on the wrong side of the very debates that it has spent so much of its energy partaking in, opposing computationalism and pragmatism when both are, in fact, built into its very nature. Put bluntly, LOT has been its own worst enemy. But we now know that these commitments are unnecessary—indeed, ill-fitting—elements of the LOT approach. And shedding them has facilitated solutions to the three problems. So let us be done with them. Herein I have seen fit to rethink LOT's approach to both computation and symbols. In so doing, I've rebuilt LOT from the ground up.

# References

Anderson, J. 2007. *How Can the Human Mind Occur in the Physical Universe?* Oxford: Oxford University Press.

Arjo, D. 1996. Sticking Up for Oedipus: Fodor on Intentional Generalizations and Broad Content. *Mind & Language* 11 (3): 231–245.

Armstrong, D. M. 1997. *A World of States of Affairs.* New York: Cambridge University Press.

Aydede, M. 1997a. Has Fodor Really Changed His Mind on Narrow Content? *Mind & Language* 12: 422–458.

Aydede, M. 1997b. Language of Thought: The Connectionist Contribution. *Minds and Machines* 7 (1): 57–101.

Aydede, M. 1998. Fodor on Concepts and Frege Puzzles. *Pacific Philosophical Quarterly* 79: 289–294.

Aydede, M. 2000a. Computation and Intentional Psychology. *Dialogue* 39: 365–379.

Aydede, M. 2000b. On the Type/Token Relation of Mental Representations. *Facta Philosophica: International Journal for Contemporary Philosophy* 2: 23–49.

Aydede, M. 2005. Computation and Functionalism: Syntactic Theory of Mind Revisited. In *Turkish Studies in the History and Philosophy of Science,* edited by G. Irzik and G. Guzeldere. New York: Springer, 177–204.

Aydede, M., and Robbins, P. 2001. Are Frege Cases Exceptions to Intentional Generalizations? *Canadian Journal of Philosophy* 31: 1–22.

Baars, B. J. 1988. *A Cognitive Theory of Consciousness.* Cambridge, MA: Cambridge University Press.

Baars, B. J. 1997. *In the Theater of Consciousness.* New York: Oxford University Press.

Baars, B. J. 2002. The Conscious Access Hypothesis: Origins and Recent Evidence. *Trends in Cognitive Sciences* 8 (1): 47–52.

Baars, B. J. 2007. The Global Workspace Theory of Consciousness. In *The Blackwell Companion to Consciousness,* edited by M. Velmans and S. Schneider. Oxford: Blackwell.

Baars, B. J., and Franklin, S. 2003. How Conscious Experience and Working Memory Interact. *Trends in Cognitive Sciences* 7 (4): 166–172.

Baars, B. J., and S. Franklin. 2009. Consciousness Is Computational: The IDA Model of Global Workspace Theory. *International Journal of Machine Consciousness* 1 (1):23–32.

Baddeley, A. 1986. *Working Memory.* Oxford: Clarendon Press.

Baddeley, A. 2003. Working Memory: Looking Backward and Looking Forward. *Nature Reviews: Neuroscience* 4 (Oct).

Baddeley, A. 1992. Working Memory. *Science* 255 (5044): 556–559.

Bickhard, M. *The Whole Person: Towards a Naturalism of Persons.* In manuscript.

Bickhard, M. 2001. Why Children Don't Have to Solve the Frame Problems: Cognitive Representations Are Not Encodings. *Developmental Review* 21: 224–262.

Blackburn, S. 1992. Filling in Space. *Analysis* 52 (2): 62–63.

Block, N. 1986. Advertisement for a Semantics for Psychology. In *Midwest Studies in Philosophy.* vol. X. ed. P. A. French, et al., 615–678. Minneapolis: University of Minnesota Press.

Block, N. 1991. Troubles with Functionalism. In *The Nature of Mind*, ed. D. M. Rosenthal, 211–228. New York: Oxford University Press.

Block, N. 1993. Holism, Hyper-analyticity and Hyper-compositionality. *Mind & Language* 8 (1):1–27.

Block, N. 1994. Advertisement for a Semantics for Psychology. In *Mental Representations: A Reader*, edited by S. Stich and E. Warfield. Cambridge: Blackwell.

Block, N. 1995. The Mind as the Software of the Brain. In *An Invitation to Cognitive Science*, edited by D. Osherson, L. Gleitman, S. Kosslyn, E. Smith, and S. Sternberg. Cambridge, MA: MIT Press.

Block, N. 1995. An Argument for Holism. In *Proceedings of the Aristotelian Society* XCIV:151–169.

Block, N. 1998. Holism, Mental and Semantic. In *The Routledge Encylopedia of Philosophy*, edited by E. Craig and L. Floridi. New York: Routledge.

Braun, D. 1998. Understanding Belief Reports. *Philosophical Review* 107: 555–595.

Braun, D. 2000. Russellianism and Psychological Generalizations. *Noûs* 34: 203–236.

Braun, D. 2001a. Russellianism and Explanation. *Philosophical Perspectives* 15: 253–289.

Braun, D. 2001b. Russellianism and Prediction. *Philosophical Studies* 105: 59–105.

Burge, T. 1979. Individualism and the Mental. *Midwest Studies in Philosophy* 4: 73–121.

Buxhoeveden, D., and M. Casanova. 2002. The Minicolumn Hypothesis in Neuroscience. *Brain* 125 (5): 935–951.

Calvert, G., Spence, C., and Stein, B. E., eds. 2004. *Handbook of Multisensory Processes*, Cambridge, MA: MIT Press.

Carey, S. 1985. *Conceptual Change in Childhood*. Cambridge, MA: MIT Press.

Carruthers, P. 1996. *Language, Thought and Consciousness: An Essay in Philosophical Psychology*. New York: Cambridge University Press.

Carruthers, P. 2003. On Fodor's Problem. *Mind & Language* 18:502–523.

Carruthers, P. 2005. Distinctively Human Thinking: Modular Precursors and Components. In *The Innate Mind: Structure and Content*, edited by P. Carruthers, S. Laurence, and S. Stich. Oxford: Oxford University Press.

Carruthers, P. 2006. *The Architecture of the Mind: Massive Modularity and the Flexibility of Thought*. Oxford: Oxford University Press.

Carruthers, P. 2008. On Fodor-Fixation, Flexibility, and Human Uniqueness. *Mind & Language* 23: 293–303.

Chalmers, D. 1995. Facing Up to the Hard Problem of Consciousness. *Journal of Consciousness Studies* 2 (3): 200–219.

Changeux, J. P., and Michel, C. M. 2004. Mechanisms of Neural Integration at the Brain-Scale Level: The Neuronal Workspace and Microstate Models. In *Microcircuits, the Interface Between Neurons and Global Brain Function*, edited by S. Rillner and A. M. Graybill. Cambridge, MA: MIT Press.

Chomsky, N. 1975. *Reflections on Language*. New York: Pantheon.

Churchland, P. M. 1995. *The Engine of Reason, the Seat of the Soul*. Cambridge, MA: MIT Press.

Churchland, P. M. 1998. Conceptual Similarity Across Sensory and Neural Diversity: The Fodor/Lepore Challenge Answered. *Journal of Philosophy* 95: 5–32.

Churchland, P. M. 2005. Functionalism at Forty: A Critical Retrospective. *Journal of Philosophy* 102 (1): 33–50.

Crane, T. 1990. The Language of Thought: No Syntax Without Semantics. *Mind & Language* 5 (3): 187–212.

Crane, T. 2004. Review of *Hume Variations*. *Times Literary Supplement*, May 7.

Crimmons, M. 1992. *Talk About Beliefs*. Cambridge, MA: MIT Press.

Crimmons, M., and Perry, J. 1989. The Prince and the Phone Booth: Reporting Puzzling Beliefs. *Journal of Philosophy* 86: 685–711.

Cummins, R. 1983. *The Nature of Psychological Explanation*. Cambridge, MA: MIT Press.

Cummins, R. 2000. 'How Does It Work?' Versus 'What are the Laws?' Two Conceptions of Psychological Explanation. In *Explanation and Cognition*, edited by F. Keil and R. Wilson. Cambridge, MA: MIT Press, 114–144.

Dehaene, S., and Changeux, J. P. 2004. Neural Mechanisms for Access to Consciousness. In *Cognitive Neurosciences*, 3rd ed., edited by M. S. Gazzaniga. Cambridge, MA: MIT Press.

Dehaene, S., and Changeux, J. P. 2005. Ongoing Spontaneous Activity Controls Access to Consciousness: A Neuronal Model for Inattentional Blindness. *PLoS Biology* 3 (5): 141.

Dehaene, S., and Naccache, L. 2001. Towards a Cognitive Neuroscience of Consciousness: Basic Evidence and a Workspace Framework. *Cognition* 2: 79.

Dehaene, S., Sergent, C., and Changeux, J. P. 2003. A Neuronal Network Model Linking Subjective Reports and Objective Physiological Data During Conscious Perception. *Proceedings of the National Academy of Sciences of the United States of America* 100 (14): 8520–8525.

Dennett, D. C. 1984. Cognitive Wheels: The Frame Problem in Artificial Intelligence. In *Minds, Machines and Evolution*, ed. C. Hookway, 129–151. Cambridge: Cambridge University Press.

Dennett, D. C. 1993. *Consciousness Explained*. New York: Penguin Books.

Dennett, D. C. 2001. Are We Explaining Consciousness Yet? *Cognition* 79: 221–237.

Dennett, D. C., and M. Kinsbourne. 1995. Time and the Observer: The Where and When of Consciousness in the Brain. *Behavioral and Brain Sciences* 15 (2):183–247.

Devitt, M. 1991. Why Fodor Can't Have it Both Ways. In *Meaning in Mind: Fodor and His Critics*, edited by B. Loewer and G. Rey. Oxford: Blackwell.

Devitt, M. 1995. *Coming to Our Senses: A Naturalistic Program for Semantic Localism*. Cambridge: Cambridge University Press.

Dreyfus, H. 1972. *What Computers Can't Do: A Critique of Artificial Reason*. New York: Harper Collins.

Dreyfus, H. 1992. *Being in the World*. Cambridge, MA: MIT Press.

Egan, F. 1992. Individualism, Computation, and Perceptual Content. *Mind* 101 (403): 443–459.

Egan, F. 1995. Computation and Content. *Philosophical Review* 104 (2): 181–203.

Elman, J. 1998. Generalization, Simple Recurrent Networks, and the Emergence of Structure. In *Proceedings of the 20th Annual Conference of the Cognitive Science Society*, edited by M.A. Gernsbacher and S. Derry. Mahwaw, NJ: Lawrence Erlbaum.

Fodor, J. A. 1975. *The Language of Thought*. Cambridge, MA: Harvard University Press.

Fodor, J. A. 1981. The Present Status of the Innateness Controversy. In *RePresentations: Philosophical Essays on the Foundations of Cognitive Science*, 257–316. Cambridge, MA: MIT Press.

Fodor, J. A. 1983. *The Modularity of Mind: An Essay in Faculty Psychology*. Cambridge, MA: MIT Press.

Fodor, J. A. 1985. Fodor's Guide to Mental Representation: The Intelligent Auntie's Vade-Mecum. *Mind* 94:76–100.

Fodor, J. A. 1987. *Psychosemantics: The Problem of Meaning in the Philosophy of Mind*. Cambridge, MA: MIT Press.

Fodor, J. A. 1990. Substitution Arguments and the Individuation of Belief. In *A Theory of Content and Other Essays, J. Fodor*. Cambridge, MA: MIT Press.

Fodor, J. A. 1991. You Can Fool Some of the People All of the Time, Everything Else Being Equal: Hedged Laws and Psychological Explanations. *Mind* 100: 19–34.

Fodor, J. A. 1994. *The Elm and the Expert: Mentalese and Its Semantics*. Cambridge, MA: MIT Press.

Fodor, J. A. 1998a. *Concepts: Where Cognitive Science Went Wrong*. Oxford: Oxford University Press.

Fodor, J. A. 1998b. *In Critical Condition*. Oxford: Oxford University Press.

Fodor, J. A. 2000. *The Mind Doesn't Work That Way: the Scope and Limits of Computational Psychology*. Cambridge, MA: MIT Press.

Fodor, J. A. 2003. *Hume Variations*. Oxford: Oxford University Press.

Fodor, J. A. 2004. Having Concepts: A Brief Refutation of the Twentieth Century. *Mind & Language* 19 (1): 29–47.

Fodor, J. A. 2005. Reply to Steven Pinker, 'So How *Does* the Mind Work?' *Mind & Language* 20 (1): 25–32.

Fodor, J. A. 2008. *LOT 2: the Language of Thought Revisited*. Oxford: Oxford University Press.

Fodor, J. A., and LePore, E. 1992. *Holism: A Shoppers' Guide*. Oxford: Blackwell.

Fodor, J. A., and McLaughlin, B. 1990. Connectionism and the Problem of Systematicity: Why Smolensky's Solution Doesn't Work. *Cognition* 35: 183–204.

Fodor, J. A., and Pylyshyn, Z. 1995. Connectionism and Cognitive Architecture: A Critical Analysis. In *Connectionism: Debates on Psychological Explanation,* Volume Two, edited by C. Macdonald and G. Macdonald. Oxford: Basil Blackwell.

Frege, G. 1892. Über Sinn und Bedeutung (On Sense and Reference). Zeitschrift für Philosophie und philosophische Kritik C: 25–50.

Frege, G. 1980. *Philosophical and Mathematical Correspondence*, ed. G. Gabriel et al. Chicago: University of Chicago Press.

Gazzaniga, M., Ivry, R., and Mangun, G. 2002. *Cognitive Neuroscience*. 2nd ed. New York: Norton.

Gopnik, A., and A. N. Meltzoff. 1997. *Words, Thoughts, and Theories*. Cambridge, MA: MIT Press.

Gopnik, A., and H. Wellman. 1992. Why the Child's Theory of Mind Really Is a Theory. *Mind & Language* 7:145–171.

Hagmann P., Cammoun, L., Gigandet, X., Meuli, R., Honey, C. J., et al. 2008. Mapping the Structural Core of Human Cerebral Cortex. *PLoS Biology* 6 (7).

Hardcastle, V. 1996. *How to Build a Theory in Cognitive Science*. New York: SUNY Press.

Harman, G. 1973. *Thought*. Princeton: Princeton University Press.

Harnad, S. 1990. The Symbol Grounding Problem. *Physica D. Nonlinear Phenomena* 42: 335–346.

Hatfield, G. 2009. *Perception and Cognition: Essays in the Philosophy of Psychology*. Oxford: Clarendon Press.

Haugeland, J. 1989. *AI: The Very Idea*. Cambridge, MA: MIT Press.

Hawkins, J. 2005. *On Intelligence*. New York: MacMillan.

Heidegger, M. 1972. *Being and Time*. Oxford: Blackwell.

Heil, J. 2005. *From an Ontological Point of View*. Oxford: Oxford University Press.

Horgan, T., and Tienson, J. 1996. *Connectionism and the Philosophy of Psychology*. Cambridge, MA: MIT Press.

Kaplan, D. 1977. Thoughts on Demonstratives. In *Demonstratives*, edited by P. Yourgrau. Oxford: Oxford University Press.

Keil, F. 1989. *Concepts, Kinds and Cognitive Development*. Cambridge, MA: MIT Press.

Kim, J. 1998. *Mind in a Physical World*. Cambridge, MA: MIT Press.

Kim, J. 2005. *Physicalism, or Something Near Enough*. Princeton: Princeton University Press.

Kim, J. 2006. *Philosophy of Mind*. 2nd ed. New York: Westview Press.

Kripke, S. 1979. A Puzzle about Belief. In *Meaning and Use*, edited by A. Margalit. Dordrecht: Reidel, 239–283.

Kripke, S. 1980. *Naming and Necessity*. Cambridge, MA: Harvard University Press.

Kunda, Z. 1999. *Social Cognition: Making Sense of People*. Cambridge, MA: MIT Press.

Laurence, S., and Margolis, E. 1999. Concepts and Cognitive Science. In *Concepts: Core Readings*, edited by E. Margolis and S. Laurence. Cambridge, MA: MIT Press, 3–81.

Laurence, S., and Margolis, E. 2002. Radical Concept Nativism. *Cognition* 86: 25–55.

Levine, A., and Bickhard, M. 1999. Concepts: Where Fodor Went Wrong. *Philosophical Psychology* 12: 5–23.

Lewis, D. 1983. New Work for a Theory of Universals. *Australasian Journal of Philosophy* 61: 343–377.

Lin, L., Osan, R., Shoham, S., et al. 2005. Identification of Network-Level Coding Units for Real-Time Representation of Episodic Experiences in the Hippocampus. *PNAS* 102 (17).

Lin, L., Osan, R., Shoham, S., Jin, W., Zuo, W., and Tsien, J. Z. 2005. Organizing Principles of Real-Time Memory Encoding: Neural Clique Assemblies and Universal Neural Codes. *Trends in Neurosciences* 29 (1).

Loar, B. 1996. Social Content and Psychological Content. In *The Twin Earth Chronicles*, edited by A. Pessin and S. Goldberg. London: M. E. Sharpe.

Loewer, B., and Rey, G., eds. 1993. *Meaning in Mind: Fodor and His Critics*. Oxford; Cambridge: Blackwell.

Ludwig, K., and Schneider, S. 2008. Fodor's Critique of the Classical Computational Theory of Mind. *Mind & Language* 23: 123–143.

Macdonald, C., and Macdonald, G. 1995. *Connectionism: Debates on Psychological Explanation*. Vol. 2. Oxford: Basil Blackwell.

Machery, E. 2009. *Doing without Concepts*. New York: Oxford University Press.

Marcus, G. 2001. *The Algebraic Mind*. Cambridge, MA: MIT Press.

Margolis, E. 1998. How to Acquire a Concept. *Mind & Language* 13: 347–369.

Margolis, E. and Laurence, S., eds. 1999. *Concepts: Core Readings*. Cambridge, MA: MIT Press.

Marsland, T. A., and Schaeffer, J., eds. 1990. *Computers, Chess, and Cognition*. New York: Springer-Verlag.

McLaughlin, B. 2007. Type Materialism About Phenomenal Consciousness. In *The Blackwell Companion to Consciousness*, edited by M. Velmans and S. Schneider. Oxford: Blackwell Publishers.

Miller, G. 1956. The Magical Number Seven, Plus or Minus Two: Some Limits on Our Capacity for Processing Information. *Psychological Review* 63: 81–97.

Millikan, R. G. 1993. On Mentalese Orthography. In *Dennett and His Critics: Demystifying Mind*, edited by B. Dahlbom. Cambridge, MA: Blackwell, 97–123.

Mountcastle, V. B. 1997. The Columnar Organization of the Neocortex. *Brain* 120: 701–722.

Murphy, G. L., and D. L. Medin. 1985. The Role of Theories in Conceptual Coherence. *Psychological Review* 92: 289–316.

Newell, A., and H. A. Simon. 1972. *Human Problem Solving*. Englewood Cliffs, NJ: Prentice-Hall.

Newell, A. 1980. Physical Symbol Systems. *Cognitive Science* 4:135–183.

O'Reilly, R., and Munakata, Y. 2000. *Computational Explorations in Computational Neuroscience*. Cambridge, MA: MIT Press.

Peacocke, C. 1992. *A Study of Concepts*. Cambridge, MA: MIT Press.

Peacocke, C. 2004. Interrelations: Concepts, Knowledge, Reference and Structure. *Mind & Language* 19 (1): 85–98.

Perry, J. 1977. Frege on Demonstratives. *Philosophical Review* 86: 474–497.

Perry, J. 1993. *The Problem of the Essential Indexical and Other Essays*. Oxford: Oxford University Press.

Pessin, A. 1995. Mentalese Syntax: Between a Rock and Two Hard Places. *Philosophical Studies* 78: 33–53.

Pessin, A., and Goldberg, S., eds. 1996. *The Twin Earth Chronicles*. London: M. E. Sharpe.

Pietroski, P., and Rey, G. 1995. When Other Things Aren't Equal: Saving *Ceteris Paribus* Laws from Vacuity. *British Journal for the Philosophy of Science* 46: 81–111.

Pinker, S. 1997. *How the Mind Works*. New York: Norton.

Pinker, S. 2005. So How Does the Mind Work? *Mind & Language* 20 (1): 1–24.

Pinker, S., and Prince, A. 1988. On Language and Connectionism: Analysis of a Parallel Distributed Processing Model of Language Acquisition. *Cognition* 23: 73–93.

Prinz, J. 2002. *Furnishing the Mind: Concepts and Their Perceptual Basis*. Cambridge, MA: MIT Press.

Putnam, H. 1975. The Meaning of Meaning. In *Philosophical Papers*, Vol. 2 of *Mind, Language and Reality*. Cambridge: Cambridge University Press.

Putnam, H. 1983. *Realism and Reason. Philosophical Papers*. vol. 3. Cambridge: Cambridge University Press.

Putnam, H. 1988. *Representation and Reality*. Cambridge, MA: MIT Press.

Pylyshyn, Z. 1986. *Computation and Cognition*. London: MIT Press.

Pylyshyn, Z., ed. 1987. *The Robot's Dilemma: The Frame Problem in Artificial Intelligence*. Norwood, NJ: Ablex.

Quine, W. 1953. Two Dogmas of Empiricism. In *From a Logical Point of View*. Cambridge: Harvard University Press.

Ramsey, W., Stich, S., and Garon, J. 1990. Connectionism, Eliminitivism, and the Future of Folk Psychology. *Philosophical Perspectives* 4: 499–533.

Rey, G. 2009. Review of Eduard Machery, *Doing without Concepts*. *Notre Dame Philosophical Reviews* July 15. Available at: http: //ndpr.nd.edu/review.cfm?id=16608.

Rey, G. 1997. *Contemporary Philosophy of Mind*. London: Blackwell.

Richard, M. 1990. *Propositional Attitudes: An Essay on Thoughts and How We Ascribe Them*. Cambridge: Cambridge University Press.

Rives, B. 2009. Concept Cartesianism, Concept Pragmatism, and Frege Cases. *Philosophical Studies* 144: 211–238.

Rosch, E. 1976. Basic Objects in Natural Categories. *Cognitive Psychology* 8: 382–439.

Rosch, E. 1978. Principles of Categorization. In *Cognition and Categorization*, edited by E. Rosch and B. B. Lloyd. Hillsdale, NJ: Erlbaum. Reprinted in E. Margolis and S. Laurence, eds. 1999. *Concepts: Core Readings*. Cambridge, MA: MIT Press.

Rosch, E., and C. B. Mervis. 1975. Family Resemblances: Studies in the Internal Structure of Categories. *Cognitive Psychology* 7: 573–605.

Rupert, R. 2008. Frege's Puzzle and Frege Cases: Defending a Quasi-syntactic Solution. *Cognitive Systems Research* 9: 76–91.

Salmon, N. 1986. *Frege's Puzzle*. Cambridge, MA: MIT Press.

Salmon, N. 1989. Illogical Belief. *Philosophical Perspectives* 3: 243–285.

Schiffer, S. 1991. *Ceteris Paribus* Laws. *Mind* 100: 1–17.

Schiffer, S. 1992. Belief Ascription. *Journal of Philosophy* 89: 499–521.

Schneider, S. 2003. *Meaning and the Computational Mind: The Relation Between Intentional and Computational States in a Scientific Psychology. Ph.D. diss.* Rutgers University.

Schneider, S. 2005. Direct Reference, Psychological Explanation, and Frege Cases. *Mind & Language* 20 (4): 223–247.

Schneider, S. 2007a. Daniel Dennett's Theory of Consciousness. *The Blackwell Companion to Consciousness*, edited by M. Velmans and S. Schneider. Oxford: Blackwell Publishing.

Schneider, S. 2007b. Yes, It Does: A Diatribe on Jerry Fodor's *The Mind Doesn't Work That Way. Psyche* 13 (1): 1–15.

Schneider, S. 2009a. The Language of Thought. In *The Routledge Companion to Philosophy of Psychology*, edited by P. Calvo and J. Symons. NY: Routledge.

Schneider, S. 2009b. LOT, CTM and the Elephant in the Room. *Synthese* 170 (2): 235–250.

Schneider, S. 2009c. The Nature of Symbols in the Language of Thought. *Mind & Language* 24 (4): 523–553.

Schneider, S. 2010. Conceptual Atomism Rethought. *Behavioral and Brain Sciences* 33: 224–225.

Schneider, S. Forthcoming. *The Mind-Body Problem: Rethinking Solution Space.* Oxford: Oxford University Press.

Searle, J. 1980. Minds, Brains and Programs. *Behavioral and Brain Sciences* 3 (3): 417–457.

Segal, G. 2000. *A Slim Book on Narrow Content.* Cambridge, MA: MIT Press.

Shanahan, M. 1997. *Solving the Frame Problem: A Mathematical Investigation of the Common Sense Law of Inertia.* Cambridge, MA: MIT Press.

Shanahan, M. P. 2008a. Dynamical Complexity in Small-World Networks of Spiking Neurons. *Physical Review E: Statistical, Nonlinear, and Soft Matter Physics* 78: 041924.

Shanahan, M. P. 2008b. A Spiking Neuron Model of Cortical Broadcast and Competition. *Consciousness and Cognition* 17: 288–303.

Shanahan, M. 2009. The Frame Problem. In *The Stanford Encyclopedia of Philosophy* (Winter 2009 Edition), edited by E. N. Zalta. Available at <http: //plato.stanford.edu/archives/win2009/entries/frame-problem/>.

Shanahan, M. 2010. *Embodiment and the Inner Life*. Oxford: Oxford University Press.

Shanahan, M., and Baars, B. 2005. Applying Global Workspace Theory to the Frame Problem. *Cognition* 98 (2): 157–176.

Shanahan M. P., and Connor, D. Forthcoming. Modeling the Neural Basis of Cognitive Integration and Consciousness. *Proceedings A Life XI*.

Shoemaker, S. 1984. Causality and Properties. In *Identity, Cause and Mind*. Cambridge: Cambridge University Press.

Smith, E. E., and D. L. Medin. 1981. *Categories and Concepts*. Cambridge, MA: Harvard University Press.

Smolensky, P. 1988. On the Proper Treatment of Connectionism. *Behavioral and Brain Sciences* 11: 1–74.

Smolensky, P. 1995. Reply: Constituent Structure and Explanation in an Integrated Connectionist/Symbolic Cognitive Architecture. In *Connectionism: Debates on Psychological Explanation, Volume Two*, edited by C. Macdonald and G. Macdonald. Oxford: Basil Blackwell.

Soames, S. 1988. Direct Reference, Propositional Attitudes, and Semantic Content. In *Propositions and Attitudes*, ed. N. Salmon and S. Soames, 197–239. Oxford: Oxford University Press.

Spence, C., and Driver, J. 2004. *Crossmodal Space and Crossmodal Attention*. Cambridge, MA: MIT Press.

Sperber, D. 2005. Modularity and Relevance: How Can a Massively Modular Mind Be Flexible and Context-Sensitive? In *The Innate Mind: Structure and Content*, edited by P. Carruthers, S. Laurence, and S. Stich. Oxford: Oxford University Press.

Sporns, O., Honey, C. J., and Kötter, R. 2007. Identification and Classification of Hubs in Brain Networks. *PLoS ONE* 2 (10).

Sporns, O., Chialvo, D., Kaiser, M., and Hilgetag, C. C. 2004. Organization, Development and Function of Complex Brain Networks. *Trends in Cognitive Sciences* 8: 418–425.

Sporns, O., and J. Zwi. 2004. The Small World of the Cerebral Cortex. *Neuroinformatics* 2:145–162.

Stein, B., Stanford, T., Wallance, M., Vaughan, J. W., and Jiang, W. 2004. Crossmodal Spatial Interaction in Subcortical and Cortical Circuits. In *Crossmodal Space and Crossmodal Attention*, edited by C. Spence and J. Driver Cambridge, MA: MIT Press.

Sterelny, K. 1980. Animals and Individualism. In *Information, Language, and Cognition*, edited by P. P. Hanson. Vancouver: University of British Columbia Press.

Stich, S. 1983. *From Folk Psychology to Cognitive Science: The Case Against Belief*. Cambridge, MA: MIT Press.

Stich, S. 1993. Narrow Content Meets Fat Syntax. In *Meaning in Mind: Fodor and His Critics,* edited by B. Loewer and G. Rey. Oxford, UK; Cambridge: Blackwell.

Turing, A. 1936. On Computable Numbers, with an Application to the Entscheidungsproblem. *Proceedings of the London Mathematical Society*, 42 (series 2): 230–256; reprinted in *The Undecideable: Basic Papers on Undecidable Propositions, Unsolvable Problems and Computable Functions*, M. Davis (ed.), Hewlett, NY: Raven Press, 1965.

Turing, A. 1950. Computing Machinery and Intelligence. *Mind* LIX (236).

van Gelder, T. 1990. Why Distributed Representation is Inherently Non-Symbolic. In *Konnektionismus in Artificial Intelligence und Kognitionsforschung*, edited by G. Dorffner. Berlin: Springer-Verlag, 58–66.

Vision, G. 2001. Flash: Fodor Splits the Atom. *Analysis* 61 (269): 5–10.

Watts, D. J., and Strogatz, S. H. 1998. Collective Dynamic of 'Small-world' Networks. *Nature* 393: 440–442.

Wermter, S., and Sun, R. 2000. An Overview of Hybrid Neural Systems. In *Hybrid Neural Systems*, edited by S. Wermter and R. Sun. Heidelberg: Springer.

Wermter, S., and R. Sun, eds. 2000. *Hybrid Neural Systems*. Heidelberg: Springer.

Wettstein, H. 1986: Has Semantics Rested on a Mistake? *Journal of Philosophy*, 83 (4): 185–209.

# Index

Pragmatist dimension of LOT, appreciating the, 159–175
Pragmatist theory, LOT as a, 162, 175–180
Pragmatist views
  defined, 5
  Fodor on, 5
  LOT and, 5
Prefrontal cortex (PFC), 18
Prinz, Jesse, 149, 164, 165n, 166, 170, 171n3
Productivity/productive nature of thought, 9, 10
Properties
  causal powers, 123
  global, 31–32
  nature of, 123
  syntactic, 67–68, 98
Prototype theory, 167–168
Psychological explanation (PE), 16–17
Psychological generalizations, 15, 108, 138, 152, 218, 225
Psychological states, individuation of, 108, 119, 130n, 131, 147, 213
Psychology. *See* Broad psychology; Narrow psychology
Publicity
  vs. externalist explanation, 137–140
  in terms of functional analysis, 140–142
Publicity requirement (theories of concepts), 164–165, 167
Putnam, Hilary, 192

Ramsification, method of, 121–122, 124
Referential generalizations, 138, 139, 150, 220
Referential individuation, 100
Referentialism, 16–17, 17n. *See also* Co-referentiality/co-reference
Referents and symbols, "locking relation" between, 14–15, 96, 173, 174
Relevance problem, 30, 32–35
  as an in principle difficulty, 41
Representational nature of thought, 3
Rey, Georges, 96, 175–176
Robbins, Philip, 209, 210
Rosch, Eleanor, 144, 168
Russell, Bertrand, 16
Russellian propositions, 183
Russellianism, 16n. *See also* Neo-Russellianism

Scientific properties. *See* Properties
Scope requirement (theories of concepts), 170
Semantic generalizations, 137–138
Semantic properties of thoughts, 12
Semantic proposal, 99–101
Semantics, 15, 16
  combinatorial, 12
  conceptual-role, 105, 137, 218, 220, 221
Shanahan, Murray, 30, 46, 52